MY FRIEND TOLD ME ABOUT THE GOSSIP AT HIS POKER TABLE.

"One of the players had just returned from the Bellagio, home of the world's best poker players. In the poker room, he saw 'the son of a poker world champion' and 'some Texas banker' playing heads-up Hold 'Em with over $15 million on the table.

"The amounts simply would not register in my mind. I tried writing this off as an urban legend in the making. I remembered stories about Doyle Brunson and Puggy Pearson playing rounds of golf for more money than Jack Nicklaus and Lee Trevino made in a year. I overheard pros describing their winnings in inches of hundred-dollar bills. But $15 million on the table? This much cash would weigh over 250 pounds."

—From

The Professor, the Banker, and the Suicide King

"A quick, entertaining read . . . Craig plays his winning hand with aplomb."

—SI.com

"Riveting."

—The Onion

"Very intriguing . . . tremendous insight . . . well worth the read."

—ESPN.com

"A good bet."

—New York Daily News

more . . .

"A brisk story."
—Wall Street Journal

"A knowledgeable and observant chronicle . . . Readers will be awed."
—Publishers Weekly

"This book plants the reader ringside for history's richest poker game, then won't let go until we know the hearts and minds of the world's greatest players, and the soul of the billionaire amateur who dared challenge them for everything they owned."
—Robert Kurson, *New York Times* bestselling author of *Shadow Divers*

"A remarkable story . . . more twists and turns than a bestselling thriller. Even non-poker fans will be fascinated by the compelling battle of wits."
—*Register Pajaronian* (CA)

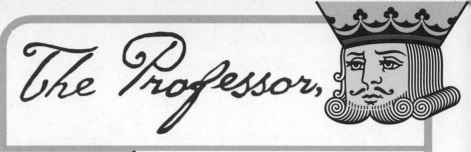

The Professor,

the Banker,

and the Suicide King

Inside the Richest Poker Game of All Time

Michael Craig

GRAND CENTRAL PUBLISHING

NEW YORK BOSTON

For Jo Anne, Barry, Ellie, and Val

Four Aces

Grand Central Publishing
Hachette Book Group USA
237 Park Avenue
New York, NY 10017

Visit our Web site at www.HachetteBookGroupUSA.com.

Printed in the United States of America

Originally published in hardcover by Hachette Book Group USA.
First Trade Edition: June 2006
10 9 8 7 6 5 4

Grand Central Publishing is a division of Hachette Book Group USA, Inc.
The Grand Central Publishing name and logo is a trademark of Hachette Book Group USA, Inc.

The Library of Congress has cataloged the hardcover edition as follows:

Craig, Michael
The professor, the banker, and the suicide king : inside the richest poker game of all time / Michael Craig.— 1st ed.
p. cm.
Includes bibliographical references.
ISBN 0-446-57769-3
1. Poker—Tournaments—Nevada—Las Vegas. 2. Beal, Andy. 3. Poker players—United States. I. Title.
GV1254.C73 2005
795.412—dc22 2004029464

ISBN 978-0-446-69497-1 (pbk.)

Book design by H. Roberts Design
Book composition by E. T. Lowe
Cover design by Brigid Pearson
Cover illustration by Daniel Pelavin

Contents

Preface

Pocket Kings

"Show us your pocket kings."

If the cowboy at the other end of the table had pulled out a knife I would have been less unnerved. But he had shown me something more lethal than a blade: a professional poker player's powers of observation.

I had started playing Texas Hold 'Em, the most popular form of poker, in 1992. For a year, I cleaned up in low-stakes Las Vegas games and fantasized about my future as a free-wheeling, high-living professional poker player.

Texas Hold 'Em seems so simple that such delusions are common. The goal is to make the best five-card poker hand out of a combination of a player's two concealed cards, also called *hole cards*, and five communal cards, called the *board*. The first round of betting follows receipt of the hole cards. Because betting position is so important and remains the same through the hand, a large disk, called the *dealer button* (or just the *button*), passes clockwise around the table, one player per hand, denoting who acts last. To stimulate initial action, instead of antes, hold 'em imposes mandatory bets, known as the *blinds*, on the two players to the left of the button. The first player to the left of the button posts the *small blind,* half an opening bet. The next player posts the *big blind,* the size of the opening bet.

After the first round of betting, the dealer turns over the first three communal cards, called the *flop.* After a second round of betting, the dealer turns over the fourth card, known as *fourth street* or the *turn.* A third betting round ensues, after which the dealer turns over the last card, *fifth street* or the *river.* The remaining players bet once more, and turn over their cards.

Generally, the casino dealing (also called *spreading*) the game specifies the betting limits. A $3–$6 game, for example, would have opening bets and raises in increments of $3 in the first two betting rounds and $6 in the last two rounds. Texas Hold 'Em can also be played without betting limits, meaning that although the big and small blinds are set, the players may thereafter bet any amount, including everything they have on the table. No-Limit Texas Hold 'Em is only occasionally played in cash games, but is extremely popular in tournaments. (Virtually all poker games are played for *table stakes,* meaning the players cannot bet more than they have on the table. They can't reach into their pockets or borrow more in the middle of a hand. But if someone bets more than an opponent has at the table, the opponent can't be forced to *fold.* They can go *all-in,* covering as much of a bet as they have in front of them. Except for unfriendly private games and bad poker movies, no one has to cover a bet for more than they have on the table by putting up their car, house, wedding ring, or fiancée.)

I considered myself so proficient at the game by the summer of 1993 that all I needed, to my reasoning, was to step up in class, repeat my stellar low-stakes results, and begin my new life as a globe-trotting professional gambler.

Or should I say *our* new life? I had a wife, two children, a law partner, and a busy practice. No one was going to encourage (or allow) me to bet the vast sums contested in the top games. I would have to prove my mettle in a poker tournament, demonstrating to all the family, friends, and colleagues who thought I had a screw loose that I was, indeed, pro poker material.

This brought me, in July 1993, to the Aladdin Oasis Poker Tournament and to the dead-eyed cowboy. The Aladdin of 1993 was not the posh mega-resort of today but a relic of the Rat Pack days brought forward three decades without, it seemed, a fresh coat of paint or a carpet shampoo. The decision to schedule three weeks of poker tournaments in Las Vegas in July was exactly the kind of thinking that consigned the original Aladdin to oblivion. Still, the tournament circuit in those days—before ESPN, Fox, the Travel Channel, and Bravo ran poker shows several times a week—had a big gap during the summer, so a cadre of hard-core pros attended, including World Series of Poker champions Tom "Grand Rapids" McEvoy (who was sitting to my immediate right), Thomas "Amarillo Slim" Preston, Walter "Puggy" Pearson, Johnny "Orient Express" Chan, Berry Johnston, Jack Keller, and Brad Daughterty. I also recognized, from old World Series of Poker videotapes I studied like the Rosetta Stone, perennial tournament winners Hans "Tuna" Lund, T. J. Cloutier, and John Bonetti.

The no-limit hold 'em event was contested by eighty-six of these pros, plus me. Thoroughly intimidated, I blundered about for a couple hours, mostly too scared to play and, therefore, get myself in serious trouble. In middle position, I looked down at my hole cards and saw two black kings. This was my best hand of the tournament. Everybody between the blinds and me had passed, so I raised the $100 and $200 blinds to $500. I tried to remain as still and calm as possible, a blank wall.

The remaining players to the button passed. The cowboy in the small blind studied me a moment and threw in his cards. The

Asian kid in the big blind peeked at his cards and immediately, forcefully, shoved all his chips in the center. "All in."

Could he have two aces?

How was I supposed to know? Two kings was a great two-card hand, and being all-in would obviate the need to make decisions about the hand in later betting rounds. I called his bet, pushing my chips to the middle.

The current rule is that when someone is all-in and no further betting is possible, the players immediately turn up their cards. This prevents a cheater from passing his chips to a compatriot by calling an all-in bet, seeing his cohort's hand at the end, and throwing in his cards unseen. But that rule did not exist in 1993 so everyone directed their attention to the empty space in the center of the table where the dealer would display the board.

The flop produced nine-nine-six. Since I was worried that my opponent had an ace, I viewed this as positive. The turn brought the king of hearts. Even if the kid had two aces, I was home clear. This gave me a five-card hand of king-king-king-nine-nine, a full house. The river card, however, was an ace. Still, unless my opponent had ace-ace or nine-nine in the hole, he couldn't beat me.

To the shock of everyone at the table, the kid turned over a six and a nine. He was bluffing but he made a full house (nine-nine-nine-six-six) on the flop.

That's when the cowboy plunged the dagger into my neck.

"Show us your pocket kings."

I can still hear that sneer today, as if I was carelessly playing the game with my cards face up.

I sheepishly turned over my winning king-king. Morosely stacking my chips, I broke protocol and asked the cowboy, "How did you put me on kings?"

"When the suicide king came on the turn, I thought I saw your Adam's apple move a little."

It wasn't until years later that I learned the king of hearts was known as the suicide king. If you look at him, he holds his broadsword behind his head (or, perhaps, pointed at it).

Needless to say, I did not win the Aladdin Oasis no-limit hold 'em tournament, or make it as a professional poker player. If I wanted to experience the thrills of poker at the highest level, I would have to do it from the rail, like all the other suckers.

Over the next decade, I gave up poker, and then took it up again. While playing $10–$20 hold 'em at the Mirage in October 2003, my friend Ted told me about the gossip at his table. One of the players had just returned from the Bellagio, home of not only a huge Impressionist art collection, couture shops, and a brilliant fountain display, but also the world's best poker players and highest-stakes poker games. In the poker room, he saw "the son of a poker world champion" and "some Texas banker" playing heads-up Texas Hold 'Em with, according to a floorman present, over $15 million on the table.

The night before, at the Mirage showroom, on his fifty-ninth birthday, illusionist Roy Horn had been mauled by a white tiger only a couple hundred feet from the poker room. The next day, the poker players in the room couldn't have cared less, other than to grab the previously issued Siegfried & Roy $5 chips before the dealers took them out of circulation. The mauling being discussed in the room was between the bulldog of a pro and a banker, not a tiger and a magician.

The son of the world champion had to be Todd Brunson. Todd's father, Doyle Brunson, won the Championship Event of the World Series of Poker in 1976 and 1977. Todd was a poker prodigy, always the youngest at the table in the big cash games.

The amounts simply would not register in my mind. I remembered, from my earlier poker days, stories about Doyle Brunson and Puggy Pearson playing rounds of golf for more money than Jack Nicklaus and Lee Trevino made in a year. I overheard pros describing their winnings in inches of hundred-dollar bills.

But $15 million on the table? This much cash would weigh over 250 pounds. (Don't ask how I know this; suffice to say that people who weigh bundles of $100 bills keep a low profile.) Although they were using chips and not bushels of currency, it just seemed like more money than even a phenomenal poker player could accumulate, much less risk, in one game.

Even the banker's place in the game didn't make sense. "But he's a billionaire," another player told me when I tried writing this off as an urban legend in the making. He said it as if being a billionaire was something that came automatically with being a Texas banker, and billionaires automatically played poker for astronomical sums. Bill Gates had been known to stop by the Mirage poker room when he was in town, but he played $3–$6 hold 'em. Even if the banker *could* throw around that kind of money, why *would* he?

That curiosity started me on the road to the richest poker game of all time, and took me inside the world of high-stakes poker. For most of a year, I learned about the unusual and impressive skills that separate the best players from the rest of the field, the enormity of their successes and failures, and their shortcomings, which almost always stemmed from their strengths as poker players and gamblers.

I also had the privilege of witnessing the problem-solving skills of the Texas banker, Andrew Beal. Beal, one of the great entrepreneurial minds of the Information Age, has accumulated great wealth, yet managed to remain almost completely anonymous. (In fact, the Bellagio allowed him to register under the name "Anonymous.") From the time he was an eleven-year-old buying broken televisions for a dollar from the Salvation Army and fixing and selling them for $30–$40, to purchasing hundreds of millions of dollars of bonds in California utilities and airlines when most investors were writing off those businesses, he has never been afraid to venture into new areas, teach himself the rules, challenge the experts and the prevailing wisdom, and measure the results.

His approach to poker, and to risk itself, is unique. By ignoring, and even contradicting, conventional wisdom, he became extremely wealthy. His hobbies made him an important and credible figure in science and mathematics, areas in which he had no formal education. As I learned more about his improbable career and unique approach to financial and intellectual issues, I wondered, why *can't* a wealthy, smart, determined person figure out a way to compete on an even footing with top professional poker players?

Most important, I learned what a capricious game poker can be, and what a difficult profession it can be for even its expert practitioners. In fact, when I started, I thought the central question of the book would be why Beal would attempt something so apparently foolhardy, taking on the best in the world at their game. By the end of the story, the more pertinent question is why the professionals continued to take up his challenge. By the time the stakes reached their peak, the pros were potentially risking everything on an edge they realized was virtually nonexistent.

The game went on at irregular intervals in an upstairs corner of the poker room at the Bellagio, in the heart of the Las Vegas Strip, for over three years. Sometimes, Andy Beal would come to town for business and play poker for a day or two. Most of the time, he came solely to test himself against the pros, staying for as long as two weeks. Occasionally, especially at the beginning, he would play a full-table (or *ring*) game. But mostly, he played the pros one-on-one (known in poker as *heads up*). He played poker in Las Vegas on ten occasions between February 2001 and May 2004.

Because of the size of the stakes and the interest in accommodating Beal's request to play heads up, the players—anyone willing to post $100,000 to $1 million to purchase a share and play

Beal on their collective bankroll—formed a group, taking turns playing Beal and sharing in wins and losses. The composition of the group changed during the three years. If a player was not physically present handing over their share of the bankroll before the first match, they were out. The group was composed of as few as eight players and as many as seventeen. On every occasion, it included a lineup of the world's most skilled poker players. Every time Beal came to town, he played in the highest-stakes game of all time. After his first few visits, the only competition for highest stakes of all time was his previous visits. In fact, based on the final matches between Andy Beal and the pros, it is extremely unlikely that a bigger poker game will materialize for several decades.

So what was the outcome? You'll have to read on to find out, but let me assure you, fortunes were won and lost. Although a weapon in the arsenal of every good poker player—and these pros are the best in the world—is an indifference to the stakes, and their opponent was one of the wealthiest men in Texas, the outcome hanging in the balance made the game's participants at different times sick with worry, angry with themselves (and, in the case of the pros, each other), elated, filled with self-doubt, overtaken by greed, petty, disgusted, thrilled, paranoid, and relieved.

But reporting on a three-year series of poker games is not like reporting on three baseball seasons, or three years on Wall Street. The American obsession with numbers has pulled tournament poker into the twenty-first century. There are now tours and circuits with money rankings, player ratings, championships, and player-of-the-year awards. But the high-stakes cash games still adhere to rules reminiscent of the Old West. Rules like, "Keep your back to the wall" and "Keep your mouth shut."

There are numerous obstacles to finding out who won and who lost (and how much), some even more imposing than the beefy security personnel who magically appear if someone lingers too long on the rail of a high-stakes game. For numerous reasons, it is bad business to reveal the results of poker games. No one wants to brag lest the IRS be within earshot. (Most of these players are pretty honest when it comes to reporting poker income, evidenced by the meticulous records I saw of some of the players, the modern casino and Treasury Department rules for recording transactions of the size necessary for these players to take money out of play, and Doyle Brunson's decades-long admonition that a poker player can never accumulate wealth if he doesn't pay his taxes.)

Bragging is also bad form. Nobody wants to rile either the losers or the poker gods, or alert the legions of cash-poor poker players looking for an easy touch. In addition, it's hard enough for the top players to find opponents without spelling out how successful they are at relieving opponents of money. Chip Reese, a regular in the world's biggest games for thirty years, told me that he loves it when people write about his losses, even better when they get the facts wrong and he actually won.

But the opposite situation also creates a problem. We are all familiar with how the big loser in a $3–$6 game will say that he "lost a little" or "just about broke even"? (Of course, *we* have never done that, but you know what I'm talking about.) I can let you in on a secret: The high-stakes pros are *exactly* the same way. With few exceptions, neither the pros nor Beal was especially forthcoming about losses.

All this led to some difficult reporting work. For example, I had five sources tell me different stories about one of Andy Beal's trips:

Source 1: Beal and the group played six $1 million freeze-outs. (A *freeze-out* is a game that continues until one person has all the chips.)

Source 2: Only two players opposed Beal in heads-up matches on that trip.

Source 3: One player won $2 million in one match.

Source 4: One player in addition to the two listed by Source 2 played Beal and won.

Source 5: They weren't freeze-outs.

Believe it or not, I was able to reconcile all this. In such situations, however, if some immaterial details could not be verified, or were in dispute, I omitted them. Every significant win and loss is described in detail, and most of the other matches are summarized. But on several trips, Andy Beal would play someone for a half-hour while waiting for his designated opponent to arrive. Or he would play someone not a part of the pros' group for a little while for smaller stakes. While all the important battles are fully covered, these minor skirmishes are merely summarized.

Whenever I cite a specific result and amount, I have either multiple sources independently reporting the number, or one extremely reliable source (someone present who I had already determined kept meticulous and reliable numbers) and agreement by others present and the opponent, or a lack of any basis to dispute the amount. There were no important results for which I did not get extremely specific information.

But there are gaps—not material gaps, or gaps that interfere with sharing the story with you, but gaps just the same. Even though it has been over sixty years since Joe DiMaggio hit in fifty-six consecutive games, fans can access a list of his statistics for every one of those games. But this is poker, not baseball. If you are comfortable with that, you will not be disappointed.

Finally, the story is about more than dollar amounts. The willingness of the world's best poker players to risk everything is both impressive and alarming. Doyle Brunson, a legendarily successful poker player and ambassador for the game, told me, "It takes kind of a sick person to play the way we do. I'm convinced we're all compulsive gamblers. We just find a way to win." Howard Lederer, also a tremendous presence in spreading a positive image of poker players, agrees: "Most of us, maybe all of us, have a little of the sickness in us. . . . The guys that end up in the biggest games are the ones that have a little too much gamble in them, but they've managed to figure out how to use it to their advantage."

This is their story.

Introduction

Ted Forrest's Wild Ride

March 2001

An hour outside Las Vegas, Ted Forrest called the Bellagio poker room. This call was part of a ritual whenever Ted returned from California. If the action was big enough, he would drive straight to the casino and play. Otherwise, he would go home and call again that evening.

Ted Forrest was a professional poker player, and he played for the highest stakes in the world. Even though he lived in Las Vegas, he chased the action around California, along the East Coast, and sometimes through Europe. The biggest games in Vegas were $1,500–$3,000, or maybe $2,000–$4,000, but those games popped up only occasionally. To keep himself in action, he commuted almost weekly to L.A. to the Bicycle Club, the Commerce Club, *Hustler* publisher Larry Flynt's house, or Flynt's Hustler Casino, for high-stakes poker.

When a poker player is playing well, every game looks like a good game, and Forrest was playing very well. He had won over $2.3 million in the first ten weeks of 2001. Most people would say there is no way such results could continue. What distinguishes a professional like Ted Forrest, however, is his focus on making those results continue for as long as possible. He did not want to turn down any opportunities to play while things were going so well.

His car, a Lincoln Mark VIII, was practically destined for this route. Tom McEvoy, the 1983 World Champion, won the car as the best all-around player at the Bicycle Club's Diamond Jim Brady Tournament in 1994. Phil Hellmuth, the 1989 World Champion, was backing McEvoy at the time and ended up with the car. Ted later staked Hellmuth, and bought the car from him.

Ted Forrest possesses the perfect disposition for this lifestyle. On the outside, nothing about Ted gave the impression that he was one of the best poker players in the world. He was thirty-six, of average height and weight. His face was youthful, his features unlined. His brown hair was always neat, though he sometimes grew it a little long. He almost never raised his voice or got angry. He looked like a new teacher at a prep school. Even at the poker table, his blank expression and vague smile confused opponents and onlookers. He looked like he didn't have a care in the world, or like he was stoned.

This exterior package hid that Ted Forrest was not someone to be trifled with, physically or mentally. He could do a standing back flip, run a marathon, or drink ten beers in thirty minutes. (He did all these things to win bets.) When he could find an opponent who was willing, he would play poker for over 100 hours at a stretch. He called these "death matches."

Only Ted's eyes hinted at the fires burning within. They were narrow and gray and, though he did not try to stare down opponents, those beady pupils behind the slits made the rest of Ted's appearance look like a mask he was peering through.

"High brush, please."

Ted did not have the poker room on his speed dial, but he dialed it so frequently he could push the buttons on his cell phone without taking his eyes off the road. The Bellagio spreads games of many different sizes, and different employees have the responsibility over different parts of the room. In one corner, up two steps, is the high-limit area, and the floorperson (nicknamed the *brush* after the floorperson's unglamorous responsibility of cleaning up messes at the table) supervising these five tables is known as the *high brush*.

"What's the biggest game in the room?" Ted expected to hear that an afternoon \$400–\$800 game was getting started, which would have been just big enough to draw him into the room.

After a pause, the floorman said, "Ten-and-twenty-thousand Texas Hold 'Em."

Ted must have heard wrong. The biggest game ever at the Bellagio had been \$4,000–\$8,000, and this was more than twice that size. A game that large doesn't just materialize on a Wednesday afternoon.

"Are you sure that's right? Ten-and-twenty *thousand*?"

"Yeah," the floorman answered, unemotional. "That's what they're playing."

Ted struggled to clear his head as he drove toward the Bellagio. His palms had gone cold and clammy.

Am I going to play? Am I going to play? I don't know if I'm going to play.

But in Ted's heart, he knew the answer. He was a gambler, and this was the gamble of a lifetime. It didn't matter that Ted had no idea who was playing in the game. It didn't matter that the consensus among poker players was that Texas Hold 'Em was not Ted's strongest game. (None of the three World Series championships he won in 1993 had been in hold 'em, and he had largely given up playing in tournaments after that.) No one would challenge that he was one of the best Seven Card Stud and Seven Card Stud Hi/Lo players in the world, but the rap on Ted was that hold 'em was just not his game. He disagreed with this assessment, but never made it a point to argue. He was not confrontational, except at the poker table, and having opponents underestimate him was rare and welcome.

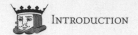

This was more action than Ted had ever seen before, and he craved action. The creeping doubts were merely the functioning of a highly developed brain. The heart, however, was that of a gambler.

He pulled the Lincoln into the South Garage, rode the elevator up to the casino, strode the short distance across the Starting Line bar, past the opening to the sports and race book, and into the poker room. Once in the room, he made a beeline for the cashier's cage.

On weekends and evenings, the room's thirty tables were filled and aisle space was nearly nonexistent. Between the narrow passageways and the traffic of players, cocktail waitresses, chip-runners, dealers on shift change, floorpeople, and supervisors, walking from one end of the small room to another could take several minutes and violated all tenets of personal space.

The high-stakes players usually didn't subject themselves to the stop-and-frisk of the room's main thoroughfares. The high-limit area was located in the back left corner of the poker room, up two steps. Three entrances serviced these five tables: one on the left, by the cashier's cage; one accessed through the middle of the poker room; and one on the right, accessed via a ramp from the sports book. The area upstairs was less crowded, received more attention from casino personnel, and offered easy access to an exit and the restrooms in the sports book and the cashier's cage.

As Ted asked for his safe deposit box, he stole a glance at Table Seven, the upstairs table closest to the cashier's cage, where two men played Texas Hold 'Em in silence. David "Chip" Reese sat in Seat Four (meaning four seats to the left of the dealer, who sits in the middle of one of the long sides of the table). Chip Reese was considered by many to be the best all-around poker player in the world, taking on all comers in all forms of poker (along with gin rummy and backgammon) for over twenty-five years. Reese, chunky, still blond, still boyish at fifty, spent a summer in Las Vegas between Dartmouth and Harvard Law School. He never made it to Harvard. Forrest did not recognize the man sitting in Seat Two. He looked to be in his mid-forties, tall, heavyset, neat dark hair, a white dress shirt. A businessman.

A businessman with a lot of money. The only chips on the table were white, with blue and red markings on the edges. The players called these *flags,* and they were $5,000 denomination chips. Forrest estimated that each man had a million dollars in chips.

His brain was still not committed to play as he examined the contents of his box. There were some loose chips of different denominations, but the main contents lay in a clear plastic five-column chip rack. One hundred flags: $500,000. Despite winning over $2 million at the poker tables in ten weeks, between money taken out for investments, taxes, living expenses, staking other players (bankrolling them for a share of the profits), money on deposit at California casinos, and irregular but occasionally substantial donations at the craps tables, this was the money Ted Forrest had to play poker.

His heart was pounding, as if to drown out any remaining doubts. He had just enough money—his entire bankroll—to buy into the biggest poker game of his life and be at a significant disadvantage in chips.

Five hundred thousand dollars sounded like a lot of money, but it wasn't. When it came out of the box, it was income. You could buy things with it, invest it, even give it away. Then, it was a lot of money. While it was in the box, however, it was working capital, and even mom-and-pop operators would tell you that a half-million dollars was not much working capital for a capital-intensive business.

Poker is the most capital-intensive business in the world. Like banking or securities trading, the commodity is money. But while technology and innovations like margins and interbank lending have supplanted the need for physical cash in the financial world, monetary transactions in the poker world have a medieval flair. Although pros are forever loaning, borrowing, staking, and trading pieces (exchanging with another player a percentage share in each other's results), their ability to compete is closely related to what they have in the box.

David Sklansky and Mason Malmuth, two expert poker players and writers with strong backgrounds in mathematics, have written on several occasions about capital requirements for professional poker players. To overcome the roller coaster of short-term fluctuations, an excellent player needs to have a bankroll equal to about 300 upper-limit bets in his regular game. A player of Ted Forrest's ability could have theoretically gotten by with less, but his regular game ranged between $400–$800 and $2,000–$4,000, with as much time as possible spent at the higher limits. In addition, many of his most frequent opponents were themselves among the best players in the world.

If Ted lost this money, he would be broke. "Broke" means something entirely different in poker than anywhere else. Poker players are gamblers and they train themselves to make the proper plays, regardless of whether those plays actually work out. Every great poker player has run through their playing bankroll, most of them many times. Going broke is both a rite of passage and a badge of honor, a reminder that they live life on the edge. Most of the highest-stakes players, through their years of success, have deliberately kept themselves undercapitalized, because they have been aggressive about trying to shelter as much money from poker as possible, buying property, starting businesses, and investing in the stock market. Of course, they obtained and maintained those assets by keeping their bankroll intact.

More often, a poker player on "broke street" simply borrows from other players and repays them when his bankroll has been rebuilt. But this is stressful and can lead to self-doubts and further losses. In this instance, Ted Forrest was one of the world's best poker players, on one of the biggest heaters of his life. How could his finances ever be secure if he went broke *now*?

Immediately to the right of the cage was an unmarked door. Inside, monitored by cameras every moment of every day, players accessed their safe deposit boxes. The cashier would move along the continuation of the counter to the other side of that door and receive the player's key. The player would sign a card acknowledging receipt of the box, and check its contents. Ted removed the rack from the box, handed the box back to the cashier, signed the card acknowledging return of the box, and waited a moment to receive his key back.

Ted exited the room and walked up the two steps to Table Seven. He saw a game going on at Table One, the corner table usually spreading the highest stakes, but he averted his eyes. He did not want to give himself a chance to choose another game.

Ted took a better look at Table Seven. Regulation 23 of the Nevada Gaming Commission and State Gaming Control Board required that the rules of each game be posted at the table. This meant the Bellagio always had a plastic card to the dealer's left stating the game, the stakes, the blinds or antes, and the rake (the portion taken by the casino for spreading the game). There had never been a poker game this big, so the Bellagio did not have a placard with that information. Someone taped a piece of paper over another placard, writing "$10,000–$20,000 Texas Hold 'Em," "minimum buy-in $100,000," and blinds of "$5,000–$10,000."

Ted sat down in Seat Six, to Chip Reese's left and across from the dealer. The best seat was the empty seat between the stranger and Chip, Seat Three. Position is important in Texas Hold 'Em and Seat Three would put Ted to the left of the stranger, acting after him throughout the hand, two-thirds of the time. Forrest and Reese would be trying to win money from each other, but they had played each other for years and knew each other's expert skills. Both expected their profit to come from the businessman. Reese, however, obviously left Seat Three open to give him and the stranger a little space, not as an invitation for someone to take over that prime position (as if anyone other than Ted Forrest would just wander into a $10,000–$20,000 poker game).

Ted decided not to start the game with a confrontation. Anybody with the minimum buy-in could sit in any open seat in the Bellagio poker room. Reese would have objected, however, and it wasn't worth starting the game with a fight. It was enough that Ted felt the butterflies in his stomach he hadn't felt since his $15–$30 stud days, when he was putting most of his bankroll on the line whenever he played.

Against an unfamiliar opponent, Ted Forrest tried to keep an open mind. He respected their bets until he learned how they played. This was not a matter of courtesy. For Ted, it was good strategy. Too many pros assumed an unfamiliar player didn't know how to play, refusing to give him credit for having a big hand when he led the betting. In the end, the pro would learn the new player's style and adjust, but underestimating a new player's ability was the more expensive error. If he overestimated a player's skill, he would get that money back when the player continued believing he could bluff Ted Forrest off his hand. Not giving the new player proper respect, however, could cost a lot of bets in the short term.

In $10,000–$20,000 Texas Hold 'Em, the blinds are $5,000 and $10,000. With three players, it was costing Ted a minimum of $15,000 every three hands just to sit at the table. It was an excruciatingly expensive way to get a read on the new player, a Texas banker named Andy Beal. Beal was very aggressive, playing nearly every hand, raising most of the time. It was costing Ted $20,000 per hand to see the flop, and his bankroll was taking a beating. After twenty minutes, Ted was down to his last $100,000, and he hadn't even gotten involved in many pots.

Oh, my God, he thought, what am I doing? Why did I sit down?

Part I

The Live One

1

Flipping Pennies

February 2001

In early February 2001, Andy Beal was having a fun evening during his first visit to the Bellagio poker room. The forty-eight-year-old owner of Dallas-based Beal Bank had finished his day's business and found himself with nothing to do. He did not chase women or enjoy showrooms, and he was traveling alone.

More than twenty years earlier, when he was just out of college and starting his real estate business, he would travel to Las Vegas to play blackjack. He counted cards, treated the trips like missions, and won as much as $50,000 in a weekend. He had even gotten barred from some casinos on the Strip, an experience more fun in the retelling than when it had actually happened.

Winning like that was exhilarating, but he was a different person then. Though he did not spend lavishly on most things, he had long passed the time when making $50,000 was worth the effort a professional card counter would have to expend to win that much.

Unlike counting cards at blackjack, playing poker was not

work. He had not read any books, practiced with any computer poker programs, and had played poker in a casino only once before. He just walked in, sat down at a $15–$30 Texas Hold 'Em game, won a few hundred dollars, and moved to the smallest game in the high-limit area, $80–$160 hold 'em.

Amid the fun time, Andy Beal understood the real game being played. At $80–$160, his opponents were all professional poker players who saw him as easy pickings. He was just killing an evening, relaxing. If they could figure out how to get a few thousand of his dollars, good for them. He played aggressively, by instinct, and his wary opponents usually afforded the newcomer a wide berth until they figured out how he played. So he continued to win.

Andrew Beal's physical appearance was a study in contrasts. He was tall and broad, with a large head balanced on wide shoulders. The features of his face, however, were thin in profile: a long, angular nose and an angular chin. He was also quiet and soft-spoken, preferring listening to talking. His stare could be piercing, and once he developed an opinion and chose to express it, the quiet reserve vanished. He could bludgeon opponents into submission with the force of his reasoning or, just as easily, probe someone with superior information with endless questions. He had little use for idle chat but could see the routine absurdity of everyday life.

These characteristics, coincidentally, were ideal for a poker player: physical strength, initial reserve, courage of convictions, focus, and a sense of humor. But in February 2001, Beal was playing poker in Las Vegas for only the second time. He had spent nearly twenty-five years in real estate and banking, and became one of the great entrepreneurial success stories of the last quarter of the twentieth century. Nevertheless, he was virtually unknown, which suited him just fine.

The professionals made casual conversation. Naturally, they

had an ulterior motive; they wanted him to give away some information about himself that would help them take his money. This was a lark to Andy, and he was having a good time, so he told them he was a banker from Dallas who was giving up blackjack for poker.

His opponents were working professionals trying to eke out a decent living in a capricious business. The $80–$160 game was a way station for most poker players—a place to build a bankroll to challenge a bigger game, rebuild after losing at the bigger games, or recover from a serious reverse on borrowed money. These men were grinders and their civility only barely covered the tension of their daily lives, exacerbated by an obvious novice winning. "Always be nice to the live one" was a universal rule of professional poker players, however, so they were unfailingly polite, civil, and complimentary to the newcomer.

This delicate balance—simultaneously casual, civil, friendly, competitive, intense—was shattered by the arrival of Mike Laing, who sat in Seat Seven. Laing, a professional poker player the same age as Beal, was his opposite in every way imaginable. While Beal radiated robust good health, Laing's pallid complexion and the bloating of his once long face and narrow features, the consequence of years of heavy drinking, made him look unhealthy.

Beal would prefer to listen than talk; one of Laing's principal weapons was his nonstop chatter at the table: small talk, trash talk, boasting, insults, self-deprecating humor, and drunken raving.

Andy Beal built a financially sound professional life for himself by managing risk. Mike Laing, in the poker business, was almost always broke, despite some great successes and an uncanny ability, especially in the late stages of big tournaments, to read his opponents. Laing won $212,000 in the $2,500 Limit Hold 'Em event of the World Series of Poker in 1994, in front of one of the largest crowds to gather for a final table of a preliminary event. Most of those watching, it turned out, were Mike's creditors. Despite his status as a frequent borrower, however, he was diligent about paying back his lenders. Within a week, he paid back everybody he had borrowed from, and had less than $2,000 left.

Andy was intensely private, building his real estate fortune, banking business, and other interests without accessing public capital markets, making no more than the required minimum public financial disclosures, and without courting the press and drawing attention to himself. Laing regularly brought his dysfunctional world to the poker table. Between hands, he would borrow and repay (and, on the rare occasions when he had it, loan) money around the poker room. His ex-wife would sometimes show up on the rail, heckling him. She actually left him and delivered the news during the night of his World Series win. With some Jack Daniel's and a pep talk from Vince Burgio, a fellow professional who, like many of Laing's contemporaries, saw him as a good person with great talent despite his flaws, Laing dominated the final table. Then, of course, there was the heavy drinking, which was part of virtually all the seemingly endless stories about Mike Laing.

On this particular night, Laing was returning to the Bellagio for the first time after the greatest success of his professional career. On January 26, 2001, Mike won the main event of the inaugural World Poker Challenge at the Reno Hilton. (This was one of the most prestigious poker titles outside Binion's Horseshoe's annual World Series of Poker. The Reno event has ridden the stratospheric rise in poker's popularity and is now televised as part of the Travel Channel's coverage of the World Poker Tour. First place in 2004 paid over $600,000; it may pay $1 million in 2005.) Laing outlasted a glittering final table including Scotty Nguyen, Daniel Negreanu, and Amarillo Slim to win $331,000, the biggest payday of his life.

Laing won in his unique fashion. At a significant disadvantage in chips against his last opponent, he repeatedly went all-in with hands like trey-deuce and nine-four, then showed his bluffs when his opponent folded. The next time he went all-in, his opponent called, only to find Laing holding two aces.

He also made a bizarre proposal at the final table. Because of the steep payout structure and the large blinds and antes at the end of tournaments, players would frequently propose deals to divide the top prizes more evenly, and play out the tournament for a smaller sum, as well as the right to be called champion. When there were four players left, all roughly equivalent in chips, Mike Laing suggested that they each take $20 and play one hand for the remaining $600,000 in prize money.

The gallery laughed, but Laing would have done it. Another player once said that "Mike Laing lives like he is allergic to money," and few would dispute the characterization.

Laing came into the Bellagio's poker room that night in February 2001 with over $300,000 in cash. Unlike the period following his World Series win, he did not have a long list of creditors. In fact, his small safe deposit box at the Bellagio would not hold all the cash, so he walked around the poker room looking for something to do with fistfuls of hundred-dollar bills, banded together in stacks of $5,000. (Putting the money in a bank was apparently never a consideration.) He had also been drinking.

In the corner of the high-limit area at Table One, he saw Jennifer Harman waiting for a game to start. Harman, a regular in the highest-stakes cash games, knew Mike, but everybody knew Mike. "Jennifer," he asked, "I don't have room in my box. Can you hold $25,000 for me?" Without waiting for her reply, he shoved five stacks at her and walked to the next table, still $15,000 in his hands.

He saw two pros, Marlon and Irish, playing Pot Limit Omaha. It was an expensive game, and not Mike's specialty. (Omaha, like hold 'em, requires players to make the best possible hand from their hole cards and five community cards. The main differences are that players receive four cards instead of two, and the five-card hand must be made from exactly two hole cards and three community cards. *Pot limit* means that players could bet an amount equal to whatever was in the pot at any time, leading to an exponentially rising betting structure.) Receiving congratulations and trading barbs as he worked the room, he sat down and played a hand, winning it. Then he got up and walked away.

The Irishman, a former world champion in Pot Limit Omaha, naturally started verbally jabbing at Laing for winning one hand and leaving. Big mistake.

"How much you got in front of you?" Mike asked him.

"About five thousand," Irish responded.

"I'll flip you a coin for it."

When Irish declined, it became Laing's turn to unload, which he did with gusto as he walked to the nearby \$80–\$160 hold 'em table and sat down at Seat Seven, two seats to the left of Andy Beal. Still holding \$15,000 in cash plus the handful of chips won during his one hand of Omaha, he ignored congratulations on his Reno victory and instead told his colleagues how he put the Irishman in his place. He asked around the table for someone to sell him a rack of \$20 chips, exchanging \$2,000 for a rack.

Catching Andy Beal's eye in the Five Seat, Mike Laing said, "You want to flip for a rack?"

Certain the pros were on to his style of play, Andy had started playing more conservatively. It was getting boring, folding hand after hand. He appreciated that the clownlike pro wanted to shake things up. Gamble.

"Sure."

Mike fished through his pocket, pulled out a penny, and passed it across to Andy. "You flip, you call."

The dealer and the other players watched as Andy flipped the penny in the air and called heads. It bounced on the green felt and turned up heads.

Mike Laing pushed Andy the rack of chips. Then he separated $2,000 from his cash and pushed it over to Andy to rebuy that rack of chips.

But before the dealer could start the hand, Mike said, "I want to do it again."

Andy Beal quickly agreed. "Okay, heads." He tossed the penny in the air and the result was the same. Two more times, they repeated the process.

One of the other players grumbled, "Damn it, we're here to play poker. If you want to flip a coin, do it on your own time." Action stopped at other nearby tables as players turned to watch Mike Laing lose $8,000 in coin flips.

Finally, a floorman came by to restore order. "Come on, Mike. Let's get back to the game, okay?"

Mike stood up and handed him his stack of yellow $20 chips, $400. "Just one more, for eight thousand. Double or nothing?" The floorman quietly walked away.

Andy agreed to one more flip, but there was a question about whether Mike had enough cash left to cover a loss. Just then, Jennifer Harman came by to give Mike his $25,000 back. She was leaving and told him she didn't want to hold on to his money.

Andy flipped the penny in the air and, like the previous four flips, called heads. This time, however, he tossed the penny much higher. It hit the padded rail, bounced on the floor, and rolled beneath the table near Andy. The penny joined the eclectic collection of items that find their way under poker tables: chip racks, empty water bottles, straws, swizzle sticks, the *Daily Racing Form, Card Player* magazine, sports parley cards, and candy and gum wrappers.

As the other players scrambled under the table to see the coin, Mike Laing knew if he could not see the coin, he should call off the action. He would call off the bet and demand a new coin flip.

But he was drunk, and he could not put his thought into words fast enough. Andy Beal looked under the table, called, "Tails, you win," and scooped up the penny before anyone had a chance to see it.

Mike Laing kept his mouth shut. Andy handed back the $8,000 in cash Mike lost to him over the previous three minutes. The dealer began the next hand, and players from other tables returned to their games. Neither man remembered anything about the $80–$160 game that followed, but they gave everyone in the room a story they were sure to repeat for years.

The next day, the two men met again in the poker room. A new $80–$160 hold 'em game was about to start and both arrived in time to play in it. Mike Laing approached Andy Beal and introduced himself and Andy did the same as they shook hands; they hadn't learned each other's names the previous evening.

"I was kind of drunk last night, Andy, but I'm dead sober today. A lot of people would have taken advantage of the situation when that coin rolled under the table. I want you to know that I think you are an honorable person and a true gentleman—"

Andy muttered his thanks.

"—and if you ever get yourself broke in this town, you can count on me for $10,000, no problem."

It was a sincere offer. Even though Mike Laing was almost always broke and scrounging for a stake or watching from the rail, he would still lend an outrageous sum of money to a stranger if he had a good feeling about the guy.

Mike eventually lost all that money from the Reno tournament, but he never had to loan it to Andy Beal. Mike's instinct for a good credit risk was as good as his card-reading skills.

Andy soon became bored with the size of the stakes in the $80–$160 game, and moved to a $400–$800 hold 'em table. Even at these stakes, where players regularly won or lost $20,000 in a session, Andy was getting restless. Waiting for a good hand was becoming a chore. In blackjack, you made financial decisions every hand. In poker, it seemed to be fold-fold-fold while you waited for cards.

It was late, and Andy should have gone to bed, but he never slept well in Vegas so he stayed up and played. As players left to go home, the game became more interesting. Down to three players, Andy started playing more hands, recognizing that he no longer had to wait for premium cards. In addition, if he represented a big hand early, his opponents (who were also not waiting for premium cards) could fold, increasing the value of aggressive play.

Against two world-class pros, Andy played in a style he described as "wild-man": playing nearly every hand, always raising. The Irishman, Mike Laing's foil from the evening before, had joined the game because he saw the newcomer, and was getting the worst of it. Andy was running over him, and when the pro made a stand with a decent hand, those turned out to be the occasions when Beal had big cards or outdrew him. After a few hours of three-handed, Irish lost all the money he had in front of him and left.

Andy was also winning money from his other opponent, Todd Brunson. Brunson, thirty, was one of the youngest of the high-stakes professionals. His father, Doyle Brunson, was one of the world's best and most famous poker players. Never completely escaping the shadow of his famous father, Todd nonetheless worked his way up the poker hierarchy on his own, rung by rung, winning some big tournaments and establishing himself as a first-class money player, especially in Texas Hold 'Em.

Todd had left a bigger game at Table One as it was breaking up to get a seat in this smaller game with the newcomer. Even when the game came down to heads up—one-on-one—he could not make a dent in Beal's growing stacks of chips.

As the poker room started emptying out, they played on, talking a little.

"I want to play higher," Andy told Todd.

"Okay," Todd said, "I'll play you higher."

"No, not this time. I'd like to come back and play a lot higher, like $10,000–$20,000."

Todd didn't think he was serious. This $400–$800 game was not particularly large by Todd's standards, but this guy wanted to play for twenty-five times as much.

"If you come by tomorrow afternoon, they'll get a bigger game going in the corner. And I can talk to some people about getting you a big game next time."

They played heads up for a few hours before Andy decided it was time to try to fall asleep. He won money from Todd, and cleaned out the Irishman, so it was a successful night. He wanted to get some rest before coming back the next afternoon and trying the game in the corner.

When Andy got up, they shook hands and introduced themselves. "I'll see you around," Andy said as he left.

Todd thought, This guy must be full of shit.

Andy Beal had his bank wire more money to the Bellagio, and he played at Table One over the next two days. The regular game at Table One was usually a $1,000–$2,000 (or more) mixed game, where the players starting the game choose various forms of poker to play in ten-hand rotations.

This was the site of the biggest game in the room and, usually, the biggest game in the world. Winning a high-profile poker tournament brought a big payday and a measure of fame, but the *best* players were those who would risk $100,000 or more every time they sat down at that table. They also excelled at all forms of poker, so the mix would usually include, along with Texas Hold 'Em, some forms of Omaha (with a high-low version where the *worst* hand wins half the pot), Seven Card Stud, Seven Card Stud Hi/Lo, some low poker (like Razz, which is played like Seven Card Stud but the worst hand wins, or forms of single- or triple-draw poker like Ace-to-Five and Deuce-to-Seven), and something exotic, like Chinese Poker (which is rarely played except in high-stakes games, where four players receive thirteen cards and receive points by making three hands of three-to-five cards and comparing them with their opponents' hands).

It was so rare that a completely new player would play for such high stakes, however, that the pros would play whatever game he wanted. When Andy arrived, he and three other pros started playing $1,000–$2,000 hold 'em.

By the next day, the table filled up and there was a list of players waiting to play. One high-stakes pro drove through the night from California to get in the game. He heard about Andy Beal late at night, too late to catch the last flight out of L.A. He didn't want to wait until the next morning and risk arriving too late to get an open seat.

By the second day, Andy Beal was facing a lineup of the best big-money poker players in the world: Doyle Brunson, Chip Reese, John Hennigan, Jennifer Harman, Chau Giang, and Todd Brunson.

Doyle Brunson was poker's equivalent of Babe Ruth, a larger-than-life character who shaped the game's history. He had done it all: back-to-back world championships (the main event of Binion's Horseshoe's World Series of Poker is universally regarded as poker's world championship), eight World Series bracelets (winning any event comes with, in addition to the cash, a gaudy bracelet, and Series records are measured in bracelets), destroyer of Texas road games, author of the best strategy manual, and a fixture in the biggest cash games in Vegas and around the world going on forty years.

Unlike baseball's Bambino, Brunson in his late sixties was still a threat to hit the ball out of the park. He had largely given up playing in tournaments, but still played in the biggest cash games, the higher the better, and still won. A fierce competitor and a phenomenal athlete as a young man—he had been scouted by the Minneapolis Lakers in the early 1950s before suffering a crippling leg injury in an industrial accident—he remained one of the world's highest-stakes golfers until his bad leg finally forced him to retire for good. For good, that is, until some of the young Turks in the golf-poker group started offering propositions: They'd give him a stroke per hole, he could have someone tee up every shot, he could tee off from the forward tees. He finally shut the kids up by agreeing to a nine-hole match play contest, winning the first five holes, and never playing again.

Chip Reese was the only professional within two decades of Brunson in age, achievement, and experience. Reese took Vegas by storm in the 1970s and was now considered the best all-around big-money poker player in the world, and high on the list of gin rummy and backgammon players as well.

Doyle and Chip had played in the biggest poker games ever contested. During the 1970s, they played in the wild games built around casino owner Major Riddle and drug dealer Jimmy Chagra. Chagra would toss $20,000 blind bets into the pot. Riddle, advanced in age, once played for twenty-four hours straight and quit only because he had to attend a board of directors meeting at the Dunes. Trying to recoup his massive losses in the game, he made the other players promise they wouldn't quit while he was gone. They won enormous sums of money in those games. They played the legendary "Frenchman," Francis Gross, even traveling to Paris for one final game when he was too sick to travel. (The Frenchman went out in style, winning over a million dollars from his visitors before peacefully expiring.) Chip also played against Archie Karas, the daring gambler who turned a $5,000 loan into more than $10 million during an amazing run at pool and craps. They both played with George the Greek, the colorful, volatile tycoon who once set his cards on fire in anger at the Mirage. (Mike Laing, in a similar fit, once *ate* one of his cards.)

John Hennigan learned his gambling in Philadelphia, where he started as a professional pool player and turned to poker when he ran out of opponents. Nicknamed Johnny World because of his willingness to bet on anything, he once took a bet that he couldn't live within the Des Moines city limits for a month. (There were different stories about how that bet concluded, but Hennigan did not last the month.) Hennigan was part of the new breed of high-stakes pros in their thirties. He was an erratic player, but his A-game had even the top pros in awe.

Chau Giang, Jennifer Harman, and Todd Brunson had all arrived at Table One by the same route, but by overcoming different obstacles. Giang, forty-six, had left his native Vietnam with almost nothing in the late 1970s and settled in Colorado Springs as a cook in a Chinese restaurant. Unable to make ends meet, he started making money in local low-stakes poker games. He moved to Las Vegas and worked his way up, like Brunson and Harman, level by level, until he was a premier player in the highest games. In fact, he was establishing himself as the biggest winner at Table One. He was so skilled that a few other players believed he might be using voodoo, a belief he was aware of and did nothing to discourage.

Jennifer Harman, a small, attractive blonde in her mid-thirties with delicate features, was the only woman who regularly played and won at such high stakes. She had no role models or mentors and was naturally slower than her peers to become part of the all-male Vegas poker subculture. Gradually, she won their respect, which was inevitable when she won their money. She also had to deal with being estranged from her father for many years as a result of her career choice.

Among the top players, few of them had families initially supportive of their decision to become professional gamblers. Even Todd Brunson, whose father was Doyle Brunson, had trouble at home with the decision. While players would snidely remark that his famous father's money and instruction paved his way to Table One, the opposite, in fact, was true.

If Andy Beal was intimidated by the quality of his opposition, he did not show it. In fact, he insisted on raising the stakes, from $1,000–$2,000 to $2,000–$4,000, $3,000–$6,000, and finally $4,000–$8,000 by the end of the second day, making it the highest-stakes game since the Bellagio opened in 1998.

As the game filled up, it became less fun for Andy, and he kept raising the stakes to maintain his interest, as well as to test the professionals. Jennifer Harman had never played this high and noticed everyone was playing tighter than usual, saving bets, and abandoning the aggressiveness that was the hallmark of the highest-stakes professionals.

Andy Beal is backing down the best players in the world by raising the limits, she thought. This is unbelievable.

Andy won over $100,000 in a game filled with the world's top money players. He was flabbergasted. Maybe I'm actually a good poker player, he thought. But he also realized that he had a lot more fun playing three-handed against Todd Brunson and the Irishman, then heads up against Todd, going wild-man.

He returned to Dallas and the professionals knew little more about him than when he arrived. But they were sure of one thing.

He would be back.

2

Heads Up

March 2001

Andy Beal felt uneasy on the American Airlines flight from Dallas to Las Vegas. The more he thought about his success at poker the month before, the more he realized he had simply gotten lucky. To succeed this time, he would need more than luck. He would need to attack the edge the professionals typically enjoyed. And he would have to be careful.

Upon his return from the previous trip, he asked an assistant to order the fifteen best-selling poker books on Amazon.com. He had been reading them, but they offered only a little help. He agreed with the books that the concept of pot odds was of paramount importance, but they did not give enough attention to the statistics.

Pot odds are the payout offered by the pot expressed in comparison to the price to call a bet. For example, if there was $100 in the pot and the player had to put in $20, the pot was offering 5-to-1 odds. These odds were then compared to the likelihood the player making the decision would win the hand, either by having the best cards or drawing to the best hand. When it came to figuring out what hand an opponent had, pot odds became subjective. If a player had two pair and a straight draw (four cards to a straight), the likelihood of winning the hand depended on whether the player needed a straight to win. But Andy found the books deficient in presenting objective information. He knew mathematical tables weren't for everyone, but the key to the game was understanding the probabilities. Without knowing them, all the strategies advocated by the authors would be less effective.

The basic strategy advocated in these books was too conservative. Sure, you should raise with a pair of aces, but you could expect them only once in 221 hands. There just wasn't enough action in the waiting game. Finally, the books devoted almost no attention to shorthanded games. If Andy could arrange it, he would play with just a few opponents or heads up.

Andy also had conflicting thoughts about the character of his opponents. They had been nothing but friendly and gracious to him, but he did not really know them or their world. Could they have been letting him win? Were his winning sessions just their way of baiting the hook, keeping him interested? Somehow, he doubted that they would give away over $100,000 on just a hint of a greater return. He also had to consider that it was unlikely he was being hustled because he was the one who wanted to keep increasing the stakes. Still, he wanted the stakes high enough that no one would toss him an occasional win.

He was more concerned about the opposite situation, being cheated. Again, everything about them and the game seemed aboveboard, but they were all intimately familiar with both one another and all the angles, while he was the only outsider in their game.

Beal was only vaguely aware of poker's seamy past. No one liked to talk about the details, but before 1980, some players would hold out cards and slip them back into play at opportune moments. Unscrupulous casino personnel would occasionally collude with players, putting marked cards in the game, readable only by highly trained cheats. Most of these practices developed in the era when the mob had a big presence in the operation of casinos. (Even the mob, however, could get cheated in a poker room. Doyle Brunson told a story in *Gambling Wizards*, a series of interviews with gamblers conducted by Richard Munchkin, about the late Johnny Moss, who won the World Series of Poker championship three times and was hailed, by the end of his life, as the "Grand Old Man of Poker." Back in the 1950s, Moss had told Brunson, he tried to cheat Flamingo owner Gus Greenbaum by having compatriots peeking at his opponent's cards through a hole in the wall. He was discovered, barely escaped with his life, and stayed away from Vegas for nearly two decades.)

At least in Las Vegas, that era ended long ago. The new generation of players around 1980, including Chip Reese and Eric Drache, started running card rooms themselves, stamping out such practices and letting the old-time cheaters die out. In the ethic of the times, they usually let the known cheaters play if they promised not to cheat. Eric Drache swore that the cheaters usually honored their promise. According to Reese, the cheaters, when they weren't cheating, were the worst players in the game and they were desperate to gamble whether they could cheat or not. The ones who didn't die off simply lost all their money.

The influx of corporate investment in Las Vegas, first from Howard Hughes in the 1960s, then from Hilton, Holiday Inn, Sheraton, and Mandalay Resort Group (originally Circus Circus) and high-profile individuals like Kirk Kerkorian, drove out the dirty money and created an incentive to clean up unsavory practices. A company like MGM Mirage (made up of pieces of Kerkorian's holdings, plus the former Golden Nugget/Mirage public company) made hundreds of millions of dollars per year from its gaming licenses. There was too much money to be made honestly, far more than could be made cheating on poker or even risking the taint of a cheating scandal.

In fact, several casino operators were high-stakes players. Bellagio president Bobby Baldwin was the 1978 World Champion and played in a $4,000–$8,000 game with Doyle Brunson, Chip Reese, and a few others during each year's World Series. Another regular in that game was Lyle Berman, a founder of the World Poker Tour and a principal in several companies that operated casinos. These men would be putting too much at risk to participate in a game where cheating was a possibility. The caliber of players in the biggest games also made cheating less likely in those games than anywhere else. The best players didn't need to cheat and were the least likely victims because of their observational skills. The highest-stakes players also policed their games. Nothing could kill a poker game faster than the possibility of cheating.

Nevada gaming regulations, technology, and the desire to remove all doubt about the honesty of the games created an entirely different atmosphere compared with Vegas's Wild West days. Take the playing cards. Dealers would change the deck every half-hour and the setup (the two different-colored decks at each table) every hour. The decks were kept in a secure location, under constant surveillance. Kem, the company that sold the Bellagio poker room thousands of decks of cards per year, placed an extra seal on each deck, which was broken in view of the players. Dealers were trained in a detailed ritual of spreading, counting, making available for inspection, and handling the deck.

In addition, dealers changed tables every thirty minutes and were randomly assigned. They never knew before their shift at which tables they would be dealing. Cameras kept the poker room and the area around it under constant surveillance. This included the areas immediately outside the room: the entrances from the casino, the Starting Line bar, and the sports book; the offices; the area where the dealers took their breaks; the cashier's cage and the privacy room where players opened their safe deposit boxes. A camera was trained on every table twenty-four hours a day.

The only cheating even remotely possible in a Las Vegas poker room was when two players, without the knowledge of the casino or other players in the game, colluded to signal their cards and manipulate the betting. It was almost unheard of in big games, but theoretically possible.

Throughout the two-and-a-half-hour flight, Andy Beal struggled, both to fit his six-foot, two-inch frame comfortably in the cramped coach seat, and to figure out how to prevent the possibility that some of the pros might team up against him. The ideal situation, he realized, was to play heads up.

He had broached the subject during his February trip. On a short break, he saw Jennifer Harman standing in the sports book. Jennifer was on the waiting list for Andy's game and was just killing time.

"Jennifer," he had asked, "how about you and I play heads up for a little while?"

It was difficult to explain to Andy why she couldn't do that. If they started another game, it would immediately fill up with players on the waiting list or players from his original game following him to the new game. The prospect of taking Andy's money packed the poker room's high-limit tables. Jennifer could not separate Andy from the herd without repercussions.

"Then how about we break up the game into two tables and play shorthanded?"

Beal did not quite understand that any game he played would fill up, even if he kept raising the stakes. The Bellagio was a public place of business. You could not keep players from sitting down at a table, and if Andy and his money were there, players definitely would have taken all the empty seats.

Andy had called Doug Dalton, the manager of the Bellagio

poker room, and asked for an accommodation. Dalton explained that anyone could sit at any game in the poker room if they had the minimum buy-in, so he could not exclude anyone who wanted to play.

"Look," Andy said, getting frustrated, "I'll pay the time charge for every other seat at the table. But if I can't play heads up, I'm going to play somewhere else."

Dalton said, "I'm sorry but I can't do anything about it."

Beal was furious. He was aware of the outrageous demands that casinos fulfilled for big players. Maybe they just didn't take him seriously yet.

He made up his mind. He would raise the issue again with Doyle Brunson, and not take no for an answer. He had wired several million dollars to the Bellagio earlier in the day. If that didn't show how serious he was, perhaps he would have to find another poker room and other players.

If a blackjack or craps high-roller had asked for a private table, the casino would have accommodated him. If he brought a seven-figure bankroll to gamble, they would probably get Wayne Newton to pull his chair out when he sat down. But poker was different.

Casinos made very little money directly from their poker operations. Nevada gaming regulations limited the Bellagio to raking 10 percent of the amount wagered per hand. Based on the structure established by the poker room, the house usually raked much less, on a scale based on the size of the pot, with a maximum of $3–$5, depending on the game. This was the arrangement for games at limits of $15–$30 and below. For higher-stakes games, the Bellagio took even less, in the form of a time charge every half-hour of $6–$10, depending on the stakes. Unlike the other games in the casino, where the Bellagio was betting against the player, the casino bore no risk of loss, so running a poker room provided a reliable, steady profit, assuming the room was busy and management kept costs under control. But casinos *wanted* to risk losing to the players in exchange for the chance at greater profits. The odds were in their favor, and any casino could make more from rows of slot machines than it could from poker tables.

Before the current poker boom, the stereotypical view of poker by casino management was that it was an unwelcome distraction or, at best, attracted tightfisted locals who dressed sloppy, complained a lot, and wanted everything for free. Until 2003, the Las Vegas resorts were closing their rooms and the new properties never bothered offering poker. Five men share the credit for keeping poker alive in Las Vegas until the current frenzy reversed the course and found casinos scrambling to open and even expand their poker rooms: Jack Binion, Steve Wynn, Eric Drache, Bobby Baldwin, and Doug Dalton.

The 1970s were, in a sense, the "bad old days," with the threat of cheating, but poker also flourished. Bill Boyd, considered the greatest Five Card Draw player in history, had run the Golden Nugget's poker room for over thirty years, keeping a commitment in Las Vegas to honest poker. The Horseshoe did not have a poker room but hosted the World Series of Poker and spread poker during the Series. The Dunes, Stardust, Flamingo, Sahara, MGM Grand, Aladdin, Silver Bird, and Caesars Palace all had substantial poker rooms at various times during the 1970s. Johnny Moss, Chip Reese, Doyle Brunson, Bobby Baldwin, and Eric Drache all managed or hosted rooms.

Steve Wynn, the charismatic CEO of the Golden Nugget and a poker player (he could be seen in a crude video of an early World Series of Poker playing in the main event, wearing what looks like a Confederate soldier's uniform), began monopolizing poker talent. Wynn looked for management talent in different places than his competitors, but he saved poker in Las Vegas during the process.

Wynn hired Eric Drache to run the Golden Nugget card room. Drache, in turns both cultured and street-savvy, discovered poker in Las Vegas on a weekend trip in 1970 and never left. (Serendipity had always played a large role in guiding Drache's professional life. He dropped out of Rutgers when he found out after a day at Freehold Raceway that he had missed a chemistry exam.) Drache ran the World Series of Poker from 1973 to 1989 for the Binion family and kept the tournament afloat in the early years. (The incident that led him to offer his services to the Binions illustrated the level of professionalism in the pre-Drache years: He showed up for the Seven Card Stud championship only to be told it was postponed for a day "because Johnny Moss was up all night playing.")

Drache not only turned the Series from a gathering of gambling buddies to the international event it remains, but he pioneered satellites, minitournaments in which players put up a fraction of a regular tournament buy-in with the winner getting a spot in the main tournament. Satellites were the reason the main event grew from 102 participants in 1982 to 631 in 2002. The skyrocketing attendance at the main event—2,576 entries in 2004—had been the result of online poker sites running World Series of Poker satellites.

Eric Drache had a deal with his friend Bobby Baldwin. Whichever one of them got a job running a poker room first would bring in the other. Steve Wynn, therefore, hired Baldwin as the poker host. Baldwin, an intense young Oklahoman nicknamed "The Owl," was a top high-stakes poker player. Baldwin had so impressed Wynn that Wynn promoted him out of the poker room and into management at the Golden Nugget. Baldwin later became president of the Mirage, chief financial officer of Mirage Resorts (the public company acquired by MGM Grand in 1999), chief executive officer of Mirage Resorts after the acquisition, and president of the Bellagio.

Drache ran the Golden Nugget poker room until it closed in 1989, then opened the Mirage poker room nine months later. He was the poker manager at the Mirage until 1993. He later worked with longtime poker enthusiast Larry Flynt, publisher of *Hustler*, on purchasing a casino in Los Angeles. While waiting for the casino to open—a process that took several years, because it needed to be rebuilt—Eric organized a Seven Card Stud game at Flynt's home that eventually ran for 400 nights before moving to the Hustler Casino. Stakes rose from $400–$800 to $2,000–$4,000, making it one of the highest continuing games of all-time, rivaling Bellagio's Table One.

Despite Drache's youthful appearance—he still wore his graying hair in the Beatle style he favored thirty years ago—he emerged from the poker boom as an elder statesman for the business. The new owners of the Golden Nugget hired him to consult in 2004 when they reopened their poker room. He also worked on a variety of other projects, including arranging some of the one-time televised poker tournaments that have sprung up during the current craze, including Fox's Poker Superstars Invitational.

But during the 1990s, poker in Las Vegas was dying. To some degree, the Mirage's commitment to poker (and the Horseshoe's emergence as the downtown poker destination for the low-stakes locals) pushed out some marginal poker rooms. For the most part, however, the Mirage was dominating a market no one else wanted.

The Mirage became the home of many of the world's best poker players, but even Steve Wynn's commitment to poker was put to the test. Wynn became furious when he learned that one of his biggest baccarat players, George the Greek, had started splitting his time (and his money) between the baccarat pit and the poker room.

Steve Wynn is a bottom-line sort of guy. A $1,000–$2,000 poker player pays the house a maximum of $10 per half-hour to play; wins and losses are between the players, not (as in the table games) between the players and the house. A $2,000-per-hand baccarat player, facing a 1 percent disadvantage, is theoretically giving the house that much per hand. At 100 baccarat hands per hour, the casino expects to make $2,000; when that player goes into the poker room, the casino gets $20.

When Wynn heard that George had gone off for a big number in a poker game, he was beyond arguing about theoretical loss rates. He wanted to close down the poker room. "I didn't build this place to make Doyle Brunson and Chip Reese richer," he said. It took all of Bobby Baldwin's persuasive ability to keep the room open, and to keep Wynn from adopting his other sanction—barring Brunson and Reese from the property.

Ultimately, keeping the room open was a wise decision. George the Greek was originally a Caesars Palace customer. Caesars had closed its poker room when the Mirage opened. Even though George originally played poker for relatively low stakes, he took his action next door because Wynn's property allowed him to play both baccarat and poker. The Mirage, and then the Bellagio, also built by Steve Wynn, in part out of the Mirage's profits, have made large sums of money because big players have checked out the poker room and lost in the pits before returning to their "regular" place, or switched allegiances to the casino offering them poker along with their favorite pit games such as craps, blackjack, baccarat, or roulette. In addition, the big winners in the poker room frequently gave their profits back to the casino in the pits. Many poker pros have kept the Bellagio from winning customers' money by taking it off them in the poker room, only to lose gigantic amounts at blackjack, craps, and sports betting.

Wynn's last big deal at Mirage Resorts (the name of the public company after it outgrew Golden Nugget Corporation) was building the Bellagio. Wynn was not completely committed to putting a poker room in the new resort, which would be one of the most expensive and lavish ever built in Las Vegas. Baldwin and Doug Dalton, who ran the Mirage poker room after learning the business in the 1970s and 1980s in various rooms operated by Reese, Brunson, and Drache, lobbied hard for a poker room in the new property. Dalton believed he could run poker rooms at both the Mirage and the Bellagio, and fill them both. Baldwin trusted his judgment, and argued to Wynn that poker contributed indirectly but significantly to the Mirage's bottom line and the company's best property, attracting its highest rollers, should have the best poker room.

Wynn relented, and Dalton proceeded to make the poker room into a marketing tool for the resort. The carpeting and wall murals gave the room the feel of a luxurious English parlor room from the nineteenth century. Dalton promoted the room around the world, attending poker tournaments and encouraging the top players to visit.

Dalton also brought in Jack McClelland, another Las Vegas veteran who worked with Eric Drache and Jack Binion on the World Series of Poker, as well as pioneering poker tournaments at other venues. They played an important part in starting the World Poker Tour, establishing the Bellagio as the host of the first WPT event and as the home of the season-ending WPT Championship. Dalton and McClelland had the Bellagio host other poker tournaments to show off the property and promote poker. In the current environment, the Bellagio was the closest thing poker had to a home field.

Steve Wynn no longer has a place in this empire. He left after MGM Grand acquired Mirage Resorts in 2000. But Wynn's influence is still apparent and many of his chief lieutenants stayed on. For Doug Dalton, Wynn's presence is more tangible. He snagged Wynn's last office chair from storage for the tiny office he maintains behind the poker room. The chair is so nice that Kerry Packer, the Australian media billionaire who occasionally drops by the Bellagio to gamble astronomical sums at blackjack, specifically requests it for his room.

Despite the tremendous growth in poker's popularity, its hold in the casino has always been tenuous. That Andy Beal wanted to play for the highest stakes in history at the Bellagio added to the poker room's reputation, but it was still making only $20 per hour off the millions he was willing to bet. (The time charge later increased to $100 per hour, plus a similar amount to tip the casino staff. It was still just a fraction of what the casino would expect to earn if he brought, say, one-tenth the bankroll to the Bellagio, but bet it at craps, blackjack, baccarat, or roulette.)

Kerry Packer could *have* Doug Dalton's chair. For Andy Beal, Doug Dalton would *get up* from his chair, but only to tell Beal that the Bellagio would not change its rules for him. What he wanted interfered with Nevada regulations and the prevailing practice in Las Vegas for over thirty years. And the people most likely to complain were the high-stakes pros shut out of whatever exclusive game Beal wanted to stage, and some of them were the casino's best customers.

Doyle Brunson came up with the solution. Even at very high stakes, a lot of players wanted to be in a game with Andy Beal. The waiting list from the $4,000–$8,000 game the month before proved that. At those stakes and higher, players would simply sell a percentage of themselves to get into the game. Professional poker players were the ultimate independent businessmen. They had no bosses, no employees, and no set hours. But they were thinly capitalized—more so in the highest games than at the lower rungs—and their bankroll requirements could vary drastically. No one regularly played at Table One on other people's money, but players would sometimes take a financial partner for a higher-stakes game.

What if all the players who wanted to play Andy took a piece of one another and he played just one of them (or several of them, one at a time)? If everyone who might sit down at the table was part of the group, Andy and one player could play undisturbed. This also provided the players a financial cushion, though a few of them might play Andy at the stakes he sought on their own bankrolls and others would have simply found nonplaying financial backers.

Doyle did not have much time to arrange this. Andy pressed his demand when he arrived at the poker room and, though he sat down to play a ring game for a little while, he insisted that he wanted to play $15,000–$30,000 and would do so only if he could play heads up. In fact, if he couldn't play heads up, he might just go back home to Dallas.

Brunson canvassed the other players in the game, and then called around town to reach others who could conceivably sit down in a game that size. His goal was to keep players from walking in on the game, not spreading the wealth or creating a fraternity of high-stakes players. He limited his efforts to Las Vegas players, not even inviting Todd to join because he was out of town.

The business of presiding over a group of poker players was not something Brunson wanted to do. He took the task reluctantly and only because the circumstances required it. Beal was a new face in the poker room, someone clearly capable of losing a lot of money. Many players wanted a shot, but Andy threw a wrench in the meritocracy by insisting on playing heads up.

If someone didn't take charge, it would be bad for poker. First, Beal could leave town, giving up high-stakes poker forever or until he could get what he wanted. Apart from Brunson's economic motive to keep that from happening, it was antithetical to how poker players operated to let anything get in the way of a game. A poker player who knows he has an edge considers his flexibility an important tool of the trade.

Second, for Beal to get what he wanted, he risked getting hustled, which was bad for poker, bad for Beal, and bad for pros like Brunson who felt the way they comported themselves affected how other players behaved, and generally set the standard for the business. Without some means of organizing, individual players might approach Beal about playing him heads up. Because, as Jennifer Harman recognized, that wouldn't fly in a public room, these would be private games, without the security offered by the Bellagio.

In addition, even if everyone proposed honest heads-up contests with him, it would be open season on Andy. Some players would call him in his room to beat the competition. The next time, a player who missed out would wait in the lobby. Then someone would get a leg up by meeting him at the airport. That player would lose out to those who called him in Dallas. Yet another player might camp out in his bank's parking lot to preempt the others. Such a competition would probably cost everybody money, especially because it is hard to imagine a new, wealthy player remaining keen on playing after such a display.

It would be an understatement to say, however, that poker players are difficult to manage. Most chose poker because they didn't want to be subject to anyone else's rules. Every one of them was idiosyncratic about making financial and scheduling commitments. Although they tended to agree on strategic matters, that was merely because they all had phenomenal capacities for strategic thought. They generally had few opportunities to exchange opinions and rarely had to give in to someone else's authority.

Despite Brunson's position of seniority and universal respect, he did not consider himself management material. Most of the other players weren't even born the last time he held a conventional job. Doyle and those who loved him got a kick out of telling stories about his shortcomings in adapting his tremendous poker talents to seemingly mundane business and financial matters.

But Doyle was the man for the job. He was regarded by

friends and detractors (of which there were few, but poker players can't agree on *anything*) as the king, the godfather. Now he would add another unofficial title: CEO.

The most he could mount was a haphazard effort. Andy wanted to play at noon the next day, Wednesday, March 7, so Doyle had only Tuesday night to reach other players. Although many of the top players are friends, seeing each other several times a week and talking on the phone about travel plans, business ventures, or golf matches, poker players keep odd hours and are just not reachable sometimes. Doyle contacted and received commitments from Chip Reese, Jennifer Harman, Howard Lederer, John Hennigan, Chau Giang, and David Grey.

He decided they should pool together $1 million. Those in the group, if they were not playing that night, had to retrieve the chips from their safe deposit boxes and give them to Doyle before noon the next day.

That evening, Brunson explained the situation to Beal. He contacted everyone he thought might be a threat to get into the game, and though Beal would play only one opponent, that opponent would be playing his or her own money plus the money of other players in the group. This disappointed Andy a little, because he knew that even the professionals, at a certain level, would feel the pressure of the stakes, and joining forces would minimize their exposure. But his main objective was to play heads up, and he was getting his wish.

They argued over the details. Andy wanted to choose his opponents. Doyle gave in, but asked if Chip Reese could play him first, because the match would be the next day and there was only so much time to make sure the player was available. Andy agreed.

Andy wanted both sides to bring $1 million to the game, and Doyle agreed. He was willing to give Beal just about whatever he wanted; he expected they had a huge edge over Andy and wanted him to feel comfortable in the game. Doyle did, however, hold the stakes down to $10,000–$20,000. Those stakes would make the game the biggest ever played, but Andy had raised his demand to $15,000–$30,000, primarily because when he suggested $10,000–$20,000, the players didn't seem especially worried. The pros were famous for being unconcerned with the size of the stakes, and he hoped he could get an advantage by *making* them concerned. But Doyle insisted on this, and Beal gave in.

Before they parted for the night, Doyle reminded the banker that certain parts of this arrangement were beyond their control. The Bellagio poker room was open to the public. It was unlikely someone would just sit down at those stakes, especially because all the most likely players to do that were part of the group, but it could not be prevented.

The next day, that is exactly what happened. Ted Forrest was one of those rare gamblers willing to bet everything on the right situation, and Doyle never reached Ted because he was in California. Unaware of the negotiations or the financial arrangements among the players, Ted sat down in Seat Six just after 1:00 P.M. simply because it seemed like a good game, a moneymaking opportunity.

Almost instantly, he regretted the decision. The $500,000 he brought to the table was his entire bankroll, and he lost 80 percent of it in twenty minutes, and didn't even get much action for his $400,000.

Besides repeatedly wishing he had not sat down at this game, Ted also reminded himself to remain calm. Look for a good situation where you can make a stand and hopefully win a pot.

He found such a situation, got his money in, and won. He was still down $270,000, but he was finding a comfort zone. He got into the rhythm of the game, won a few pots, and was soon even.

Then he went on a tear—good cards, good draws, good bluffs—and Chip Reese couldn't do much but stay out of the way while Ted manipulated Beal, getting the most out of his good hands, scaring Andy out of some situations where Andy had the better hand, and conceding some small pots.

Andy was out of money before dinnertime. Without talking to Chip or the stunned onlookers at Table One, Ted Forrest left the table with more than three racks of flags, a profit of $1,035,000.

He walked to the cage, requested his box, and dumped the three racks inside. He did not request a check (a regular practice when cashing out a large amount in chips). He already figured some of that money would be in action at the craps tables over the next few days.

Then he retrieved the Mark VIII from the garage and went home.

That night, Ted received two interesting telephone calls. In the first call, he learned about the group, Brunson's earlier negotiations with Beal, and how sick everybody was that Ted walked in and won all the money.

There were no hard feelings. As Doyle told Andy, it was a public room. Ted had the balls and the money to sit down and play, and reaped the rewards. The players wanted that money for themselves, and believed Ted kept Chip Reese from getting it, but they admired him for it.

In fact, they wanted to prevent the situation from happening again. Would Ted like to join the group? Ted agreed, and then found out that Andy wanted a rematch, just the two of them, the next afternoon.

The second call came from Eric Drache. Drache probably had the biggest Rolodex in the poker world. He knew Ted because he was responsible for getting Ted into Larry Flynt's game. Drache worked for Flynt in setting up the game, though he turned down numerous opportunities to profit from it. Even though Drache rode the financial roller coaster more than most poker players, his sense of ethics would not allow him to profit in this fashion. On the other hand, he would *borrow* money from anyone and everyone. He was responsible for the adage "Only a fool plays poker with his own money."

Drache knew nothing of the poker game with Andy Beal and Chip Reese. Part of his daily routine, however, was calling around to borrow money and it was Ted's turn to get a call.

"Ted, I don't know if you've got any money these days, but I could really use the help. Could I borrow $12,000 from you?"

Ted laughed. Ted Forrest has said of Eric, whom he likes and respects, "Eric lives the best out of anybody who's broke. Many times on a plane, I've walked past him on the way back to coach, where I'd sit between two 300-pound people, and see Eric, who has $17 in his pocket, sitting in first class."

"Eric, I was coming back from California this morning and I was low on cash, but you're in luck. I found a game at the Bellagio where Chip Reese and a stranger were playing $10,000–$20,000 hold 'em, and I just won a million dollars. I think I can help you out."

Andy Beal and Ted Forrest met the next afternoon for a rematch, this time heads up. No one joined the game this time (or ever again). Andy came out firing chips, even more aggressive than the day before, if such a thing was possible. Forrest had his opponent sized up, however, and rolled over him. On drawing hands, he would accommodate Beal and trap him. In mixing up his play, he noticed that the banker would not be bluffed. Consequently, Ted realized that if Andy had any kind of hand at all—even ace-high—he would stay in to the end, checking and calling. Although the pro would still throw in an occasional bluff attempt, just to keep the novice's distrust level high, this allowed Forrest to get the maximum from his strong hands.

Andy also continued to agitate to raise the stakes, this time to $20,000–$40,000. Ted obliged and won $2 million for the group.

Jennifer Harman was feeling the pressure, but it had nothing to do with the stakes. After spending a couple of days in the poker room playing one game while she and the other players craned their necks to watch another game, she decided to wait at home for her turn. Andy was choosing his opponents, so she had no idea whether she would play him or when.

She would be playing stakes of at least $10,000–$20,000, more than double the highest she had ever played, and ten times the size of her regular game. Nearly all the money belonged to her friends and peers. Playing on her colleagues' bankroll made her much more nervous than the size of the stakes. The waiting, however, was worst of all.

Jennifer Harman did not look like a poker player. She looked more like an actress; think of Helen Hunt or Meg Ryan, sweet and likable, but much tougher in adversity than you would expect. Writers have frequently described Harman with references to actresses, which was ironic because she played a poker player in the independently produced film *The Big Blind*. Jennifer was just five-two and 100 pounds, with blond hair and delicate features.

Away from the table, unless she was angry, she projected a frailty inconsistent with the stereotypical view of the world's best players. In a game, however, she looked completely at home. She played with tremendous confidence, maintained the balance between being responsible with her money and being indifferent to losing, and had an intensity (and accompanying poker stare) as intimidating as any male player.

Of course, part of the struggle of Jennifer's career had been that women were not expected to be poker players. Poker could be such a lonely occupation, and the low periods could be so devastating, that seeing how players in your situation have succeeded could be an important sustaining force. Howard Lederer, for example, struggled several times as a young poker player in New York in the mid-1980s. But playing at the Mayfair Club in New York, with players who had won at the World Series and played and won in big games in Vegas, convinced him at least that it was possible. When Ted Forrest moved to Las Vegas with a few hundred dollars and the crazy idea that he could make a living playing poker, some dealers at the Palace Station poker room helped him along and even taught him to deal, an experience he credited with teaching him his talent for reading opponents.

Jennifer had no one like that.

No one could really understand how difficult it was for Jennifer Harman to become one of the best poker players in the world. Disguising your feelings, or just not showing them, is an elemental part of poker. But Jennifer seemed like a person forced to make her way alone.

Jennifer Caramello grew up in Reno, in a very close-knit family. The family played games together and she learned to play poker when she was only eight. She took to the game so well that by the time she was twelve, she would play for her father in his home game if he was losing. She was precociously talented at reading other players and benefited—not for the last time, by a long shot—from older men underestimating her ability. She never failed to win her father's money back.

When Jennifer was a teenager, a hereditary kidney condition took her mother's life and required that Jennifer receive a kidney transplant. Jennifer went to college to study medicine, but her poker talent intervened. She started playing locally and her father thought it was interfering with school.

"If you play poker, you won't get anything from me," she recalled him saying. She later realized now that his stubbornness was just fear. "I wanted to be a doctor and now I'm a poker player? What is that? He was scared. 'She's going to throw away her life.'

He comes from Reno. 'All the gamblers I know are broke and living on the street.'" Her father finally accepted her career choice in 1997. He had great respect for her abilities—as he did when she was twelve—and now realized that this was the work she was meant to do. But who could have predicted such a thing? They went several years without speaking.

Between 1989 and 1995, Jennifer played \$50–\$100, \$75–\$150, and \$100–\$200 Texas Hold 'Em in Reno, Los Angeles, and Las Vegas. The first time she saw the big game at the Mirage in the early 1990s, a \$300–\$600 game, she thought, I want to play in *that* game.

Finding a game she could beat was never her goal. She wanted to become good enough to play in the biggest game in the room and win.

This began a pattern that lasted from the late 1980s to 1997. Every time Jennifer would build her bankroll, she would take a shot at the \$200–\$400 or \$300–\$600 game, lose all her money, then start building her stake back up again. She moved to Las Vegas in 1993 so she could take a shot at the bigger games at the Mirage, and went broke. Harman was devastated. She hated borrowing money, having to rely on someone else. But she swallowed her pride, borrowed \$50,000, and drove herself even harder to pay the money back and prove she could succeed in Las Vegas. (She repaid the money in four months.) Every attempt to move beyond the \$100–\$200 hold 'em game, however, ended in failure. At least eight times, by her count, she moved up and lost enough to be forced back into the lower game. She can still remember the stress of sitting down to a game with her entire bankroll on the line.

By 1997, however, Jennifer Harman finally broke through. She started winning at the bigger games, and spent a year playing in the \$400–\$800 game, as well as learning other forms of poker. Although hold 'em was by far the most popular game in Las

Vegas—Seven Card Stud remained extremely popular in California and on the East Coast, and Europeans increasingly preferred Omaha—the highest-stakes games in Las Vegas were mixed games, so moving up required playing all the games, and getting your education against the toughest competition you have ever faced.

By the time the Bellagio opened in 1998 and Mirage Resorts (now MGM Mirage) moved the high-stakes poker room to the new property, Jennifer moved up to the biggest game in the room, usually $800–$1,600. As the games got bigger, she kept her place at Table One. Although she would occasionally have someone take a piece of her action in a particularly large game, she preferred to play her own money. "I think it's very important to play with your own money because you just have more heart." In addition, even in the environment of the Bellagio poker room, where money passed so easily between players, habits of self-reliance died hard. "I was always too shy to ask somebody to take a piece of me."

There are, at most, 100 to 200 players in the world who play at least occasionally in a $1,000–$2,000 game. Jennifer regularly played in the toughest game at those stakes, the mixed game at the Bellagio. Only a dozen or so could win regularly at that level and compete on the rare occasions when the stakes rose even higher. Jennifer was also in that select group. A few players, like Doyle Brunson and Chip Reese, had been winning at those stakes longer, and they and a few others were more likely than Jennifer to play in the games above $1,000–$2,000, so it would be overstating her position to say she was *the best* poker player in the world but she was unquestionably one of the best. Because of her painstaking rise to the top of the poker world, she was not an underdog to anyone in the world at any stakes at limit hold 'em. But she also had a unique qualification when it came to ranking players in other games, or evaluating all-around poker skills.

Jennifer won her first World Series bracelet the previous May in the $5,000 buy-in No-Limit Deuce-to-Seven Single-Draw championship. After the main event, Deuce-to-Seven was the most coveted bracelet among the top professionals. The game was rarely spread except in occasional high-stakes mixed games, so the only players entering were high-stakes pros. The Horseshoe ran no satellites for this event, and rebuys were allowed for the first two hours, so entrants might spend more on this tournament than the $10,000 buy-in championship event. The list of Deuce-to-Seven champions was more impressive than the winners of the main event. Jennifer not only became the first woman to win No-Limit Deuce-to-Seven, but she won it the first time she ever played.

The goal in Deuce-to-Seven is to make the lowest possible five-card hand. Because aces are high, pairs are bad, and straights are worse, the best possible low hand is 7-5-4-3-2. There are multiple versions of Deuce-to-Seven, the most notable being Triple-Draw (played in a structure similar to hold 'em with blinds, betting limits, and four betting rounds) and No-Limit Single-Draw. The former is an "action" game that has become popular in high-stakes games within the last few years. The latter is almost never played, except in the $5,000 buy-in World Series event. It takes an enormous amount of games-playing skill to excel in a form of poker that is practically extinct. Jack McClelland, when he was the tournament director of the World Series, was once asked the average age of Deuce-to-Seven players. "Deceased," he answered.

There is a sharp debate over whether Deuce-to-Seven is a game requiring tremendous skill and flair, or a card-drawing contest. Most of the top pros swear by the game, pointing out that, with no exposed cards, players must be adept at reading their opponents. Some high-stakes pros who are not Table One regulars are not so enamored. This group includes excellent poker players who don't play the World Series event and are critical of the sudden high-stakes popularity of the Triple Draw version of the game.

Mike Matusow, a regular in the Bellagio's $400–$800 games

and holder of World Series bracelets in hold 'em and Omaha, doesn't mince words. "Triple Draw is a game for morons!" He will tell this to anyone who will listen, including an open microphone during the 2004 World Series of Poker. Beyond Matusow's bluster is a serious point: Though the lack of exposed cards requires high-level skills at reading opponents, this also makes it difficult to give credibility to a bluff based on exposed or community cards.

Matusow has an aphorism: "If you can't steal, it ain't poker." Mike's poker nickname is "The Mouth," so his opinions are sometimes viewed as ranting.

Although Matusow's criticisms generally apply primarily to Triple-Draw, the lack of exposed cards in both forms of Deuce-to-Seven gives his point some validity. For example, a hold 'em player who checks and calls suddenly leads the betting after an ace appears on the turn. Does he have a hidden ace, or is he bluffing? The art of the bluff is elevated by exposed cards.

Still, whether it was because of the game or the caliber of the players, most of the top pros played only two events in the World Series in 2001: Deuce-to-Seven and the main event. Players of the caliber of Doyle Brunson, Chip Reese, Barry Greenstein, and Howard Lederer were tournament stars by 2004, but that was only because of the recent explosion of televised poker and the opportunities it provided.

Before 2003, ESPN or some lesser cable sports network showed just an hour or two of the main event of the World Series. There was no World Poker Tour on the Travel Channel until late March 2003. ESPN offered seven hours of World Series coverage in 2003 and more than three times as much in 2004. In 2003 and 2004, it reran the coverage dozens of times. Consequently, tournament purses used to be a fraction of those now contested, and those smaller fields were a mine field of hard-bitten tournament pros.

Until recently, high-stakes cash games had been more lucrative. Making it to the final table of a tournament could take two to four days. Apart from the increased luck factor in tournaments—in a freeze-out, one bad hand or lucky draw hurts much more than in a cash game—a pro playing well enough to beat 95 percent of the competition could win many hundreds of thousands of dollars with that quality of play in a cash game. In fact, if the cash game player making it to the final table did not finish first or second, the prize money could prove to be less than the amounts contested in the individual pots of big side games.

This changed with the success of the World Poker Tour and the poker orgy the World Series of Poker has become. Not only have the swollen fields increased prize money—while adding a lot of mediocre players to the field—but the publicity generated by tournament wins could lead to endorsements and sales of books and instructional videos. But that was still a few years away when Jennifer Harman won her Deuce-to-Seven championship.

Jennifer wanted to play Deuce-to-Seven because all the regulars in her Bellagio game were entering. "I really want to play," she told Annie Duke, who rose through the ranks of the Mirage's hold 'em tables with her for several years.

"Then why don't we play it?"

"Right," Jennifer said. "I've never played it in my life and I'm going to start now!"

"I haven't played it either. We'll get a lesson from Howard."

Howard was Howard Lederer, Annie's brother and a friend of Jennifer's. (They had dated briefly a few years earlier.)

Howard gave them a five-minute lesson, explaining the hand quality needed to play in different positions. Deuce-to-Seven, because there were no exposed cards, had a lot more to do with feel than strategy, and Jennifer demonstrated her feel for the game by winning the tournament, beating Lyle Berman heads up. Berman, who played in only the biggest cash games in the world, had won three World Series bracelets, including Deuce-to-Seven.

* * *

Harman had been so successful in such a difficult game that the only basis for a debate over who was the best female player in the world was ignorance. Annie Duke was better known, but that was because she finished tenth in the main event of the World Series in 2000 while eight months pregnant, juggled poker with raising a family, was close to her Ph.D. in psycholinguistics at the University of Pennsylvania, and was the sister of Howard Lederer and Katy Lederer, a poet and author who chronicled their remarkable family in *Poker Face*. But it had been several years since Annie had played in the cash games Jennifer played, and Jennifer was the winner of those games. Annie played primarily in tournaments, and even then Jennifer Harman had a more impressive record.

To kill time while waiting for a call to play Andy Beal, and to adjust to the stakes and the heads-up format, Jennifer and her husband, Marco, broke out the play chips and practiced a million-dollar freeze-out. Cash games are usually not freeze-outs, but the game with Beal contained some elements of the format. On this trip, Andy and his opponent each brought $1 million to the table and generally played until one side had all the chips. But either side could rebuy or end the game by leaving.

Marco Traniello married Jennifer just five months before, and his initiation into the poker world was rough.

During their courtship—three months—Jennifer went on an unbelievable winning streak. On any night, Marco might ask, "How much did you win tonight?"

"Fifty thousand."

"Oh, only fifty thousand? That's it?"

It was a joke they shared, but between the winning streak and the new romance, the pessimist in Jennifer kept asking herself, What happens when I go on a losing streak?

As they pretended to play poker for a million dollars, their marriage was experiencing that first losing streak. After months of practically never seeing Jennifer lose, it was becoming a regular occurrence.

Jennifer had been riding this roller coaster for fifteen years and was not concerned. She could not, however, get Marco to understand it. He grew up in Italy, half a world away from Reno and Las Vegas, and had played poker only a few times in his life. The outrageous sums his wife gambled *when she won* jarred him. Nothing could prepare him for an extended period in which she lost those amounts. And in the midst of this losing streak, she was going to put up a substantial portion of her depleted bankroll to have other people play poker, and she would then play their money for the highest stakes of her life.

The mood in the Traniello home was glum when the high brush from the Bellagio called. Marco had just won their freeze-out.

"You have to come down here and play poker against Andy. You have to leave *now*." Shortly after hanging up the phone, she received five phone calls, all from other members of the group. The message was always the same. "Get down here. Get down here. Get down here."

As Howard Lederer and Ted Forrest gave her a pep talk in the moments before starting the poker game against Andy Beal, she could think only negative thoughts.

Everyone else is counting on me.

I've just been defeated by my husband, who has played poker about four times ever.

I'm going to play in the biggest game of my life for a million dollars of my friends' money.

Everybody has beaten him and I'm going to be the big loser. (In fact, Andy Beal had played some heads-up poker for smaller stakes on the trip against pros that weren't in the group, often while waiting for his next opponent to arrive. He did much better in those matches.)

The next thing she knew, she was seated at Table Seven, with ten neat stacks of $5,000 flags, twenty chips per stack.

I must be out of my mind.

But Jennifer Harman only *seemed* brittle. The stress, the nerves, and the doubts were all caused by the uncertainty of waiting. Once the game started, it wasn't about a million dollars, or the responsibility of safeguarding the money of her friends and peers.

It was about making smart decisions and Jennifer did not become one of the best poker players in the world by being cute or sweet or vulnerable. She got there by making smart decisions a remarkably high percentage of the time, under a variety of trying conditions: folding a strong hand to an opponent's stronger hand, even though the opponent has yet to show strength; raising with a weak hand and continuing the bluff when it is clear the opponent would call, to set up future plays where monster hands could be played in precisely the same way; and countless other plays. Every play, every trick, every decision in poker had already been tried. The reason the pros were *the pros* was because they made those plays (and detected them in their opponents) more successfully than anyone else.

Jennifer was in control from the start. But every time she had the match nearly closed out, Andy Beal would get the lucky card he needed to win a big pot and keep the game alive.

Finally, after ten hours, Jennifer had twenty stacks of flags, and Andy had only green felt in front of him. The other members of the group left their game at Table One and surrounded Jennifer, but she couldn't make out what they were saying. She couldn't talk. She had used every ounce of mental energy on the match, and was completely exhausted.

Somehow, she made it home, and immediately fell asleep.

* * *

The last player Andy Beal faced in this series of matches was Howard Lederer. Lederer delivered the coup de grâce during a weekend session.

Andy Beal towered over most of his opponents at the table but he looked in danger of being swallowed up by Howard Lederer. Howard was a bear of a man, six and a half feet tall, weighing over 300 pounds, the bottom of his wide face obscured by a heavy black beard.

The bear was almost always in repose. Although Howard's competitive fire may have burned hotter than any of the other elite players, he was always quiet, cool, and analytical. Leaning far back from the table with his arms folded on his chest, he more resembled a chess player studying the board than a poker player in the heat of battle. Howard started as a chess player, running away from home as a teenager to play chess for money on the streets of New York. Poker just happened to get in the way.

A few years later, when a girlfriend made Howard start attending Columbia College, poker again came calling. It would have been interesting to see what kind of impact a computer science major in 1985 with Howard's drive (he maintained a 3.5 GPA his freshman year while making his first $100,000 at poker) could have had at the dawn of the Personal Computer Age, but he gave up the academic life to become "The Professor of Poker."

Ironically, despite Lederer's obvious intelligence and manner (plus the nickname), he spent less time in college than nearly all of his colleagues. Barry Greenstein has only to revise and defend his long-completed dissertation to receive his Ph.D. in math from the University of Illinois. Doyle Brunson received his master's degree in education nearly fifty years ago. Chip Reese graduated from Dartmouth. Ted Forrest quit Le Moyne College, where his father had been a professor, just short of graduation after a dispute with a professor who had feuded with his father. Jennifer Harman and Todd Brunson spent more time in college than

Howard, studying to someday become, respectively, a doctor and a lawyer, before they chose poker.

Howard Lederer came from a remarkable family. His parents were both brilliant academically and very competitive. He grew up on the campus of an elite prep school in New Hampshire, where his father was an English teacher. (Richard Lederer has written, edited, or co-written more than twenty-five books about the English language.) The family had serious contests with puzzles, card games, and board games. The most serious were the chess matches between Howard and his father.

His mother was an alcoholic, and Howard's and his father's attempts to make her stop drinking caused so much tension that he ran away to New York. He was eighteen, a giant of a young man with little money and no plan. But he had an intellectual certainty in the correctness of his actions and an overwhelming desire to succeed.

He did not succeed for a long, long time. At the chess club, he discovered the poker games in the back room that started late in the day and went on through the night. Poker replaced chess as his obsession, but there was one problem: He wasn't any good. He lost every night.

After Howard went through the little money he had, he was homeless for about ten days. He scraped together whatever he could by running errands for players in the poker game, then losing it back to them. He would wander the streets until morning, then lie in the grass at Washington Square Park and sleep for a few hours. He was determined not to call his father for bus fare back to New Hampshire.

He convinced the owner of the club to let him sleep on the couch in exchange for cleaning up the place. But there was still the problem of finding money to play poker.

"I probably borrowed two bucks more than anybody ever," Lederer explained years later, when he could laugh about being so poor for so long. "I would run errands for the games and I'd make enough in tips so I could buy into this one-and-two-dollar game. Invariably, at the end of the night, I'd be broke and I'd borrow two bucks, enough for a pack of cigarettes and a souvlaki sandwich. That would hold me over to the game that night and I'd run errands, pay back the two bucks, and have fifteen bucks or so to buy into the game. Go broke, borrow two bucks again. I did that for two years."

After several months, Howard's father tracked him down and, after talking to the owner of the club, actually supported (or at least did not try to oppose) Howard's decision. It took a great leap of faith by Howard, his father, and the owner of the club, but, for some reason, they all believed Howard was good enough to give this a try.

Slowly and painfully, Howard Lederer learned how to play poker. In 1982, there were no books from which he could soak up some knowledge. All he could find was a collection of tall tales by Amarillo Slim, full of stories about characters with names like Texas Dolly, Treetops, and Puggy, and poker games with names like Deuce-to-Seven No-Limit Draw. It all seemed a million miles away.

After two years, he started beating the $1–$2 game, then the $3–$6 game. The year his girlfriend made him attend college was a grind, but a great learning experience. He would wake up at seven, be at school by eight, arrive at the Mayfair Club (then the best of New York's underground poker clubs) by four, play until midnight, do a little homework and sleep a few hours, and start again. But the real education took place at the Mayfair. He was beating up the $50–$100 game and learning from opponents like Jay Heimowitz, Steve Zolotow, Erik Seidel, Dan Harrington, and Noli Francisco. Erik, a close friend of Howard's, went on to win six World Series of Poker bracelets. Heimowitz came close to winning the championship a couple times in the 1970s and also went on to win six bracelets. Dan Harrington won the world championship in 1995 and made it to the final table on three other occasions.

In 1987, Howard went to Vegas to play in the World Series and finished fifth to Johnny Chan in the championship, becoming the youngest ever to make the final table. (To Howard's chagrin, it proved to be his only final table appearance in the main event.) The next year, Erik bettered his friend, finishing second to Chan. Howard started beating the Mayfair Club game consistently and moved to Las Vegas permanently in 1992. Continuing to move up, by 2001, he was a regular in the biggest games in Vegas.

Howard made short work of Andy, winning a million dollars in less than three hours. Howard played heads-up hold 'em even more aggressively than Andy, and the banker found himself increasingly checking and calling when Howard came charging at him. Doyle Brunson had called Lederer the best limit hold 'em player in the world a few years earlier, and he demonstrated why. If it wasn't clear to Andy Beal before, it certainly was by now: He was far, far behind the poker professionals in every area that counted for this game.

As Andy Beal left town, it seemed everything had gone as the professionals expected. Beal had a lot of money and "a lot of gamble"—which is a huge compliment for gamblers to pay—but not much skill. To paraphrase the namesake of the Bellagio's next-door neighbor, Caesars Palace, "He came. He saw. He was conquered."

3

The Thursday Game

Late March 2001

In late March 2001, about three weeks after his pasting by the poker pros, Andy Beal was back in Las Vegas. He had some bank business in town and decided to drop by the Bellagio poker room.

No one knew he was coming, but word spread fast. Because so few new players simply dropped in to play in the highest games, members of the poker room staff would call the local pros. Many players would also alert their friends.

To outsiders, this might sound like collusion or hustling but, in fact, the opposite is true. Players like Andy Beal want to play the top players. On a Wednesday afternoon, the biggest game in the room could be \$80–\$160. Beal wanted to play much higher, and he specifically wanted to test himself and his developing theories against the best players.

When the poker room calls the top players and they call one another, it also prevents hustling. Among the pros, if everybody finds out when a new player is in town, the field among them is level. The competition to get the new guy's money is open and fair. No one can try to arrange a private game or separate the newcomer from the others. Any possible collusion among players is also headed off by the other top pros playing in the game. If a couple of poker players want to get together to cheat an outsider—something today's top pros, at least the ones who are the subject of this book, simply don't do—it would be a lot easier in a shorthanded game: easier to keep secret, fewer people with whom to coordinate the cheating, and fewer confederates among whom to divide the spoils. If everybody knows that the wealthy outsider is coming to play, potential cheaters would have to either include everybody or hide their cheating from their world-class colleagues.

A $2,000–$4,000 hold 'em game materialized for Beal as if by magic and quickly filled up. The waiting list grew, even as the stakes rose to $3,000–$6,000 and $4,000–$8,000. The game broke up with plans to reconvene Thursday afternoon with limits of $10,000–$20,000.

Why didn't Andy Beal insist on playing heads up, as he had on the previous trip (and would on all future trips)? He had not really prepared himself for the mental combat of playing heads up. He dropped by the poker room on a whim because he had an afternoon free, and then extended his trip by a day. He was still torn about how much he wanted to commit himself to poker. He relished the mental challenge of planning and executing a heads-up poker strategy but he hadn't put in the hours to feel he had any better chance than he did three weeks earlier. In addition, he won money in the February ring games, in contrast to his performance in the heads-up matches.

He wanted to make sure he wasn't making a mistake by insisting on playing heads up. Finally, the stakes of the $10,000–$20,000 ring game would affect the pros more than playing at those stakes heads up. Although the pros told him that some players in the game would be playing the money of nonplayers in addition to their own, he imagined they had much more financial exposure than they did when he faced one opponent playing everyone's money.

The Thursday game was, by far, the highest-stakes full table poker game of all time. Amazingly, there was a waiting list. Players flew in from California, only to find they were too late to get in. They played a $2,000–$4,000 game at a neighboring table, hoping to get a seat, but no one wanted to leave.

Ted Forrest made it back from California in time to get in. Johnny Chan, two-time World Series of Poker champion and one of the most famous players of the last twenty years, had to put his name on the list and play in the second game. (Chan lived in California but, like Ted, chased the action between Las Vegas and L.A.) Barry Greenstein also flew in from L.A., only to find the big game already filled.

If you saw Barry Greenstein at a poker table, you'd probably want to shake him and tell him to go outside and have some fun. With his deep-set eyes, dark brows, undergrowth of beard, and long features, he could pass for a badly overworked accountant on April 14. Away from the table, however, he was one of the most charismatic figures in poker.

At forty-six, just a couple years younger than Andy Beal, Barry considered himself in his prime as a poker player, but remained uneasy about his decision to make poker the focus of his life. It was common for top pros to begin recognizing their skills while in college, and drift toward poker until a career in gambling became inevitable. Jennifer Harman, for example, wanted a medical career. She played poker for fun while in college, but started winning and improving. When asked how she chose to become a poker player, she has replied, "Poker chose me."

Not so for Barry Greenstein. He took ten years to complete

his work for a Ph.D. because central Illinois's poker games were too lucrative to leave behind, but his résumé hints at worlds beyond poker: Ph.D. candidate in mathematics at the University of Illinois, one of the first programmers hired by Symantec, a one-man wrecking crew of no-limit hold 'em in Northern California, one of the top cash game players in Los Angeles, mentor to several high-stakes pros. Poker was the best way to take care of himself and his family, but he always felt that he was meant to do more.

Over a decade ago, after he and a handful of other professionals won so much money in the Bay Area's card rooms that there was no one left to play no-limit hold 'em (and, according to Barry, he cleaned out the other pros), he had to play limit poker 100 hours a week to make the money he made at no-limit. Barry was very conservative in appearance, but he had always been generous to his family and always lived in nice houses and driven nice cars. He concedes, "I'm hard on money."

When bigger limit games sprang up in the card rooms around Los Angeles, he started flying to L.A. once or twice a month, playing for two days straight, before returning home. Then he did this once a week, then two or three times a week. It was a terrible way to live but he thought it was necessary to keep from uprooting his family. In 1999, he finally moved his family to L.A., and said goodbye to flying someplace just for a poker game.

But here he was, stuck in Las Vegas and he couldn't even get into the game. One table away, they were playing for the highest stakes ever, with more than $4 million on the table, another record. He and Johnny Chan joined the others at the table in watching the action between hands of their game. Their interest was more than mere curiosity.

To Andy Beal's disappointment, raising the stakes to $10,000–$20,000 in a ring game had less effect on his opponents than he had hoped. There was really no way to make the stakes too high for a professional poker player if he or she had an edge. The pros would just take on a financial partner, selling a percentage of their win or loss. The partner was always another poker player, someone who could evaluate whether, in fact, the player selling the action really had the advantage. A poker player having the best of it was trading a piece of a favorable opportunity for the security of reducing the amount of risk.

The best poker players walk a tightrope between their business sense and their passion. As professionals, they seek out the most profitable opportunities and control as many factors as possible to create a positive result. As gamblers, however, they want the risk and excitement of having something important on the line with the outcome hanging in the balance. The high-stakes professionals differ when it comes to judgment calls along the security-risk continuum.

Most great poker players share a common background, both with one another and millions of losing gamblers: competitive interests and families, a high tolerance for risk, and a lot of losing. Elite poker players are drawn from a pool of gamblers, not problem solvers or people readers. These particular gamblers gravitate toward poker (along with millions of other losing gamblers), usually at an early age, and usually showing some skill. Nevertheless, they still start off losing like everybody else.

At some point, the young professional poker player (who may not yet have realized they are on the road to becoming a "professional poker player") stops being like every other gambler. The pro is devoting a lot of time to gambling, but is winning, and developing a recognizable edge. From that point on, the poker pro has more in common with the casino than with other bettors. Like the casino, the professionals, with their edge, merely have to allow enough trials to even out the role of luck.

It's profitable being the casino, having the best of it, but is it fun? Is it exciting?

This is the paradox for nearly all the world's best poker players. They start playing poker because the gambling aspect is fun and exciting. They stick with it because, unlike other gambling activities (except for sports betting, and many high-stakes poker players are winning sports bettors), they can win. But winning removes the risk. How do they handle losing that element of excitement when poker is about controlling risks, rather than experiencing them? And how do they react when poker becomes risky?

Ted Forrest was the king of the risk-takers. "The first time I ever played $15–$30 stud," Ted explained, "my heart started thumping out of my chest. I don't get that feeling anymore when I sit down at a normal game. When I sat down at that $10,000–$20,000 game with Chip and Andy, my heart was thumping. It takes a really big game to make my heart pump like that." He had no trouble taking all the money in his safe deposit box and sitting down at that game. The difficult thing would have been to pass it up.

Frequently, Todd Brunson was at the other end of the continuum. Brunson was not part of the group organized by his father to play Andy Beal, even though he was clearly as talented as the others and considered one of the best at limit hold 'em. Todd was capable of playing poker at the highest limits, but frequently chose not to. If Table One included some live ones—there were several very successful businessmen who played for high stakes and the competition at Table One made them into good players, but they were at a clear disadvantage to the pros—he would play as high as they wanted for as long as they wanted. But if he thought there were too many pros and not enough "contributors," he would play $400–$800, usually cleaning up.

In fact, Todd didn't play very much at all. "I'm famous for

being the laziest man in poker," he admitted. He came to the poker room to win, not to gamble, and his business interests took up plenty of his time. Brunson was much more aggressive about hunting down good investments than good poker games, removing as much money from his bankroll as he could to buy stocks, homes, land, and pursue other business opportunities.

Most players were somewhere in the middle, and they usually had difficulty resolving the conflict between the love of action and the need for security. Jennifer Harman, for example, got no sensory pleasure from taking risks. She found it "stressful," not exciting, to put up the last of her bankroll to keep playing during her losing period after moving to Las Vegas in the early 1990s. On the other hand, she wasn't satisfied as a winning $100–$200 hold 'em player, losing at bigger games for years until she could figure out how to beat them. "You have to take risks," she explains, "or you'll never get there."

The willingness to gamble is a common characteristic of the top poker players, something that initially seemed inconsistent with the image of the wily professional intent on maintaining an edge. Howard Lederer, who could swing from end to end of the risk-security spectrum, explained that the urge to gamble is practically a requirement. "There are a lot of poker players who aren't gamblers. Those kinds of players tend to find the level where they can win and they make their living. But if you don't have that need for action in you, you don't push yourself to move higher up. It takes a certain amount of gambling mentality to keep pushing yourself to go beyond."

Howard knew because he was a perfect example of the calculating professional who struggled with an addiction to action, an addiction he wanted to control but not necessarily eliminate. Jennifer Harman has said of him, "Howard Lederer will play for his life. When he's hungry, he does better."

Lederer's media-created nickname, the Professor of Poker,

didn't do justice to the fierceness of his drive or the difficulty of succeeding in poker. Most of the millions of new poker players and fans who saw Howard Lederer as bulletproof would be surprised to know that he spent a significant amount of his time at the pinnacle of the poker world just one wrong move from financial ruin.

Despite Howard's careful, analytical approach and cool, detached appearance, he has always been, at heart, a gambler. Consequently, he has been broke many times during his gambling career, and pushed himself into bad financial situations, situations pure reason would have dictated that he avoid. But he wanted to gamble.

Even after he stopped being a losing player in 1985, Howard struggled periodically as he worked his way up poker's hierarchy. At each new level, there was a period where he would lose and either keep slugging it out on a depleted bankroll or move back to the lower-limit game and rebuild.

"I definitely had periods of doubt and didn't want to admit defeat," Howard recalled of those days. "I had internal dialogues saying how much regret I'd have to carry if I had to admit defeat and just say, 'I'm a two-and-four-hundred player.' I didn't want to do that." His skill and desire were so great that he persevered, but he had little to show for fifteen years of success.

Howard also financially backed numerous other poker players. Poker was such a solitary game that financing another player was a rare chance to create an atmosphere of comradeship. It was also a way for a successful player, in theory, to use his skills to invest in something he knew more about than stocks or land. (Howard admitted to chasing more than his share of bad business deals in the 1990s.)

Backing someone is what poker players do with their money until they learn better. If that isn't one of the wisest expressions regarding gambling, it should be. Many successful players have tried this form of investing but it virtually never works out over the long run. Although an excellent player can be broke and need a backer, there is usually a reason *why* he is broke. Learning this was a seven-figure lesson for Howard Lederer.

Sometime around 1999, Howard decided to change course. He thought carefully about why he was always on the brink of financial trouble, despite never having a bad year with his own gambling. He cut out the other activities, especially backing other players and the too-good-to-be-true business deals. Since then, he kept his finances in order. "At some point you have to say," he described later, "'Okay, maybe it's just time to bet on me.'"

So when the players had to decide what to do when Andy wanted to play in a $10,000–$20,000 ring game, they took their places along the continuum between risk and security. Jennifer Harman and Howard Lederer both had investors take a piece of their action, though both were uneasy about it. Ted brought his rack of white chips, still in the box from three weeks earlier, to the table. Todd wasn't playing.

Because of Andy's presence, the financial arrangements between players were made more explicit and more restrictive. To assure the newcomer that nothing underhanded was going on, it was agreed that no one playing in the game would have a piece of anyone else playing in the game. Therefore, both Jennifer and Howard, who decided to play (and sell pieces of themselves to some players not in the game), wondered if the smarter financial decision wouldn't have been to sit out the game and take a piece of several players, as Doyle Brunson had done.

This was the theory: Seven players were professionals, of approximately equal ability (or at least close enough where their skills against each other should cancel out). Andy Beal had significantly less skill. If you ran that game a million times, Beal should be the loser and, other than dividing Andy's money, the pros should break even. But you couldn't run it a million times; the game was being played only once. Rather than risk being dealt bad cards or not getting into hands with the banker, by owning a percentage of several players, you increased the likelihood of profiting from the skill advantage of the professionals.

Most of the players at the adjacent table, therefore, had a financial interest in the ring game at Table One. For Barry Greenstein and Johnny Chan, however, even that (along with their own high-stakes game) was not enough. Barry saw his friend Ted Forrest playing hold 'em and couldn't resist proposing a wager to Chan, who also knew Forrest well.

Because Forrest had been winning so big this year, Greenstein thought, he was the only one who could really afford to play at Beal's stakes. Consequently, while everyone else was playing tight and avoiding the action unless they had rock-solid cards—the size of the stakes, it turned out, had *some* effect on inhibiting the pros' natural aggressiveness—Forrest was *gambling*. It was a sound playing and marketing strategy: He was trying to show the newcomer a good time as well as loosen things up. But it wasn't working, and Forrest was losing because he kept running into strong cards from Beal or one of the other pros.

After Barry made some comments about Ted's qualities as a hold 'em player, he could see that Johnny had a higher opinion of Ted's abilities. Barry respected Ted as a poker player, too, but hold 'em was simply not his best game. In addition, Ted liked to play fast—lots of hands, maneuvers that worked best in shorthanded situations—and he thought, even with Andy Beal in the game, Forrest was an underdog to win. They made a side bet, cross-booking 10 percent of Ted's action. From that point on, if Forrest won, Greenstein would pay Chan 10 percent of the win. If Ted lost, Johnny would pay Barry 10 percent of that amount. Barry knew what a competitor Ted was, so he insisted on one condition: The bet was off if Ted found out about it during the game.

Ted promptly lost $445,000 of the $500,000 he brought to the table. Unlike the game earlier in the month with Beal and Reese, however, he knew he could take his time and wait for a good opportunity to make a stand with his last $55,000. Also, in contrast with the March 9 game, he had more chips in his box and could rebuy if he lost these. But he had to consider whether playing as loose as he had been would bear fruit. Every time he got in a hand with Andy Beal, the banker was holding strong cards. The other pros also seemed to be hanging back until they had strong cards.

On a bathroom break, he found himself next to Johnny Chan, who told him, "You have to win in this game because Barry bet me that you wouldn't."

It burned Ted that Barry Greenstein bet against him. He didn't take it personally; they were friends, loaned each other money, and even played high-stakes matches against each other's *girlfriends*. (Ted had won over a million dollars from Barry over the course of a month in 2000 at Chinese Poker. Barry's girlfriend Alexandra then played Ted in Chinese Poker and won about half of it back. Ted's girlfriend then played Barry in $1,000–$2,000 Seven Card Stud Hi/Lo in a short handicap match in which her antes were smaller and, though Ted could not coach her during the match, he could give her a three-minute lesson at the table immediately before. She played superbly and won $15,000 but Ted would not give Barry a rematch with her. Ted realized that the reduced ante, in the long run, would not have given his girlfriend enough of an advantage.)

Ted focused even more on the game to prove Barry wrong. He tightened up his play and began winning. After he had recouped his loss and gotten ahead by a couple hundred thousand dollars, Barry Greenstein exercised his option to call off the bet and take his $65,000 loss. He couldn't understand it. It was as if Ted had somehow read his mind and changed his game so Johnny Chan would beat him in the side bet.

Barry found out that Johnny Chan's chat at the urinal, not

Ted's clairvoyance, was responsible for the turnaround. He confronted Chan about violating the terms of the bet, but Chan insisted that it didn't matter. At these stakes, he claimed, Forrest had to be playing his best game the whole time. Barry was sure he was right but paid off Chan rather than fight about it further. Even though the other players at the table took his side in the dispute, he received little sympathy. "That's what you get for betting with Johnny Chan," one of them said.

When the game broke up seven hours later, Ted duplicated his result of twenty days earlier: He started the day by taking 100 flags out of the box, and ended it by putting 300 back in. Ted Forrest won exactly $1,055,000, one large bet more than the first time he played with Andy Beal.

It capped off what may have been the best month in the history of high-stakes poker. Statistics of this sort were impossible to obtain, much less verify, but few players have even played for high enough stakes to win $1 million in a session, much less repeat the feat less than three weeks later. Ted also won $2 million (for the team) against Andy Beal on March 10. With his share of the team's win, the two $1 million scores, and several other great sessions, Forrest won $4.4 million at poker in March 2001, and over $6.7 million for the first three months of the year.

Howard Lederer also won, as did John Hennigan. Howard still believed the backers, not the players, had the best of it. On the other hand, Doyle Brunson, who spread his risk among players he backed in the game, was the big loser. Chip Reese lost over $800,000 in the game, and Doyle had bought half his action.

Andy Beal, the reason for all the excitement, was the forgotten man. He broke even, playing very few hands. The whole experience was a bore, a wasted afternoon. He won some big pots because he waited, as the instructional books taught in full-table games, for premium cards. When he played a hand against opponents from the heads-up games, or players who heard about his wild-man style, they were surprised to find him always backing up aggressive betting with strong hands.

But the experience confirmed his first impression: He would have a chance to do better (and have more fun) against just one opponent. He also noticed that the pros were not as fundamentally sound as he expected. They were great at thinking and counter-thinking during the hand, at varying their play, and at reading opponents, but they seemed to get a lot of basic pot odds decisions wrong. If he made the mathematically correct move every time, wouldn't that substantially reduce or even eliminate the advantage of the professionals? And if he could get the stakes high enough, maybe he could knock the pros off their game.

4

The Poker Conjecture

Luck is the residue of design.

—Branch Rickey (1881–1965)

Conjecture (noun): inference based on incomplete evidence; guesswork.

—*The American Heritage Dictionary*

Spring 1976

Twenty-four-year-old Andy Beal sat alone in the drab Housing and Urban Development conference room in Washington, D.C. He had bid $350,000 for an apartment complex HUD was auctioning in Gulfport, Mississippi. The 5 percent deposit he left at the bidding window, $17,500, was all the money he could scrape together from ten years of hustling in business. He was used to being too young to do the things he did, but he was stepping up to an entirely bigger league. Alone with his thoughts, he was getting nervous.

The bids would be opened and the winner announced at 11:00 A.M. At 10:20, another bidder finally joined him in the conference room. The man looked professional; he wore a suit and tie, and carried a briefcase. Andy was wearing jeans. He was starting to feel out of place.

The man introduced himself and they made awkward small talk. They were both bidding on the Gulfport property.

"So," the man asked, "how much do you think it'll sell for?"

Andy felt a bit more comfortable. Though a novice in this business, he had done his homework. He had gone to Gulfport and spent several days inspecting the apartment complex. The roof leaked. It was run-down. It was only half occupied. But he was handy and fixing it up himself was how he thought he could make a big profit.

"Five hundred thousand, tops," Andy replied. "Not more than that."

"Oh, I know it will sell for more than that. We bid more than that."

Andy's stomach lurched. For some reason, he could tell the man was being honest.

He suddenly felt foolish. He had spent all this time and money, and it was not going to happen. He had imagined how to line up the financing, move to Mississippi, and immerse himself in bringing this apartment complex around.

It was just not going to happen.

He had no business being here. This was a man's game and he was just some kid from Lansing. Where did he come off thinking he knew what things were worth?

Nervous in the silence, he fiddled with the brochures on the table. HUD was auctioning two properties: the one Andy had bid on in Gulfport, and one he had never seen before, another apartment complex, this one in Waco, Texas.

I'm washed up, Beal told himself. I have no chance.

He looked at the Waco brochure.

It looked like a nice property. Eighty-five percent occupied. Why not make a bid?

An argument raged in his head.

That's absurd. You're out of your league. You gave it a shot, so just let it die and go home.

Just get off your butt and submit some nominal bid. At least that way, you've got a shot. And while you're sitting here, the clock is running.

Quickly, he thumbed through the brochure. Yearly rents were about $180,000. If he didn't bid much more than that, how badly could he get hurt?

If he knew how they would react at HUD's bidding window, he never would have had the nerve to do it.

It was past 10:30 when he cautiously approached the woman at the bidding window.

"Excuse me, ma'am. I'd like to withdraw my bid on the Gulfport property and get a bid package for the Waco property."

At the top of her lungs, it seemed, the woman yelled for her supervisor. "THIS YOUNG MAN SAYS HE WANTS HIS BID BACK ON GULFPORT, AND HE WANTS TO BID ON WACO! CAN I DO THAT?"

It sounded ludicrous.

The supervisor came out.

"Son, what is it you want to do?"

Andy explained it again.

"Well, I guess it's all right."

He decided to bid $217,500, rounding the estimated yearly rents to $200,000 and adding the amount of his cashier's check. Scrambling to finish the paperwork, he barely got the bid in on time.

It was just before eleven when he reentered the conference room. Now it was filled with businessmen. He saw the man he had spoken with earlier, who asked where he went.

"I went out and changed my bid."

The man was furious. "You can't do that. I never should have told you about our bid."

Andy tried to calm him down.

"No, don't worry. Not the Gulfport bid. I withdrew that. I put in a bid on Waco."

The man still looked angry.

The representatives from HUD filed in, and started with the Gulfport bids. The man next to Andy calmed down when his group's bid, over $600,000, turned out to be the high bid.

Andy's bid was the first opened on the Waco property.

"$217,500."

He suddenly had a chilling thought.

What if all the other bids were for just a fraction of that? How foolish would he feel about buying a property he had never seen before and paying double or triple what anyone else—anyone who, unlike him, knew what they were doing—would pay?

The second bid was $206,000.

He immediately calmed down. Win or lose, at least he hadn't overlooked some giant flaw that made him enormously miscalculate the amount to bid.

None of the remaining bids exceeded $206,000, however, and Beal had the winning bid. He was entering the big leagues of the real estate business—not in Gulfport, Mississippi, as he thought or planned, but in Waco, Texas. He had never set foot in Texas.

The apartment complex in Waco turned out to be a phenomenal deal. He found someone in his hometown of Lansing, Michigan, who would co-sign the mortgage in exchange for 10 percent ownership. He arranged the deal so it would close on the twenty-eighth of the month. In three days, he collected the first month of rent. The $15,000 repaid almost his entire deposit.

The complex was just eleven years old and in good condition. He moved to Waco to take care of it. He was, at least figuratively, finally on solid ground.

Andy Beal had always wanted to know how things worked.

When he was eleven, he and his Uncle Denny would go to the Salvation Army on Saturday mornings. Denny was good with his hands and they would buy broken television sets for a dollar or two. Denny showed Andy how to fix them. Denny would then take out an ad in the paper and sell them for $30 to $40 apiece. In 1964, most families had only one television, and it was considered a major purchase. Some sets sold to families splurging on a second set at a bargain price. Others struggling to get by could now purchase a first TV.

Andy later started fixing and reselling television sets on his own. Once, while out on a date, he persuaded the girl to join him on a detour to the home of a family that offered him their broken set. They had to lug it out to the trunk of his car so he could get it home.

His next business was purchasing kits for alarm systems, intercoms, and antennas and installing them in homes and apartments. If you lived in Lansing in the late 1960s and looked in the Yellow Pages for such a service, you wouldn't know from the listing, the name (Central Security Systems), or the person answering the phone (an answering service), that the principal owner was just seventeen years old.

Beal graduated from high school in 1971, took a year off, and started at Michigan State University in 1973. He was a good student, but he was there only because his mother insisted he continue his education. He did well in the classes he completed, but his growing business interests forced him to drop several classes, or accept grades of "Incomplete." He also took night classes at Lansing Community College in 1974 and 1975.

After turning twenty-one, Andy discovered Las Vegas and the world of gambling. Not content like some friends to go to Vegas to get drunk and crazy, he studied card-counting systems and learned he could profit from the activity. He also started a business as a very unorthodox travel agent. The Stardust Hotel and

Casino had a junket deal in the early 1970s. If a gambler would deposit $2,000, he could receive a free room and free airfare. He would also receive $2,000 in special chips. The chips could not be redeemed; they could be played only until they were lost back to the casino. (Of course, winning bets were paid with regular, redeemable chips. The nonredeemable chips were also returned with winning bets, to be bet again.) The deal assured that gamblers would gamble enough to run through the $2,000.

Beal would recruit friends (and friends of friends), who would pay him $200 and take the flight and room. He would give them the $2,000, and take the special chips. With six "customers," he would clear $1,200 up front. Andy had, however, paid out $12,000 and had that amount in unredeemable chips. If he could just break even at blackjack, he would play enough to lose the special chips and have the proceeds from the $12,000 in wins, but these would now be regular chips that he could exchange for cash. As a card counter, he usually did much better than breaking even. He won as much as $50,000 on card-counting trips.

Eventually, however, those nonredeemable chips stuck out like a sore thumb, especially when most gamblers signing up with the casino for the deal had $2,000 worth, and he had ten times that amount thanks to the virtual army of young gamblers he found around the Michigan State campus. Thus, the Stardust joined the growing list of establishments that barred the young card-counter/entrepreneur.

In addition to Central Security's work, he also started Mid Michigan Building Movers. When Andy was very young, he was fascinated by watching his Uncle Denny move a house—just lift it off the foundation, put it on a trailer, and drive it off to a new location. The expansion of Logan Street in Lansing forced many small homes on the market for under $1,000 apiece.

Andy and his uncle bought several, moved them, and sold them for a profit. They also hired themselves out to move other people's houses. On a few occasions, Andy built basements for people by jacking up their houses and digging out a basement underneath.

Eventually, he owned about fifteen houses around Lansing. He did all his own maintenance and repair work. In addition to homes that he moved out of the path of Logan Street, he began buying homes at HUD auctions. That was how he learned in early 1976 that HUD was auctioning apartments as well as single-family dwellings. He checked out an apartment building in Seattle and put in a bid, but did not succeed. That was how he felt he understood the system well enough to bid on the Gulfport property . . . and end up with the Waco property.

He sold or closed all his business interests in Lansing and moved to Waco. Still trying to appease his mother, he enrolled at Baylor University. He was too busy to thrive in the college environment. His education was taking place in the business world.

In 1979, he sold the Waco apartment complex and collected a profit of over $1 million. By that time, he was planning to move to Dallas to capitalize on another business opportunity, which also started almost by accident.

While attending a real estate seminar in Washington, D.C., in late 1978, Beal became bored and started contemplating the economics of the seminar business.

Let's see, there are 1,000 people in this room, and each paid $300 to be here: $300,000. They had to pay six speakers and one day's rental for the auditorium. After subtracting for marketing expenses, it was all profit.

He immediately ran ads in newspapers around the country, looking for former government officials who wanted to speak for pay at seminars about getting loans from the federal government. Out of several hundred responses, he found enough qualified speakers, and the National Institute for Continuing Professional Development, and its Government Loans and Loan Guarantee

Program, was born. Though he had dropped out of Baylor, a friend in Waco recommended that he seek Baylor's sponsorship. The university was expanding its professional education, and its nonprofit status could allow the NICPD to obtain a cheaper postage rate, the mass-mailing of the brochures being a significant expense.

Between 1979 and 1981, Beal's company conducted over 100 seminars, visiting just about every city in the United States with a population over 50,000. The travel burdens were so great that he needed to move to Dallas because of its better airports. He made millions in the seminar business, but shut it down after President Reagan announced the centerpiece of his plan for a smaller federal government was cutting the very programs that were the focus of the seminars.

Andy Beal returned to real estate in 1981 and bought several more apartment complexes at HUD auctions. Other than the Waco property, which he sold when he moved to Dallas, he became an accumulator, with properties scattered acround the country. Although he was located in the heart of a booming real estate market, which turned sour when the flow of easy savings-and-loan money dried up, he steered clear of the boom-and-bust cycle in Texas real estate, as well as the S&L scandal.

Beal was a bottom-feeder, a cheapskate. He had no desire to pay inflated prices for trophy properties or speculate on grand new building projects. He also avoided the quick-buck artists who operated the high-flying Texas S&Ls. They were a poor fit for his needs. They offered 100 percent financing and weren't picky about what borrowers did with the money, but insisted on hefty fees and part ownership of the deal.

In fact, he decided to get in on some of the action. After a friend chartered a savings and loan, Andy decided to do the same in 1984. His timing was excellent, though it looked the opposite at first.

His charter was granted in 1985, but he could not start banking operations until 1988. The S&L crisis was in its early stage in 1984–85, and the federal government was just realizing that its plan of deregulation had gone disastrously wrong. As increasing numbers of S&Ls failed, the government slowed its approvals for federal insurance of deposits of newly granted charters. The government never announced a formal moratorium, but Beal's institution was the first in Texas in years to receive federal deposit insurance when its application was finally approved in early 1988.

The delay, however, worked to Andy Beal's advantage. The avalanche of failing S&Ls created a demand for the kind of bargain hunting Beal and his thrift were prepared to undertake—the purchase of loan portfolios from closed banks and S&Ls. Like the HUD auctions Beal attended a decade earlier, Washington was selling assets at fire-sale prices. For a discerning buyer, there were some quality assets among the mess of the S&L scandal, and Beal could get them on the cheap.

Beal started his institution—he converted it from a thrift to a savings bank in the 1990s—with $3 million of his own money, most of his personal fortune. Focusing on sifting through the government's stockpile of seized assets, he found a large volume of loans where the borrower was still making payments, or was likely to resume making them. Nevertheless, the Resolution Trust Corporation, the government agency charged with disposing of S&L assets, offered packages of those loans at a discount. Until the RTC disbanded in 1996, this was how Beal Bank made most of its money.

By 1996, when the distressed-loan business began petering out, Beal Bank had grown to $1.2 billion in assets. In 1995, it had generated $27.4 million in income; income for fiscal 1996 was $48.8 million. In a July 1996 interview with the *Dallas Business Journal*, Andy considered the prospect of replacing that business and predicted, "We probably just won't grow as fast." He told the same reporter in September of that year, "There's a lot less product and more competition. The glory days of our business are over."

Beal Bank's profits did level off—but only after doubling again. Net income for 1999 and 2000 was just over $100 million per year. According to the bank's Web site, *American Banker* ranked it number one for return on equity among all banks for the five-year period ending December 31, 1999.

Despite his great and increasing wealth, Andy Beal never bought into the cultural equivalence of wealth and celebrity. If his money made him a public figure, it was not with his consent. To the contrary, he delighted in his relative anonymity. He rarely gave interviews (and usually regretted it afterward) and kept his business out of the public eye as much as possible. He had a strong social conscience, but there were no Beal medical centers or colleges, nor were there Beal foundations doing the good deeds he supported. He never indulged, like other members of the Texas super-rich, in a sports team, television station, or reality show. None of his companies had ever gone public, so he never had to court investors or disclose anything about his operations to them or the Securities and Exchange Commission. His financial service entities filed the reports required by government regulators and nothing more.

In the flesh, Andy Beal seems like an ordinary guy. On casual observation, it appears there is less, rather than more, than meets the eye. Taking a visitor to dinner, he drives a several-years-old clunky SUV. No chauffeur, no limousine, no Mercedes. Not even an upscale SUV like an H2 or an Escalade or a Lexus. He was almost killed by a drunk driver in 2000 and wants a lot of Detroit Iron surrounding him.

This is typical of his travel. He has never owned an airplane. The idea of spending $20,000 to fly from Dallas to Las Vegas—the approximate cost if he owned or chartered a private jet—is beyond ludicrous. American Airlines flies back and forth between the cities ten times a day and the round-trip ticket costs under $300. That is the cost of a *coach* ticket, which is what Beal purchases.

Asked about flying first class, he is incredulous. "Are you kidding? Do you know how much the airlines want for first class tickets? For a two-hour flight?"

At the restaurant, there is no special treatment by the valet or maître d' or the staff. In fact, the parking attendant criticizes him for driving in the wrong entrance, clearly a move made out of absentmindedness, not privilege.

No one treats Beal like a VIP, and he does not do anything to merit such treatment. He is not cheap but he leaves little impression when spending money, partly because he is well known among friends and business associates for carrying a ridiculously small amount of cash. It is a habit coincident of many very wealthy men, and it has caused him some embarrassment over the years.

At least once, after a losing session at poker against the group, he had to ask Doyle Brunson and Chip Reese to loan him a few chips until he could wire more money to the Bellagio; he was almost penniless.

He never played poker with or for cash, and used a credit card for everything more expensive than a newspaper. When he came to Las Vegas, he had the money wired in. At the end of his trips, it was wired back. He paid for his own room and incidentals (though the Bellagio in 2004 began comping his room) with an American Express card (Gold, not Platinum). With what cash he had in his pocket, he couldn't play the dollar slot machines for fifteen minutes.

By the mid-1990s, as Andy Beal passed his fortieth birthday, he suddenly had something that was missing from his life for the previous twenty years: time. He no longer had to be involved in every aspect of every deal. Even though the bank's business was becoming larger, more complex, and more far-flung, his investments in people and computers had paid off.

Beal finally had an opportunity to indulge in some of his passions away from business. His interests were unusual, as were his approaches to pursuing them. The only common thread was that once Andy's mind became engaged, he didn't do anything casually.

In 1993, Andrew Wiles, a Princeton mathematician, developed a proof of Fermat's Last Theorem, a problem dogging mathematicians for over 300 years. The proof received wide publicity, even though its complexity and certain flaws put Wiles and other scholars back to work.

Andy Beal joined the effort. Although his math education formally ended in high school, the news stories engaged his mind and led him to educate himself on number theory. It started with him doodling and writing lists of numbers. Then he hired a programmer to help him program the bank's fifteen computers to run numbers for thousands of computer-hours on nights and weekends. All the computer power at his disposal demonstrated that the theory Beal had been working on appeared correct. This led him in September 1994 to begin publicizing the problem he devised. Contacting mathematicians and periodicals, he heard from several respected sources that his discovery was unknown.

R. Daniel Maudlin, a professor of mathematics at the University of North Texas, helped Andy develop what was now called the Beal Conjecture into an article for the American Mathematical Society and accompanying press release, both released in November 1997. In addition, Maudlin chaired a committee that would give a prize to anyone who proved or disproved the conjecture.

Originally, Andy funded the prize with $5,000, to be increased by $5,000 a year until it reached $50,000. But the response to the announcement of the Beal Conjecture was so enthusiastic that he quickly increased the prize to $50,000. Subsequently, Andy increased the prize money again, to $75,000 and then to $100,000. The prize remains unclaimed.

In 1995, Beal read an article about the coming boom in satellite technology. He thought about the relatively few companies capable of launching satellites, and wondered if the cost of sending payloads into space could be cut substantially through greater competition.

He spent two years learning. He evaluated the debate between disposable and reusable launch vehicles. He consulted experts on different fuel mixes. In 1997, the company, now called Beal Aerospace, began scaling up. He hired an experienced core of leaders and managers. The size of the company eventually rivaled his bank.

The scope of this project was almost beyond imagination. According to published reports, their engine would be the largest developed in the United States since the Apollo space program. It would burn three swimming pools of fuel per second. A horizontal test of one of the rockets shot a 300-foot flame. To launch an object out of the earth's atmosphere would require that Beal build a city from scratch in a Central American jungle.

For three years, Beal Aerospace persevered over enormous obstacles. The U.S. State Department and an outdated missile treaty threatened plans to ship his rockets to proposed launch sites. Environmentalists and treacherous weather forced the company to abandon its first spaceport. Border politics in Central America interfered with a second site. During the entire project, Beal had to compete with Boeing, Lockheed Martin, and NASA itself, entrenched giants with government resources or rich government contracts.

 In October 2000, Beal Aerospace announced that it was ceasing operations. Andy Beal, in a statement released with the announcement, mentioned the risks faced by the project but said, "In spite of these additional risks, which we have faced for some time, we would have remained in business if the government would have simply guaranteed that NASA's subsidized launch systems would never be allowed to compete with the private sector." Whether the government's funding of NASA projects that could compete with the private sector was the main reason, or one of many reasons, the project was too ambitious to succeed. Articles describing the demise of Beal Aerospace reported that Beal spent $200 million of his own money on the project. He has refused to comment on the cost, but has maintained two things. First, he had no partners and bore all the costs, whatever they were, out of his own pocket. Second, "It was a wonderful experience, and I wouldn't trade it for anything, not even the money I spent on it."

Just four months after shutting down Beal Aerospace, he wandered into the Bellagio poker room. Small wonder, given that he returned twice in less than two months, that he committed himself to improving. If Andy Beal's history proved anything, it was that he did not attempt anything casually. He had succeeded at most, though not all, of his major projects. His successes had come against long odds. His accomplishments, even in failure, had been impressive.

He knew that challenging the best poker players in the world could end in failure. But was he less likely to succeed than in any other area where he had applied himself? Besides, he wanted to test himself, and he needed to find out how poker worked.

As much respect as Beal had for the pros, he thought their biggest weakness was the fundamental soundness of their games. In the simple math of making plays based on the proper odds, he felt they were not experts. This was understandable. First, their instincts were honed from tens of thousands of hours at the tables.

They did not need to work out the math. Second, their ability to read their opponents was so advanced that it provided a better basis for a decision than pot odds, which became increasingly subjective when it came to evaluating the probabilities based on the opponent's cards.

Andy would never be able to match them for experience and instinct. On the other hand, he felt he could match—and maybe exceed—their ability to work out the right play based on the odds with the brute force of his intellect and determination.

He wrote his own poker program in BASIC. It was very simple, dealing out combinations of the fifty-two cards in the deck and running large numbers of trials to determine the likelihood of different hands prevailing. In addition, he could set up situations and run them a million times to see the likelihood of different results.

If you dealt out a million hands of poker heads up, you found out some interesting things. The top pros knew many of these things and could intuit others, but they would probably not get perfect scores on a test like this:

1. What is the lowest high card you could have in your hand and expect to win more than half the time regardless of second card?
2. What is the unpaired, unsuited hand with the lowest high card that would win more than half the time?
3. What is the lowest suited hand that would win more than half the time?
4. What are the highest suited hands that would not win half the time?
5. What are the worst hands that would win more than half the time?

Andy Beal spent hour after hour at his desk, whenever he had some time (sometimes while he was primarily occupied on another matter), running his poker program and trying out different combinations and different developments on the board. He knew he would never have the pros' faculty for reading opponents, but he would pit himself against any of them for knowing the percentages.

After five and a half months of preparation, the terrorist attacks of September 11, 2001, reordered Andy Beal's priorities. He worried for the safety of his family, his business and employees, and his country. It was clearly not a time to be preoccupied with poker.

Although the aftermath of the attacks sent the financial markets into a tailspin, Beal Bank provided a stabilizing force, which also turned out to be profitable. For the past several years, since the drop in business of buying loan portfolios from the government, Beal Bank had been profiting increasingly from event arbitrage. When particular events dominate the news and alter values within the financial markets, there is always the question of whether the markets react appropriately to the new event, overreact, or underreact. Beal Bank, similar to its business after the S&L crisis, looked for situations where the market overreacted, discounting quality assets more than circumstances demanded. The bank had stepped in during the foreign debt crises and Long-Term Capital Management collapse in 1998 when government bond prices plummeted, buying at a discount and collecting full interest and/or reselling when the panic ended and prices climbed.

Beal had already been busy throughout 2001 as a result of the California energy crisis. The threat of bankruptcy by California energy companies, and the actual bankruptcy of Pacific Gas & Electric on April 6, 2001, caused bond prices of California energy companies to drop precipitously. Other utilities and energy companies in other states reacted, often causing their bond prices to drop. Beal Bank was analyzing as many of these situations as possible, looking for (and sometimes finding) discounted prices on debt where the danger of bankruptcy or other disruption in the debtor's ability to pay interest and principal was remote. Still other times, there was some likelihood of default, but certain bondholders were well protected because of the quality and priority of the collateral. Too often, the market was not efficient in making such distinctions. This created profitable opportunities for the bank.

The terrorist attacks, and the markets' reaction, provided numerous other opportunities. For example, after the attacks hardly anyone wanted to hold the debt of U.S. airline companies. Most were already in trouble due to price competition and heavy debt-servicing costs and every carrier was a candidate for bankruptcy.

Beal had an opportunity to set his bank up to profit tremendously, and stabilize the market at the same time. Everyone who owned the debt of U.S. air carriers, it seemed, wanted to sell, but there were no buyers. Prices would have been in free fall without buyers like Beal Bank. Naturally, the bank's analysts had determined the likelihood of carriers continuing to make payment on various forms of debt, as well as the quality of the collateral for that debt. For example, many carriers' aircraft were mortgaged. Because of the quality of the collateral—the airplanes that the carriers needed to do their job—default and even bankruptcy should not diminish the value of the debt significantly. Furthermore, to keep from having their aircraft seized as part of a bankruptcy proceeding, the airlines were motivated to make payments on this debt even when in default on other debt.

Andy Beal had a full plate through the fall of 2001, though he kept looking at those percentages. He was feeling like he had run every conceivable situation, and had done it so often that the odds were becoming second nature to him. When things settled down a bit, he would return to Las Vegas and test himself once again against the best poker players in the world. He had no reason to believe he was equal to the professionals in ability, but he was confident that he could make the mathematically proper move at all times, something he thought even the pros had not mastered.

Answers to the quiz:

1. King. King-deuce off-suit won 52.6 percent to 53.2 percent of the time. Queen-high would not always win half the time. Queen-deuce off-suit, for example, won only 48.8 percent to 49.4 percent of the time.
2. Ten-eight off-suit won 51.5 percent of the time.
3. Nine-six suited.
4. Jack-deuce suited won exactly 50 percent of the time. Ten-four suited won 49 percent to 49.4 percent of the time.
5. Several hands hover around 50 percent. In two separate million-hand trials, the following hands were the worst poker hands that still won over 50 percent of the time:

Queen-trey off-suit: 50.2 percent to 50.4 percent.
Jack-trey suited: 50.6 percent to 52 percent.
Deuce-deuce: 50.3 percent to 52.4 percent.
Jack-four suited: 50.2 percent to 50.5 percent.
Queen-four off-suit: 50.8 percent to 51.5 percent.

5

Picture Day

December 2001

Andy Beal finally returned to the Bellagio on Tuesday, December 11, 2001, nearly nine months after his last visit to the poker room. He was a welcome sight.

Following the terrorist attacks of September 11, Las Vegas struggled, along with the rest of the travel and tourism industry. In the first weeks after the attacks, the Strip looked like a ghost town. As people slowly began traveling again, the city, which obviously depended enormously on tourism, had to fight two fears: fear of flying and fear of appearing frivolous, gambling in Las Vegas while America was under attack. Traffic through McCarran Airport in November 2001 was nearly 18 percent less than the year before.

The impact reverberated through the local economy. The mega-resort across the street from the Bellagio, the Aladdin, already in financial trouble, announced that it might have to close permanently. The Las Vegas hotels laid off more than 15,000 workers and cut back the hours of thousands more.

Even in the poker rooms, where news of the outside world rarely intruded on the games, the mood was glum. The professionals considered the poker room their office. They may act unaware of what goes on in the low- and medium-stakes games, but the upbeat feel of the room—the hum of noise and flurry of movement—was gone. The high-stakes players didn't rely on the mass-market tourist trade, but the live ones also kept a low profile after September 11. If they weren't worried about their businesses and investments in the wake of the attacks, they were worried about the appearance of gambling huge sums of money in such an environment.

As the town tried to put on a brave face and drum up the interest for a New Year's Eve celebration, the poker room's biggest customer dangled an early Christmas present before them. Beal wanted to play a heads-up $20,000–$40,000 game. He even accommodated Doyle Brunson's need for time to get the players and the money together by sitting down to the ring game in progress at Table One.

There were two changes in the game: It went from a mixed game to Texas Hold 'Em, and Andy started agitating to raise the stakes beyond $1,000–$2,000. They were soon playing $4,000–$8,000, which (as Beal had hoped) took the players out of their comfort zone. That left them with two choices: take more chips out of their boxes and keep playing, or line up a partner to take a piece of their action. (Quitting the game would never be considered an option.)

For Jennifer Harman, it finally looked like her luck was going to change. Andy Beal's presence meant the chips would be flying but most of those chips flew *away* from Jennifer during his trio of visits in early 2001. Poker was just not going her way in February and March, whether it was bad luck, the wrong state of mind, or some flaws that had crept into her play—possibly all three. She struggled in the ring games and beat Andy heads up, but it was a long, frustrating, draining experience.

He had just popped into the poker room and she was already feeling the stress. She had to post her share of the group's bankroll. Then she had to play in the game where he continually hectored to increase the stakes. Of course, no one was going to refuse. The pros had the edge and this just increased their expected profit, but the higher the stakes, the bigger the short-term swings. When the stakes rose to $4,000–$8,000, they took a break and Jennifer decided to sell some of her action. They would be playing Andy heads up by Wednesday and a few big hands could create a swing of several hundred thousand dollars; it was too much to bet on so little.

Doyle, who was also trying to raise the group's bankroll for when they played heads up against Beal, said, "Todd will probably want a piece." Doyle declared him in for 25 percent of Jennifer's action. The elder Brunson did not usually play *any* role in his son's poker career but he couldn't reach him by phone and he knew what Todd would do. Todd and Jennifer moved up the ranks of the Las Vegas poker hierarchy together through the 1990s. They had tremendous respect for each other's abilities. They also had a serious romantic relationship and lived together, a situation that left surprisingly few hard feelings. They had each gotten married in the last year, remained friends (and poker competitors), and shared custody of their two dogs from the relationship.

Barry Greenstein also took 25 percent. He was back in Los Angeles, and knew Jennifer only from occasionally playing in a game with her, but Ted Forrest arranged it. Ted was in the game, wasn't selling any of his own action, and said, "Barry will probably want a piece," and made the call.

Jennifer then got those few good hands and was soon ahead $300,000. One of her partners didn't even know he was in the game and the other probably couldn't have cared less. They would get half the profits, but at least she was winning. As she took a quick cigarette break, she could be excused for thinking that, finally, she was the one catching Andy at the right time.

Top poker players have formed an uneasy truce with the concept of luck. Luck was the enemy, but it was also a necessary, though unwitting, ally. Over the long haul, luck should have no impact on a poker player's results—no *net* impact. Over a short period of time, however, a random distribution of the cards could give the worst player good enough cards to crush an expert. When Andy Beal won thousands of dollars from the Irishman and Todd Brunson in February, it was luck.

In fact, good poker players are more likely to be the victims of luck than the beneficiaries. Back in 1981, when Bobby Baldwin was earning his living as one of the world's best poker players, he made the logical case for why good players seemed to experience the worst luck. "If you are an excellent player, people are going to draw out on you a lot more than you're going to draw out on them because they're simply going to have the worst hand against you a lot more times than you have the worst hand against them."

It was hard remaining stoic when years of skill proved worthless against an inferior player, but the best pros have learned to soldier on. Howard Lederer said, "One of the things I focus on when someone shows me a ridiculous hand is, 'Okay, that's why I'm here.'"

Without luck, the better player would always win, as in chess. No intelligent poker player wants that, however, because if each game clearly distinguished the pecking order of players, the less skilled players would always lose and quickly give up hope. The pros want the live ones to get lucky sometimes and win. They just want it to happen in someone else's game.

Very few professionals associate themselves with the twin

trappings of luck: charms and superstitions. Johnny Chan may carry an orange around with him during the World Series of Poker, but that is merely to enhance the stereotype that Asian players carry some kind of mysterious Eastern luck. And that's why Chau Giang was happy to let the rumors swirl that he had voodoo working for him, even though voodoo's origins are African, not Asian.

When Harman returned to the game, Andy Beal was gone. She followed the eyes of the now preoccupied players in her game to the adjacent table, where he was playing heads up against Howard Lederer.

That fast? Damn. Maybe her luck with Andy hadn't changed. It wasn't a good omen for the week.

Howard and Andy did not play long that evening. Beal, an early riser still on Central Standard Time, tired out early and went to bed. Howard immediately realized, however, that Andy had focused a lot of attention on poker since being blown away in their last heads-up encounter. Andy was ahead when he quit, and they made plans to begin again the next morning.

Lederer won back what he lost, and a little more, but he did not have the easy time he had in March. The banker was not backing down from the pro's attempt to counter his aggression. In fact, he may have been the only player to beat Andy over the next four days.

From Wednesday through Saturday, Andy Beal systematically mowed down the best players in the world, racking up decisive wins over Todd Brunson, Jennifer Harman, John Hennigan, Ted Forrest, Chau Giang, and others. The whole room was feeling the pain. The Bellagio poker room was a pretty open place, and what the regulars didn't actually see, they learned about through an active gossip network. Especially because of the slow times, it seemed every player wanted a piece, or a piece of a piece. Some

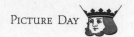

$80–$160 players tried buying 1 percent shares from individual members of the group for $1,000.

Doyle had not reached Todd on Tuesday night, so he was again excluded from the group. As Todd walked through the high-limit section a few days later, however, Beal saw him while dispatching another victim. Andy remembered Todd from the $400–$800 game on his first Bellagio trip as well as from some of the ring games.

He stopped Todd and stuck out his hand. "Todd? Andy Beal."

Todd remembered.

"How about you and me play heads up in a little while?"

The group offered Todd a freeroll—a chance to participate in the outcome of his match without putting up a portion of the bankroll—but he wanted to join as a full member. He was annoyed that he wasn't part of the group from the start. He not only played regularly in the $800–$1,600 and $1,000–$2,000 mixed games at Table One, but he practically discovered Andy Beal. He had a reputation as a hold 'em player and a heads-up player so, to him, it seemed obvious that he not only be on the team but a playing member.

He then proceeded to lose a million dollars in the fastest, ugliest way imaginable. It started when they were both dealt mediocre cards. Todd, on the button in the small blind, was dealt six-four. Todd called and put in the rest of the opening bet, another $5,000. Andy, holding ten-five, raised to $20,000. Todd called. The flop came ten-three-deuce, all different suits. This gave Andy a pair of tens, and Todd an inside straight draw. Andy bet $10,000. Todd raised, and Andy called. There was $80,000 in the pot.

Todd caught his dream card on the turn, a five. It not only filled his straight, but it made Andy two pair, tens and fives. Andy bet, and Todd raised. Andy reraised, and so did Todd. They went back and forth, each throwing eight chips into the pot, until all Todd's chips were committed. (Neither man can recall the precise number of raises, but Todd estimates at least twenty.)

The river card was another five, making Andy a miracle full house.

Todd Brunson's table demeanor is usually low-key, especially around the amateur players who give the pros action and who need luck to remain anywhere near competitive. But this was too much for him to handle. He tried to pull players in the group from the other high-limit tables to show them.

"Come on, look at this hand. Can you believe this? On a runner-runner full house?" (Runner-runner means catching perfect cards on the turn and the river to make the winning hand.)

But it didn't matter. Andy Beal pulled in the million-dollar pot and scanned the room for his next opponent.

Jennifer Harman's experience was no more satisfying. She quickly lost a million dollars to Andy but felt sufficiently in rhythm with his play that she could win it back. Like Todd Brunson, she had lots of experience in limit hold 'em, and enjoyed playing heads up. To her, it was early in the match. But Beal quit on her, so he could play a $100,000 freeze-out with another player in the high-limit section who wasn't even in the group. Her string of bad encounters around Andy continued to grow.

The pros were completely unprepared for Andy to beat them, and for him to do it day after day. They knew an inexperienced opponent could, theoretically, get lucky and win, but they didn't expect that he would do so repeatedly. Consequently, the group did not initially raise more than the $1 million it took into the first heads-up match. That amount had proved sufficient during the first games in March, when Beal never threatened to win their starting bankroll.

Every time Andy Beal cleaned out one of the pros, the team had to reconstitute its bankroll. It was a time-consuming and demoralizing experience, especially because a few players needed to be reminded to get their money down.

In addition to putting up $100,000 or more toward the team bankroll, they needed at least that much to play in their regular game. Poker players were also frequently loaning money and staking other players, plus they periodically removed money for taxes, investments, and living expenses. This did not even take into consideration the possibility of any recent losing sessions, which could have stripped the bankroll of hundreds of thousands of dollars or more. Everyone was a little light in the economic environment of December 2001, with business slow and the players watching nervously, along with the rest of the country, as their investments plummeted amid the post–September 11 uncertainty.

Everybody's week was hectic. In addition to receiving calls to post more money, the players held ad hoc meetings to discuss who was playing next, strategy, Beal's continued requests to raise the stakes above $10,000–$20,000, and who had cash available for members who were short. At first, these meetings took place after Andy went to bed. As they became more frequent and more urgent, players would just peel off to the adjacent sports book to talk.

Panic was in the air. Without exception, the players believed the tide would turn. They knew they held a huge advantage in skill and experience, but how much longer would it take to become evident? Because some of the players had sold or given away small pieces of their shares, players at lower-stakes tables had a financial interest. These players kept peering over, walking by to ask questions, even though it was clear that the answers were not encouraging.

By Saturday, the players were not even maintaining the pretense of keeping their situation from Beal. As the bankroll became depleted yet again, they met right next to the table while he was playing. In addition, there was some concern about whether Andy might take the money and run. He never said how long he intended to stay, and he had been in town since Tuesday. He was feeling sick, and had another player—a local doctor who occasionally played for high stakes—give him some antibiotics.

Although the Doc was just helping out another player in need, a physician could live comfortably off the health impact of the poker lifestyle. It was easy to accumulate bad habits in the poker room: inconsistent sleep patterns, lack of exercise, poor posture, hurried eating, and a fondness for free drinks made with milk and ice cream with whipped cream on top. Several years earlier, the Doc attended to a spectator at the final table of a poker tournament at Binion's Horseshoe who suffered a seizure and stopped breathing. (Another doctor, who was actually playing at the final table, also assisted and revived the man, who survived long enough for the ambulance to arrive.)

How much longer would Andy stay? He had given them plenty of opportunities to get their money back. They just had not capitalized.

Even when it looked like the pros would recoup their losses, their hopes were dashed. John Hennigan, potentially as much a wizard at the poker table as with a pool cue, got ahead of Beal by more than $1.5 million.

When Andy began a comeback, the other players' attention focused on the beer bottles accumulating on Johnny World's side of the table. Nobody attached any significance to Hennigan enjoying a beer while he was winning, but now it looked like he was drinking away millions of dollars. After Andy recovered his losses and steamrolled the pro for at least another million, they ended the game. While his colleagues stared from the next table, Hennigan sat alone, his shaved head in his hands, covered by a red bandanna, sunk low to the table.

* * *

Saturday started as a continuation of the same miasma the entire week had been. Ted Forrest was still playing in a game from Friday night when Andy Beal wandered into the room early in the morning. Andy and Ted were supposed to play later that day, but Andy was having trouble sleeping and, having nothing else to do in Las Vegas, wanted to get started.

Ted agreed to play, but he wasn't holding the team's bankroll. The player who had those chips on account wasn't expected to arrive for several hours. Ted called the other player and told him the starting time had been moved up, so he should come to the Bellagio and get the money from his account. In the meantime, Ted loaned the team the $240,000 he had in his box until the other player arrived.

The experience gave Ted Forrest a fresh opportunity to experience how scary it could be playing high-stakes poker on a short bankroll. Heads-up poker requires playing a lot of hands and playing aggressively, but with a bankroll of only twelve large bets, he felt like Beal was draining his chips while he waited in vain for a hand. As it was becoming certain that Andy would win the $240,000, Forrest asked Beal to front him some additional chips. Unless Andy wanted to put his heater on hold until the bankroll arrived, he would have to loan Ted some chips to keep the game going.

Andy hesitated. Did he really *know* Ted Forrest? Apart from finding him a nice guy and terrific poker player, all Andy knew was that Ted was not part of the original group. Andy just sat down and played, choosing his opponents by names and faces he could remember or recognize. He knew that his opponents were staked by one another, but no one briefed him on the team's composition or financial arrangements. What if he fronted Ted the money, Andy won it, and Doyle said that Ted *still* wasn't part of the group?

He knew he was just being paranoid. As a banker, rather than a gambler, however, their casual handling of financial transactions was alien to him. He loaned Forrest the money so they could continue playing.

But Beal made him sign a promissory note on a napkin.

And he won that money from Ted as well.

Ted lost $620,000 in two hours and let someone else take over. He couldn't shake the feeling that he was on a short bankroll, throwing around too many chips for his own good.

Between the phone calls and the visits to the poker room to post more money, it had been a stressful, chaotic week for Jennifer Harman. She tried to take a break from poker and do some Christmas shopping.

One of the fringe benefits of being a professional poker player is easy access to great shopping, dining, and entertainment. The pros generally took this for granted; after all, you could spend only so much time shopping at Prada and Armani and eating at Wolfgang Puck's. But for the holiday season, this came in handy.

She was next door to the Bellagio at the Forum Shops of Caesars Palace, getting her car from the valet, when she got the first call.

Chau is playing Andy. Surely, Chau would put an end to this and return things to their proper order.

Even among the world's best players, Chau Giang was regarded with respect bordering on awe. Like Jennifer Harman, his ascent in poker was a solo venture. Born and raised in Vietnam, he came to Las Vegas in the early 1980s by way of Florida and Colorado, and set up shop at the $20–$40 hold 'em tables. He slowly moved up. When he finally made it to the big game at the Mirage, he took his lumps in his first encounters with Doyle Brunson and Chip Reese. At one point, he blew a million dollars at baccarat.

But Chau learned from his mistakes. He plugged his leaks and improved his game with more exposure to the best players. By

2001, he may have been the player at Table One most feared by his peers.

There is probably less prejudice in poker than in most areas of American life. There are more stereotypes *about* the players than *from* them. Plenty of ignorant people play poker, so there are bigots of every type among the fifty million or so Americans playing the game. But among the professionals, as the expression went, "cards speak." An opponent's skin color, religion, or nationality would not change the cards. (Women have had some trouble getting respect, but even then, not at the highest levels. And when such dismissive attitudes do occur, high-stakes players like Jennifer Harman and Mimi Tran are happy, because it makes it easier for them to take the money.)

Many émigrés of Vietnam have excelled at poker over the past two decades, but none played for such high stakes or with as much success as Chau Giang. Ultimately, the most important reason the top pros hold Chau in such high regard is because he is so good. And, what is probably the highest compliment a professional poker player can bestow on a peer, Giang has a reputation of playing better when the stakes rise.

By the time Harman got to the Bellagio poker room, however, Chau was broke.

Jennifer could read on the long faces of the other players that something bad had happened. Chau was joining several members of the group at the adjoining table. Jennifer took a seat as well to try to figure out what was going on. Four members were playing Chinese Poker, a game in which each player receives thirteen cards and wins by getting points based on how they arrange the cards into three- and five-card hands. To all but the Table One regulars, Chinese Poker was like TEGWAR (The Exciting Game Without Any Rules), the made-up card game from the movie *Bang the Drum Slowly*. Even those few players who played it for ridiculously high stakes acknowledged that the element of skill in the game was pretty small.

What made this game even more unusual was that there were no chips on the table. Ted Forrest was keeping track of wins and losses with a pencil and a pad of paper. Everybody was out of chips.

Andy Beal walked over to their table.

"Who am I going to play next?" he asked.

Doyle Brunson looked up and gave him a wry smile. "Congratulations, Andy. We're broke. Go back to Texas."

Everybody chuckled, and Doyle said it as a joke, but it wasn't too far from the truth. Between when he arrived the previous Tuesday and that Saturday night, Andy Beal had won $5.3 million. Someone muttered something about "there won't be any more high-stakes games for a while," but Beal thought they were pulling his leg.

Finally, Doyle said, "Okay, Andy. If you want to play some more tonight, I'll play you. We just have to get the money together." Satisfied, Beal went back to his table, alone, with rack after rack of white $5,000 chips.

Everybody was in some form of financial distress. "We're broke" was not an exaggeration. What Brunson technically meant was that everyone's safe deposit box was cleaned out, or nearly so. Hence, the Chinese Poker game "on the pencil." The players had varying amounts of nonpoker assets, some of them substantial. Accessing those assets would require breaking a cardinal rule of money management: Once money leaves the room, it doesn't come back.

Professional gamblers lived and worked on a high wire, and that rule was their only safety net. The old-fashioned road gamblers were proud of going broke, even being broke. But when they wanted to let you know how well they'd really done, they told you how much *their wives* were worth. The late Johnny Moss told a story about how he won $250,000 on a monster run at the craps tables in 1939. He told his wife, Virgie, to find the nicest place she could in Dallas and he would send her the cash. That way, no matter what happened to him, she would have a home. She took a friend and they had a wonderful time, touring the grandest estates the city had to offer. When she finally picked out a home, she called and asked him to send the money. "It's gone," he told her. "You should have looked faster."

More often, the pros just borrowed the money. They were, after all, the best in the world and loaning them money was usually a good risk. Borrowing money was complicated, however, because the pressure was not merely to play well, but to *win*. Some poker players thrived in this situation. Generally, however, it was a circumstance they preferred to avoid. In addition, many of their closest friends were in the same boat. Some of their best sources, therefore, were also broke and anyone they approached could be getting hit up by the other players.

For Howard Lederer, it was a waking nightmare. He had plenty of experience being broke, and a long list of people willing to stake him or loan him money. But he had worked hard for two years to reconcile his gambling lifestyle with a responsible adult's financial discipline. He directed his energies not just to winning, but toward building a secure future. He had also gotten married just six months earlier. Somehow, despite his best efforts and all the changes he had made, he had "gotten broke."

Howard got word that if they could keep Andy in town, the plan would be for him to play Beal at eight the next morning with what might be the last $1.4 million they could gather. (Even after that, the players would not have exhausted their borrowing power or seriously hurt their nonpoker assets, but borrowing more money to play Andy Beal might have been out of the question.) Howard had to force himself to go to bed early, unheard of for a poker player. But he first had to make arrangements to borrow the money needed to post his share by the morning. Just like the rest of the team, he got the call from Doyle. "You better get your money down here or you're not in."

At least Howard was spared the bizarre scene that unfolded next.

While Andy was waiting for Doyle to get the chips to play him and the others played Chinese Poker for IOUs, he sent for the Bellagio photographer. The casino resorts on the Strip all had photographers, usually stationed around the gourmet restaurants, to take commemorative photos of the guests to mark what the casinos hoped were special occasions.

For Andy, this was a very special occasion and he wanted to commemorate it. He was sitting at a poker table with fifteen racks of chips. Each chip was worth $5,000. Each rack was worth a half-million dollars. During the half-hour he waited for the photographer, he removed the chips from their racks and stacked them in rows of twenty. He made one long horizontal row, stretching from his seat at the center of the table almost to one end. But that was fewer than four racks. So he made a second long row, then a third and a fourth. Even after that, he had two racks of chips propped up against the rail.

When the photographer finally arrived, Andy walked over to the adjacent table. He asked Doyle if he would sit for a picture Andy wanted taken. Jennifer Harman and Ted Forrest joined Doyle as they arranged themselves around the fortress of chips.

If the situation was uncomfortable for the players, it was about to get worse. As the photographer told them to hold still and smile, his flash failed to work. They had to freeze in that position as he repeatedly snapped pictures, trying to get the flash to work. Finally, after what seemed like a dozen tries, the flash popped and Beal had his picture.

Andy Beal sat in the middle, behind $7.5 million in chips. Brunson sat to his left, almost leaning away from Andy. The expression on his face is clearly half a smile, half a grimace. Harman and Forrest stood between Brunson and Beal. Jennifer, over Doyle's right shoulder, had a blank expression. Other than Andy, who looked tired and happy, only Ted was smiling. Ted looked like he had been in the room for days—a circumstance not far removed from the truth—but it could just as easily have been a picture of his great accomplishment instead of Andy's, from the expressions on their faces.

There was no sense in which Beal was trying to show up the pros. To Brunson, the man was simply proud of his accomplishment. "Why take anything away from him? If you can't do something like pose for a picture after that, you're in the wrong business." To Harman, it was simply an accommodation to a nice guy. He won all their money, but that didn't make him an enemy.

Ted Forrest agreed with Jennifer and Doyle. "I think he just wanted to have the picture to remember his friends and the trip to Vegas. That's a hell of an accomplishment if you can pull it off, to come to Vegas and play in a game bigger than has ever been played, and face seven or eight of the top twenty players in the world and win. That's one hell of an accomplishment."

And it was one hell of a picture.

Between loans and commitments to post the money by the next morning, Doyle Brunson was able to bring nearly $1.5 million in chips to take one last shot that night at Andy Beal. After the picture, however, Beal had run through his supply of adrenaline. He was exhausted, but after making Brunson and the group scramble around to get the money, he felt he had to play for a little while. It was the sporting thing to do.

After about twenty desultory minutes, Beal caught a lucky run of cards and, in a flash, was ahead $200,000. But the needle on his gas gauge was squarely on E. He made his apologies to Doyle and called for security to pick up his chips. The cashier's cage in the poker room could not store Beal's $7.5 million in chips. Two security guards, using Lucite boxes with metal handles, carried the chips through the casino to the main cage.

He felt a little awkward about not giving Doyle Brunson more play. But otherwise, he felt great. It was after 11:00 P.M., so it was too late to fly home. He would give them another chance in the morning. He fell asleep almost instantly.

6

The Last Lesson of Professor Backwards

Later That Night

It was nearly midnight when Doyle Brunson left the poker room. Before he left, he told the members of the group present—Jennifer Harman, Chau Giang, Ted Forrest—that he thought Howard Lederer was the right choice for the game the next morning.

The players were under no obligation to follow Brunson's advice. In fact, as premier players themselves, they had strong personal reasons for disagreeing. Nevertheless, they expected (and were expected) to follow it without argument. Organizationally, their enterprise was, if anything, socialist in nature. Bound by their common abilities, their trust, and their respect, they had no leaders or decision-making apparatus. They shared in what they put in, and in what they took out.

Brunson was never elected captain, nor did the players vote

on any of the decisions. It was all done informally, but that was the poker way. He was the oldest by a generation, the most experienced, and was respected among the pros above all others. Chip Reese enjoyed a similarly elevated position among his peers, but he was closer in age and background to the other players. He was also out of town this week, though his money was posted.

Doyle's recommendation was just that: his opinion. And no one saw any reason to question it. Like Chau Giang, Jennifer Harman, and Todd Brunson, Howard Lederer had moved through the poker ranks on the strength of his hold 'em game. Because Howard started so young and made his bones in the rough-and-tumble underground clubs in New York, Brunson's assessment was backed up by Lederer's deep experience, especially in difficult financial situations.

Not that anyone would explicitly concede the point; every member of the group would step forward to play Beal with their financial stability on the line rather than have it ride on someone else's shoulders. None would admit that their talent was inferior to Howard's. But it was a reasonable recommendation, and from an impeccable source.

Doyle Brunson left the details to the group, as well as who would safeguard the remaining $1.2 million of the bankroll until the match on Sunday morning. Once Brunson was gone, Jennifer Harman looked at all those chips and thought, now we can play poker! They abandoned the Chinese Poker game and started a $1,500–$3,000 mixed game. As the players got the chips broken down into smaller denominations, they established some special rules.

The chips could not leave the table at the end of the night. The losers would have to settle up separately with the winners. This was the team's bankroll and it needed to be turned over in its entirety to Howard Lederer the next morning. Likewise, anyone playing in the game who wasn't part of the group was told of the situation: Their winnings had to stay on the table as part of the joint bankroll.

Jennifer Harman was one of the winners that night. Her profit meant that she would not need to post her share the next morning. Finally, something good came of the week.

By 4:30 A.M., Sunday, she decided it was time for this long, strange day to end. Chau and Ted kept playing on with a few others. Gamblers defined their sleep needs differently from the rest of the world and those two in particular seemed to take a childlike joy in playing for days on end, as if they were kids who tricked the baby-sitter into missing their bedtime.

Just as Jennifer was leaving the poker room, Andy Beal was waking up. He could never adjust his body clock to the Pacific Time Zone, nor could he get used to the desert air. Even with the antibiotics, he wasn't feeling well. But he was wide awake with nothing to do.

When Jennifer got home, it was just after 5:00 A.M. She remembered something they needed to tell Howard. Andy had been pressuring his opponents to double the stakes, to $20,000–$40,000. The group decided that they should not give in. It would be easier for them to take advantage of their edge on the relatively short bankroll if they kept the stakes down, at least initially.

It was too early to call Lederer, so she dialed Ted Forrest's cell phone. He would probably play poker until Howard took the bankroll away.

"Remember to tell Howard we're going to start at ten-and-twenty."

"No," Ted said. "We're going to play twenty-forty."

Ted's voice seemed distant. Then it dawned on her.

"Really?" she asked a bit sarcastically. "You're already playing him, huh?"

"Yeah."

"Well, good luck." They said goodbye and hung up. So it would be Ted Forrest, who had been in the room playing for two days straight, rather than Howard Lederer, recommended by Doyle Brunson as their best hold 'em player.

Nevertheless, she fell asleep without any trouble. She was a gambler and this was a good gamble. Ted Forrest should be better than Andy Beal, and her money was down. She had the right side of the bet and there was nothing more to do.

Her husband, Marco, didn't have it so easy. He had been a wreck all week, trying to keep up with the phone calls and the meetings, how far behind they were. He tried to balance being present and supportive with giving her space and not adding his concerns to the woes of the week.

Not that his concerns would have mattered. When he married Jennifer a year earlier, he knew what he was getting: a strong-willed woman who gambled for a living. She made it clear that she was going to be part of this group until the end, no matter how it turned out. There would be no debate or discussion.

Marco Traniello could live with that. He just couldn't eat or sleep with it very well.

For Andy Beal and Ted Forrest, Sunday morning looked like a replay of Saturday morning. It was hours before the scheduled time of his game, but Andy couldn't fall back asleep. He walked into the poker room, to find Ted Forrest squeezing out the last bit of action before morning. Andy, at least, had gotten most of a night's sleep. Ted and Chau Giang looked like they had been in the room since Steve Wynn nailed the roof on.

Ted again agreed to play Andy, bypassing Brunson's recommendation and the consensus of the group. Ted and Chau gathered the chips borrowed from the group's bankroll and changed them for flags. Because Forrest was feeling a little tired, he made

Giang sit and watch, or "sweat," the game. Chau, however, was even more exhausted, so he set up a row of chairs and periodically lay across them, catching short naps.

When Beal asked about raising the stakes, Ted agreed without argument. The $1.2 million bankroll was big enough for a $20,000–$40,000 game, and Ted was from the sit-down-and-play school. In general, he did not labor over getting the largest possible edge before playing.

Professional gamblers faced this all the time, choosing between the conflicting goals of maximizing their advantage and marketing themselves so people would gamble with them. After all, if the members of the group somehow demonstrated to Andy Beal that their advantage was so big that he had no chance whatsoever, he would never sit down to play them. Likewise, if they would play only under conditions that favored them in every way, he would eventually become frustrated by their inability to give him a fair chance and give up.

Poker was a game of skill, but if you played it for a living, you also had to be willing to gamble. Someone who bet only on sure things may be smart, but they would have to work hard to find people who would bet against them. A gambler who would enter a situation where the edge wasn't clear, or when it looked like he had the worst of it, would always be in action.

The best gamblers, therefore, weren't necessarily the ones who were best at getting the edge. The true professionals—those most respected and often the most successful—were those whose carefree attitude might sometimes cost them, but who had the extraordinary instincts and management skills to handle the bad gambles while cashing in on all the favorable situations their "let's gamble" style brought their way.

As skilled as Ted Forrest was at poker, this aspect—combining socializing, marketing, having fun, the urge to gamble, and instinct—set him apart even from other top professionals. His willingness to gamble on anything, even when he appeared to be a huge underdog, had earned him the nickname "Professor Backwards" from his closest gambling buddies.

Just for the sake of action, Ted would propose and take ridiculous bets. He has a bet outstanding with Jennifer Harman that he can beat her at Ping-Pong using her cell phone as a paddle. The wager is for $500 but Harman has the option to increase the stakes to $20,000.

Ted had a bet with a friend over whether another friend would win the World Series of Poker before a major leaguer hit 100 home runs in a season. He has wagered thousands of dollars on his ability to guess how much people weigh.

He has made bets with several friends over how fast they could run a mile. If he hears someone he knows is trying to lose weight, he may make them a weight-loss bet. This led to the famous "cross-weights" bet with Mike Svobodny against Huck Seed and Howard Lederer. Svobodny was one of the world's best backgammon players. Seed, like Forrest and Lederer, was a world-class poker player who won the World Championship in 1996 along with three other World Series bracelets, as well as a tremendous athlete. All four men were action junkies.

The cross-weights bet had its genesis in the usual New Year's resolutions. Lederer wanted to lose a lot of weight. Seed, over six and a half feet tall and wiry, was going to begin weight training to bulk up. As an incentive, Forrest and Svobodny bet Lederer and Seed $50,000 each that they could not cross weights during the year. To win the bet, Huck Seed had to outweigh Howard Lederer at some time during the year. Howard started at over 300 pounds. Huck weighed 180.

Lederer and Seed had to pay off. After several months, Howard was struggling to lose weight and still had a long way to go. Seed, training regularly with weights, actually *lost* four pounds.

Forrest's devil-may-care approach masked an iron will. One night, he lost $60,000 in a poker game. This was not an extraordinary sum based on the stakes, but it especially bothered Ted for some reason. As the game broke up early in the morning, he vowed not to leave the poker room until he won back the money.

Unfortunately, the biggest game still going was $30–$60 stud. He could beat that game like a drum around the clock for months and not win $60,000. But he had made himself a promise, so he sat down. He then proceeded to get hit by the deck, the gambler's expression for getting great cards, and won $2,500 in less than an hour.

He experienced another piece of good fortune when Erik Seidel walked into the room and noticed him sitting at the $30–$60 game. Would Ted like to play some heads-up hold 'em, say $300–$600?

Ted not only took Erik up on the offer but also called their friend Howard Lederer. Ted knew that Lederer shared the opinion that Ted was not a great hold 'em player, while the general—and correct—opinion was that Seidel was an excellent hold 'em player. Seidel won three World Series hold 'em events and finished second to Johnny Chan in the world championship in 1988.

Would Howard like to book 100 percent of Erik's action?

Howard took the bet, agreeing to duplicate whatever Seidel's results were in the game.

By the time other players joined the game and they declared the bet closed several hours later, Forrest beat Seidel for over $15,000 (and an equal amount from Lederer). After another eight hours of playing in the $300–$600 ring game, Ted won enough to wipe out his $60,000 loss and claim a small profit for the session. He still does not know why he made this pledge, but he understood what he learned about himself. "If you make a promise like that and keep it, and do that several times, you gain a lot of confidence in yourself."

Ted Forrest could also extend himself physically beyond reasonable limits. He has several times played poker for 100 hours or more. Part of the lore of the Mirage poker room was the four-day $600–$1,200 game Ted played with Hamid Dastmalchi, the 1992 World Champion and a man similarly possessed of a cast-iron constitution. At the end of it, Dastmalchi was taken out of the Mirage in an ambulance. Forrest joked that it was all the bad beats he showed Hamid, but it may have had more to do with the estimated *fifty* packs of cigarettes Dastmalchi smoked during the game. "And he lit only one match," Ted noted when telling the story.

Back in July 1996, Ted jumped into a juicy-looking ultra-high-stakes game of Pot Limit Omaha and lost $250,000, the most he had ever lost in a session and his entire bankroll. He walked home from the Mirage in the middle of the night through the worst area of town he could find, hoping someone would attack him. There were no takers.

The next day, at tennis with Mike Svobodny and Huck Seed (Mike had bet Huck that Huck couldn't play tennis eight hours a day for a month), Forrest asked Svobodny if he would pay him $5,000 to run a marathon that week. The next morning, Svobodny woke him up to say the bet was on. He would actually bet Ted $6,000 that he couldn't run a marathon that day at the UNLV track, 106 laps.

"Make it $7,000 and it's a deal."

Svobodny agreed before Ted woke up enough to realize what he'd gotten himself into. It was the Fourth of July in Las Vegas, and the temperature was expected to climb above 110 degrees. The UNLV track was red, rubber urethane, which would radiate the heat.

Huck Seed showed up to run with Ted. (Huck once won a huge golf bet by shooting under 96 for four rounds in one day without a cart, using only three clubs, on one of the hottest days of the year. He not only improved his score each round, but he shot 96 in the opening round and therefore had to play five rounds that day.) He had a separate bet with Svobodny to run the marathon.

The two men were such incredible athletes that they were fine for the first fifty or so laps. They even talked about how much they might get Svobodny to bet them that they couldn't do it five days in a row. Forrest recalled: "The next six miles were a lot tougher. And the last six? It wasn't even human."

Huck finished first and the UNLV track coach, amazed that someone was out on the track, asked what Forrest was doing. "He could die out there," the coach said.

By the end, Ted was suffering from heat exhaustion. He said the sole of one of his feet actually separated from his foot and came off in his sock. He may have run two extra laps because he could no longer think clearly enough to count or make himself stop. "It was two weeks before I felt human again. Today, I wouldn't take that bet for $100,000."

So even if Forrest had been in the poker room for days on end and was not, by reputation, the best hold 'em player in the group, he brought enormous resources to the table that he could call upon in an important confrontation. This was the kind of challenge, mental and physical, that Ted craved, an opportunity to break through the walls of fatigue, doubt, and failure.

Even though he let Andy raise the stakes, and was just one day removed from the feeling that he was taking a beating for being undercapitalized, Ted Forrest had a plan. The usual strategy for heads-up poker, especially among the pros, was to play as aggressively as possible. If an opponent showed just a bit of weakness, the aggressive pro could run them over, as Howard Lederer did the first time he played Beal heads up. But Beal wasn't backing down on this trip. That meant they were playing showdown poker for a couple hundred thousand dollars per hand. Where did their edge in skill and experience go? When they played aggression vs. aggression, it was just a coin flip over who had the better cards. Beal's deeper bankroll (especially now that he had most of *their* bankroll) gave him the best of that confrontation, even if they somehow used their skill to a small advantage.

So Forrest stood the traditional strategy on its head. He would play more passively, though only by degree. The idea would be to let Andy win more pots, but use his superior skill and experience to get away from weaker hands and win most of the big pots.

The strategy immediately began paying off. The group's bankroll was not fluctuating by large amounts every single hand. The size of the average pot dropped. Fewer pots were contested to the end. Forrest was folding more hands, but mixing up his play with the hands he pushed, and took a majority of the big pots.

Andy Beal was also starting to wear down. He had done little but play poker, eat, and sleep since Tuesday and it was now Sunday. He was sick and he wasn't sleeping well. Looking back on his play, he thought he was becoming careless in handling his cards, holding them and placing them differently based on their quality. It was not a big error, but one a pro like Forrest could catch and exploit.

Beal also realized that the time he took to make a decision provided his world-class opponents with too much information. Therefore, especially as the games became a grind, he would decide quickly how to play strong cards and weak cards. Even if he played the cards contrary to their strength, he would decide quickly. With a borderline hand, however, especially after the flop, it took him a few more seconds to decide on the play. It was not a flaw obvious to most players, and Beal did not discover it until later, but it was ammunition to a player of Ted Forrest's caliber.

As it got closer to the time when Howard Lederer would be

coming to the poker room, Ted and Howard talked on the phone. How was Ted doing? How was he feeling?

"I'm winning," Ted replied.

"Then I probably won't come in until a little later."

When Howard came by later in the morning, he saw three very ragged-looking men at Table Seven: Ted Forrest, Chau Giang, and Andy Beal. Only one of them looked like he wasn't there as part of some prison sentence, the once preppy-looking man with a growing pile of flags in front of him, Ted Forrest.

Finally, around 1:00 P.M., Ted decided he felt fatigued and told Howard that he wanted him to take over. Other players had been calling in throughout the morning. As he took Howard aside to talk during a short break, he made a mental note of the chip count.

Nine racks, one stack.

Nine hundred twenty flags.

Four million six hundred thousand dollars.

Subtracting the morning's starting bankroll, Forrest had won back $3.4 million of the group's money. They were still stuck $2 million, but disaster had been averted. If things stayed as they were, the players would be looking at a loss in the area of $200,000 each, compared with over $500,000 apiece as of early Sunday morning. Almost more important, if Lederer could hold on to these chips, everyone now would have several hundred thousand dollars in their box. They could play their regular games and rebuild their individual bankrolls.

Forrest explained to Lederer his new strategy for playing Beal. This was a unique opportunity for Howard. Professional poker players did not often have the chance to discuss strategy. Occasionally, in a tournament, pros might discuss the play of a hand afterward or during a break, but that was more just chatting than a serious exchange of information. Primarily, their most frequent opponents were one another, so it obviously made no sense discussing strategy with a target of that strategy. Even talking about fairly innocuous matters could provide an opponent insight.

That was what made poker such a lonely profession. The players were bound together by their love of action and by their common skills—and among the very best, their extraordinary skills were understood by only one another—but they were adversaries and restrained from discussing the very thing that brought them together hundreds, or even thousands, of hours a year.

To keep from becoming even more maladjusted, the professionals became close friends with their adversaries, mastering the trick of separating the professional from the personal. Outsiders occasionally used the friendships and common bonds of the elite players as "evidence" that they must be ganging up on outsiders. How could they really be taking each other's money if they were so chummy away from the table?

But how could it be otherwise? It was extremely difficult for poker players at this level to maintain relationships with people outside the gambling business. If a player had to give in to animosity against all opponents, every night would be like going into battle, alone, against everyone in sight. And if the player had to treat every other player as the enemy, who could they share a ride to the airport with, or a round of golf?

Contrary to what some people would like to believe, these friends really did compete hard against one another at the poker table. One time, in a mixed game, the Table One regulars were playing Deuce-to-Seven. Jennifer Harman and Doyle Brunson were competing in a hand, heads up by the end. According to Jennifer, she turned over her hand and the dealer said "seven low," an excellent hand. Brunson mucked his hand, throwing the cards face down into the discard pile. Then he noticed that there were two deuces in Jennifer's hand. She didn't have an excellent low hand, but a pair of deuces; Doyle had thrown away the winning hand.

Brunson was furious, and he does not get angry often. He called a floorman, but he ruled as expected: once a player throws a hand into the discard pile, the hand is dead. Harman got the pot, and the force of Brunson's anger. The incident was so upsetting that she had to leave the room. Even in the days after, it was uncomfortable for them to play together.

"Jennifer," he groused, "you'd steal the quarters off a dead man's eyes."

After a week, Doyle finally got over it. But that he could get that angry—at a woman who regarded him like a father, whom he loved like a daughter, whom his son dated for over five years—provided an idea of how seriously they took the games against each other. And the closeness of the relationships away from the table, and their ability to resume them after such disagreements, demonstrated a rare ability to separate business from personal relations.

Howard Lederer appreciated the rare opportunity to share strategy with his friend-colleague-competitor. Lederer believed in a more aggressive style for heads-up hold 'em than Forrest, but his advice made sense. Howard would remain aggressive but mix up his play a bit more. He would try to keep down the fluctuations in their bankroll and aim for controlling the action after the flop and winning the bigger pots.

Not satisfied with merely maintaining the day's win and holding down the group's loss, Howard continued to attack. As the afternoon dragged on, Andy Beal's play became more erratic. He became careless and increasingly disregarded his carefully developed game plan.

Less than twenty-four hours after having his picture taken with 1,000 flags won with cunning and skill from the world's best poker players, Andy Beal had given every chip back. Almost worse for Beal, he again stayed beyond the last flight, and trudged back to his room with nothing to look forward to but another restless night.

Andy lost again before he left town on Monday, not a huge amount but enough to allow the players to claim a small profit. It was a nice Christmas present, considering how they were looking at a loss of approximately $500,000 apiece just thirty-six hours earlier. They stuck together, buoyed one another's spirits, helped one another through the financial scrapes of the previous week, and hung on long enough for Ted Forrest and Howard Lederer to finally assert the group's advantage in skill.

For Beal, the loss stung more than the amount involved, or the swing to a small loss from a $5.5 million profit. He had lost much more than that in business. This felt personal.

Like the players, he could separate his competitive feelings from his personal feelings. He was coming to like and admire the players. But the contest was more intimate than any kind of business he had ever conducted. The pros sought to expose and exploit every weakness. He did not expect to become a superior poker player in less than a year. But his four-day winning streak gave him the impression that he had made progress, that his theories for bridging the gap were correct. It was painful for it all to fall apart so fast and so decisively.

That was why Andy Beal decided before he even left Las Vegas on Monday afternoon that he had to give up poker forever.

PART II

ACTION

7

Gone

Interregnum, 2002–2003

That Monday in December 2001, Andy Beal told Chip Reese that he was through with poker, and he meant it. At least he thought he did.

Reese had returned to town and the two men had lunch before Beal went back to Dallas. People who considered professional card players somewhere between con men and crooks would say he was merely "chilling out the mark."

Such an interpretation, however, fundamentally misrepresented the scene. Beal had lost fair and square. If there was some scheme to cheat him, it was either unrealistically brilliant or unrealistically stupid, because he had won $5.5 million of the players' money before they won it back and eked out a small profit. Although Andy periodically took steps to make sure the game was on the level, he did this merely out of prudence and his thorough examinations and precautions never revealed anything that could have been interpreted as cheating.

To the contrary, Andy Beal got his money's worth. He found a group of the best poker players in the world and had them on call to play him whenever he wanted for almost a week. Even though he was a novice and they were motivated to play their best, he nearly had them pinned for the count. To be able to play—and defeat—in succession Jennifer Harman, Todd Brunson, John Hennigan, Ted Forrest, Chau Giang, and Doyle Brunson would be the experience of a lifetime for any person who played poker. If you gathered all the people in the world who could afford to spend a million dollars on a challenge or test, Beal would not be the only one to choose this experience.

Consequently, professional poker players have learned over the last twenty-five years that "honesty is the greatest hustle in gambling." (Howard Lederer said that, attributing it to London high-stakes player Ali Sarkeshik, though it could have just as easily originated with Mario Puzo, Tennessee Williams, or Fyodor Dostoevsky.) The reason a person like Chip Reese—solid in education and values from middle-class Dayton and Ivy League Dartmouth—had thrived in Las Vegas for thirty years was that he was simultaneously much more skilled than his adversaries, yet never ran out of men with money and inferior skills who would challenge him. A dishonest man in this position could have made some of the scores Reese had to his credit, but only an honest gambler could so consistently win and keep his outclassed opponents coming back for more.

Reese and his colleagues were like a casino in that regard. A casino running a crooked game would be sure of making money, but would ultimately be found out or at least suspected of cheating, which would chase away gamblers. The honest, heavily regulated modern casinos with their tiny edge make billions and sometimes have to turn people away.

Reese was a gambler's gambler, superbly skillful at the games, but also at the game of staying in action and showing his opponents a good time. Was being friendly and treating his amateur opponents with respect manipulative or cynical or hypocritical? Sure, Chip Reese was a salesman. But he was selling an honest gamble against a skilled opponent, and he did it well.

Beal told him that he was giving up poker. It was taking up too much of his time. He and his wife were expecting another child, and he had a lot going on at his bank.

"I'd appreciate it if you wouldn't call me. I don't think I want to play anymore and I don't want to be tempted."

Reese understood. A professional gambler knew that the urge to play could be irresistible. Chip had an expression for it: a gambler in heat. He worked on controlling it in himself and profiting from it in others, but was careful not to exploit it. Gambler's remorse could be powerful and it was rarely worth it to win one time and sour your opponent from coming back. You could shear a sheep countless times, but slaughter it only once.

He and Doyle Brunson would respect Andy's wishes. The men finished lunch and Reese drove Andy Beal to the airport so he could catch his flight back to Dallas.

If being nice was hustling, then Chip Reese was definitely a hustler. But he was being true to his nature and, after all, honesty was the best hustle of all.

Poker is such a stupid game, Andy thought. It has no redeeming value and takes up so much time. I'm not going to spend my life like that.

That feeling lasted several months, through the birth of Andy's son in February 2002. They were simply better than me, he told himself. I put a lot of effort into the game but I still couldn't beat them. I can do better things with my life.

Beal's sole contact with professional poker for most of 2002 was in February. It was the only time Brunson and Reese broke their promise not to contact Andy. The banker had learned while he was in Las Vegas the previous December that his new director of risk management, Craig Singer, was a poker buff. He, in turn, mentioned it in passing to Brunson. A copy of Doyle Brunson's *Super System,* autographed and shipped by the lead author, materialized on Craig's desk.

During spring 2002, the World Series of Poker started a process that fundamentally altered the perceptions of millions of people about poker. It started slowly, almost imperceptibly. The top pros, even those who didn't bother with tournaments, all played in the main event, which drew a record 631 players. Even Doyle Brunson and Chip Reese surprised everyone by entering.

The World Series was a creation of the Binion family and the pros played—usually the main event and events that functioned as reunions for the high-stakes poker fraternity, like Deuce-to-Seven and Chinese Poker, during the brief time it was an event—out of respect for the memory of Benny Binion and because of their friendship with his son, Jack. Benny Binion, of course, built Binion's Horseshoe, started the World Series of Poker, and was regarded as a friend and patron by generations of poker players.

But Jack Binion lost a family fight for control in 1998. Following Jack Binion's development of a gaming business separate from his family and various lawsuits, he sold his family stock to sister Becky Binion Behnen. Jack's ouster, followed by the dismissal of the World Series staff, led Doyle and Chip to skip the event.

For only the second time in the history of the World Series, in 2002 an amateur made off with the championship. Robert Varkonyi, an MIT-educated computer programmer working on Wall Street, won the bracelet. As word spread that an amateur had bested the pros for $2 million, more people were sure to give poker a try. The new phenomenon of Internet poker was already making the game more accessible to players who lived far from a casino or who had felt intimidated as novices by the atmosphere of a poker room.

Among the high-stakes players, the Series was most notable for Jennifer Harman. She had decided to play a few more events. She finished fourteenth out of 610 competitors in the first event of the Series, $2,000 buy-in Limit Texas Hold 'Em, and made it to the final table of a Seven Card Stud event ten days later.

On May 11 and 12, in the $5,000 buy-in Limit Texas Hold 'Em Championship, Jennifer triumphed over a talented field of 113 to win $212,440. For only the eighth time in World Series history, a woman won an open event. Twice, that woman was Jennifer Harman. Mimi Tran, Barry Greenstein's protégée—he taught her poker in exchange for her teaching him Vietnamese—finished third. Tran, a high-stakes player in L.A., was now also among the top all-time female money winners at the World Series. Ironically, the women-only event ran the same day.

John Hennigan also won a bracelet. Chip Reese even contended in the championship for a while, reaching as high as second position in chips at the end of Day Two, but was eliminated on Day Three. Otherwise, however, the World Series was a distraction for the high-stakes pros, though a welcome one because it drew together the fraternity of big-money players. The wins by Jennifer and Johnny World were significant, but most of the cash players simply didn't bother.

Less than a week after the conclusion of the Series, on May 27, 2002, the Bellagio hosted a $10,000 buy-in No-Limit Texas Hold 'Em tournament as the inaugural event of the new World Poker Tour. Back in February, documentary filmmaker Steve Lipscomb and Lyle Berman agreed to organize a series of filmed poker tournaments. (It would not be until January 2003, when half the first season of tournaments had been completed and filmed, that the WPT lined up the Travel Channel to air the episodes.)

Lipscomb brought excellent credentials and cutting-edge ideas to the project. He had filmed poker tournaments, including the World Series of Poker. He believed the key to TV poker was in a specially designed hole-card camera that would allow the television audience to see the players' hidden cards.

Nevertheless, the key to getting the World Poker Tour off the ground was the participation by Lyle Berman. He brought money (a $3.5 million investment by a subsidiary of his gaming company, Lakes Gaming), a history of success in business, and, most important for this project, credibility in the poker world.

Lyle had attended Wharton Business School at the University of Pennsylvania but was kicked out after being arrested for gambling. (Charges were dismissed.) Lyle later joined the army, then graduated from the University of Minnesota and went to work in his family's retail leather business. He expanded the business into a chain of twenty-seven stores, and sold it to W. R. Grace in 1979. He continued to run the operation, expanded it to over 200 locations, led a leveraged buyout in 1986, and resold it in 1987.

After recovering from a health scare that led him to sell the leather business (now part of Wilson's, The Leather Experts, a staple in malls nationwide), he invested in a series of start-ups, one of which became Rainforest Café. He was the CEO of Rainforest from 1994 to 2000.

In 1990, some other venture investors told Lyle about a project to build and operate an Indian casino north of Minneapolis. Berman invested $3 million and took the venture public in 1992 as Grand Casinos. Eventually, the company operated three Indian casinos in Minnesota and two in Louisiana. It also owned three Mississippi casinos, and was part owner of the ill-fated Stratosphere in Las Vegas.

The Stratosphere again demonstrated that the bonds among

poker players were strong enough to survive stresses beyond competition at the tables. The Stratosphere started as Vegas World, a casino built by Pittsburgh native and self-nicknamed "Polish Prince," Bob Stupak. Vegas World, a wacky place with a spaceman painted on a hotel tower and featuring Cher as a headliner during one of her many career slumps, was located in the no-man's-land between the Strip and Downtown. Stupak, a tireless promoter who once ran for mayor of Las Vegas, was also a high-stakes poker player. He won the Deuce-to-Seven Championship in 1989. He tried expanding his eclectic property into a first-class resort, but overextended himself. Grand Casinos provided financial help, but the project still fell into bankruptcy, and Grand took a beating. Nevertheless, Berman and Stupak remained friendly competitors at the poker table.

In 1998, Grand merged with the casino division of Hilton to form Park Place Entertainment, one of the world's largest gaming companies. After clashing with the board of directors at Park Place, Lyle began running Lakes Gaming, developing contracts to build and operate more casinos on Indian lands.

Berman's poker credentials were first-class. He started playing in Vegas in 1983 and became good friends with Chip Reese and Doyle Brunson. He was a regular part of the highest-stakes games during the World Series and whenever the biggest players congregated.

Was he a live one, an outsider the pros built a game around? The point was arguable. He did not play nearly as much as the pros, and made no secret that he didn't really like limit poker and mixed games. (He would prefer playing No-Limit or Pot Limit Omaha or Hold 'Em, though he played all the games at high limits.) Lyle could certainly *afford* to be the live one, and enjoyed the time spent with his friends, who were also very talented players.

On the other hand, he was a tough competitor with a long list of tournament successes for an occasional player: three World Series bracelets in different forms of poker (Limit Omaha, No-Limit Texas Hold 'Em, and Deuce-to-Seven), a final table appearance in the main event, and a victory in the main event of Binion's Hall of Fame Tournament in 1991, when that was the second biggest tournament of the year. In September 2002, he was inducted into Binion's Poker Hall of Fame, one of only twelve men to receive that honor in their lifetime.

Berman started putting his credibility to work by first approaching the Bellagio to be a charter sponsor of this new World Poker Tour. Berman wanted the Bellagio to host two tournaments during the first season. The new venture, World Poker Tour LLC, would charge each venue $50,000 per tournament to have its property featured. This would be a substantial sum for promotional consideration, in view of the fact that poker had never found a good TV audience, no one knew whether players would support a poker tour, and the WPT did not have a TV contract.

Doug Dalton, the director of poker operations for the Bellagio and parent company MGM Mirage, however, wanted the company to take the leap. This was exactly the kind of promotion he wanted to do for the poker room, which would in turn both attract poker players to the Bellagio (some of whom would be good customers for the casino) and show off the property wherever and whenever the tournaments aired. Bellagio president Bobby Baldwin, who knew Berman from years of high-stakes poker games, agreed to let Dalton give it a try. To seal the deal, Berman and Lipscomb agreed to charge all the charter members of the tour only half the site fee for the first season.

For Dalton, the timing couldn't be better. He had just hired Jack McClelland, longtime tournament director of the World Series of Poker, as his director of tournament operations. Between the two of them, they were able to help Berman cement the first season of the tour. Dalton lined up the Bicycle Casino in Los Angeles, and the Aviation Club in Paris. McClelland convinced Jack

Binion, owner of the Horseshoe Casino Hotel in Tunica, Mississippi, to host a WPT event. McClelland's contacts at the Commerce Casino in L.A., and online poker site UltimateBet.com also came through and they hosted events during the first season. The tour eventually lined up twelve tournaments for that season, in large part through the efforts of Dalton and McClelland.

Asking tournament players to plunk down $10,000 twice within a week may have been expecting too much, but scheduling the first event of the tour at this time benefited the non–Las Vegas players, who were still in town from the World Series. Without the luxury of preliminary events or satellites, 146 players still showed up to pay and play. Because it was Berman and the Bellagio, the high-stakes pros supported the event. Doyle Brunson and Chip Reese played, giving the tournament immediate legitimacy.

This time, Doyle Brunson took a run at this new generation of tournament players. After the first day, he was in fourth place out of 100 players still left. He was eliminated, however, on the second day of the competition. (Chip did not last the first day this time.) Lyle Berman outlasted his friends. He was in tenth position at the end of Day Two, but was eliminated on Day Three. The final table featured an eclectic mix of cash game pros and tournament specialists, including John Juanda, Freddy Deeb, Scotty Nguyen, and John Hennigan. First place and $556,000 went to Gus Hansen, a tall, angular Dane who started as a professional backgammon player and alternately awed and infuriated his competitors with his bizarre hand selection and reads on his opponents. It would be ten months before the edited version of the final table appeared on the Travel Channel, but the players were excited about the debut.

After a disappointing World Series in which he put forth little effort and had no positive results, Howard Lederer decided to change his approach to tournament poker. Other than the tradition of the no-limit championship, he had gradually cut himself off from the tournament world to focus on cash games. Though he did not regret, and in fact relished, the time spent playing the biggest games in the world with legends like Doyle Brunson and Chip Reese, he wondered if he was missing out on something by losing touch with tournament poker. More important, was he *about* to miss out on something?

He had no specific expectations for how the World Poker Tour would turn out. Still nearly a year away from actually showing up on television, it was little more than an attempt to organize and slightly expand the number of big no-limit hold 'em tournaments. But he sensed it could be the Next Big Thing and if it was, he wanted a piece. He also wanted to improve on his dismal record in the main event of the World Series: fifth place in his first try, then fifteen consecutive finishes out of the money. Lederer decided to play all the major no-limit tournaments between that summer and the 2003 World Series of Poker, and take stock afterward.

In November 2002, in the sixth event of the World Poker Tour, Lederer's efforts bore fruit. Howard won the $10,000 buy-in World Poker Finals at the Foxwoods Resort Casino in Connecticut. He defeated eighty-eight other players to win $320,000, including a tough final table featuring Phil Ivey (who won three World Series events that spring), MIT-Harvard–educated engineer–lawyer–poker player Andy Bloch, and Las Vegas tournament pro Layne Flack.

After twenty years in poker, Howard Lederer was about to become an overnight sensation.

When Andy Beal would pass Craig Singer in the hallways at Beal Bank, they would often exchange small talk about their common interest in poker. Singer was tall, approximately Beal's height, but many years younger. He had a boyish face and a serious, earnest manner. The bank hired him to direct compliance, auditing, and internal control functions. Because of Beal Bank's complex operations and position in a highly regulated environment, he always had plenty to do. Andy would usually end these brief conversations by saying, "We've got to get together and play sometime," before one (or both) of them would dash off in opposite directions.

It took almost a year, but Andy Beal's brain would not allow him to let go of poker completely. Involuntarily almost, his mind focused on trying to figure it out. He started to analyze *why* they had beaten him. He would have to identify his weaknesses and shore them up. Then he would have to figure out how to deprive the pros of their strengths and somehow take them out of their comfort zone. If he could make the contest come down to fundamentals, he might have a chance.

In December 2002, Craig Singer was working in his office. There was a board meeting the following week and he had to gather materials on accounting, internal controls, and financial results. He got a call from the boss.

"What are you doing?"

Craig explained that he was getting ready for the board meeting.

"I want to play some poker, Craig."

"Okay, how about tomorrow after work. I could get this finished—"

"No, I want to play right now."

Singer would still have to find time to finish his work. But a few minutes later, he was with Beal on the fifth floor, clearing space on a table in a nearly empty area of the bank to set down chips and cards. Then they played Texas Hold 'Em, heads up, a freeze-out for $100.

* * *

In December 2002, Marco and Jennifer Traniello flew to Italy to spend the Christmas holidays with Marco's family. The decision to spend time away from Las Vegas was not entered into lightly.

Although they had made previous trips to Italy, they had gone during the summer, the slow season in Vegas. Late December was a busy time for poker players. It was a rare concession to regimentation; like nightclub entertainers, poker players spend a lot of holidays on the job, the flip side of working at what other people—vacationing people—did for fun.

It had already been a big year for Jennifer. She won her second bracelet. The big games were getting bigger and better. Sharing the holidays with Marco and Jennifer would be a big deal for the Traniello family, and a big deal for her. They planned the trip.

While in Italy, she kept in touch with her friends back in Vegas. While talking with Chip Reese, she found out that Andy Beal was coming to town during New Year's week.

She had to leave Marco and his family behind and make the trip back to the United States. She returned only to find that Andy's plans must have changed; he wasn't coming after all. She spent New Year's Eve sleeping, jet-lagged and angry at leaving Marco and his family for a game that wasn't even happening.

She didn't know that Beal had never planned to come to Las Vegas, nor had he called anyone to say he was coming. It was a case of a practical joke gone awry. It was nearly two years before Jennifer learned of this, and she still refused to believe it.

After playing a few hours a day for about a week, Andy Beal told Craig Singer that he was thinking about returning to Las Vegas for another big game. If Craig was interested, Andy would like Craig to help him prepare. Beal did not have to state the obvious to his employee: This was not part of Craig's job and, in fact, Craig would be expected to keep on top of his work even if Beal and poker took up some of his time. Craig jumped at the chance.

The office game evolved. They covered the six-foot table on the fifth floor with felt and played there for a while. Then they played in a space adjacent to Beal's corner office on the fourth floor so he could be easier to reach for bank business. Finally, they moved the game to a second-floor conference room. They played intermittently but often, between business at the bank and on evenings and weekends when they could spare the time from their families.

Beal and Singer gradually converted the conference room into a poker room. They replaced the conference table with a regulation ten-seat poker table. They had the overhead lighting transformed with several large pieces of cardboard to approximate the lighting of the Bellagio poker room. A natural hoarder, Beal stocked cases of Kem playing cards (the same kind used by the Bellagio), plastic cut cards used by dealers, dealer buttons, and cases of bottled water.

The structure of their games was nearly always the same: Each started with 300 chips and they played 2–4 until one of them had all the chips. They always played for $100, but the experience itself (and the bragging rights for the winner) provided greater incentive to the two competitive men. Sometimes, Beal used the sessions to experiment with strategies that turned out to be disastrous. Craig also changed his play periodically to mimic the descriptions Andy had given of some of his past opponents. Andy took some pride in being ahead in the freeze-outs. Singer played strong fundamental poker, and all the practice against Andy (whose game had improved because of all his time playing the pros) had made him even more skilled. They eventually played for several hundred hours.

Howard Lederer won a second time on the World Poker Tour in March 2003, this time aboard a cruise ship. Lederer and many other pros paid $5,000 to enter the limit hold 'em tournament, but sponsor PartyPoker held online satellite tournaments responsible for bringing aboard most of the 177 entries. He took home $289,000 in the second edition of the PartyPoker Million. The tour's broadcast outlet, the Travel Channel, was less than two months from its premiere.

It also appeared that the tour had its first star. In addition to devoting himself to his no-limit hold 'em tournament game, Howard had undergone gastric-bypass surgery the previous year and lost over 100 pounds. He had trimmed his beard to a goatee, then shaved it off entirely, revealing a thoughtful, angular face. Lederer's face might not have been a window to what was going on inside, but it showed that he was intensely thinking at all times. WPT hosts Mike Sexton and Vince Van Patten had taken to calling Howard "the Professor."

Howard Lederer was not the only high-stakes pro committing himself to the developing tournament circuit. Barry Greenstein, almost by accident, had started playing more tournaments. While Lederer had early success in the main event of the World Series and won two bracelets, Greenstein never really applied himself to tournament poker. He made the final table of a few World Series events, entered because the side action looked slow at the time, and played the main event. But he had never won a bracelet, and never really cared about it. He had done enough traveling for his poker career, so he had no interest in making a five-week pilgrimage to show anybody he could play tournament poker. Fame meant nothing to him. His poker career was about chasing fortune.

Even the prospect of big money was not sufficiently fulfilling for Barry Greenstein. He had spent his adult life in a conflict between being a good provider for his family and using his talents to do the most good. That conflict had always been resolved in favor of family, and poker had been his means of providing. He spent ten years completing his work for a Ph.D. because he was making more at poker than if he completed his education and became a professor.

His only real job had been as a computer programmer in the late 1980s at Symantec, the Palo Alto, California, software developer. It was just a start-up back then and he took the job only because he was marrying a woman in a custody fight with her ex-husband. "Software developer" looked better in a custody proceeding than "poker player" when his employment became an issue.

He planned to supplement his meager start-up-company income by playing in some of the Bay Area poker clubs. The project he was working on, the landmark database program Q&A, devoured all his time. The company made him postpone a promised leave of absence that would have allowed him to defend his dissertation and get his Ph.D. He had already grown tired of the academic community and wanted the degree only to be done with it and as a stepping-stone to get into medical school and do medical research.

When Greenstein finally finished the project, he was broke and had to quit to play poker and earn enough to take care of his family. His Ph.D. was on hold, as were the plans to cure diseases. Unfortunately, the same conscience that drove him to take such good care of his extended family nagged at him for not using his talents for the public good. Throughout the 1990s, no matter how well he did in poker, however, he could never get ahead by enough to finish his degree and get on with what he believed was his destiny: to play a role in making the world a better place.

During 2002, Barry talked with his academic advisor about finally finishing his Ph.D. Because of the time off, it would take six to nine months. Perhaps he had made enough where he could spare the time away from poker. The countervailing consideration was that he was doing so well and the games were becoming so big that he would be giving up a great earning opportunity.

While he debated this, fate intervened, in the very bizarre apparition of pornographer Larry Flynt. One of the reasons Barry thought he might be able to afford to live without poker for a while was his performance in Flynt's thrice-weekly stud game, in which the stakes had risen to $1,500–$3,000. When Barry started playing in the game, he thought, like many people who didn't know Flynt but knew only *of* him, that Larry Flynt was a scumbag who exploited women. It would be a pleasure to relieve him of some of that smut money and do good things with it.

Poker players who have met Flynt almost always changed their opinion. He was soft-spoken, good-natured, funny, and kind. He made his money delivering something the public obviously wanted, with the help of women who sought him out, thousands of whom sent explicit pictures to his magazine for publication without seeking compensation.

Flynt also made his life's work fighting to preserve the American way of life, albeit from an unusual pulpit. Defenders of individual liberty in the modern age have often been the people we instinctively least admire, because they are the easiest targets of the establishment. Flynt consistently argued for freedom—not just freedom to publish and buy pornography, but freedom to criticize the government and freedom from government oppression. Most poker players did not consider themselves as libertarians but they identified with Flynt's situation: He provided something that his customers wanted yet was hounded by the government and the "morality police" over what should be a private transaction.

During 2002, Larry Flynt decided to publicize his casino with a poker tournament. The tournament finale would feature the largest buy-in ever, a Seven Card Stud Championship requiring an entry fee of $125,000. The Hustler Casino planned multiple rounds of satellites, allowing players to rise from satellite to satellite to win the gigantic buy-in.

By February 2003, not one satellite entrant had won enough

flights to raise the buy-in. Flynt appealed to the members of his game to fill at least one table. Barry Greenstein anted up, along with Flynt, Johnny Chan, Steven Wolfe, Doyle Brunson, Ted Forrest, Phil Ivey, and Lakers owner Jerry Buss.

Barry had the chip lead when he was heads up against Flynt. They agreed to split the prize, with Greenstein receiving $770,000. He did some things for his family, and then gave the rest of the money to charity. It was a staggeringly unselfish gesture, from no more complicated an idea than "this was a better use for the money than anything else I could do with it." After all, he made money the week before. He was probably going to make money the next week. If he was doing well enough to spend $125,000 to enter, he was doing well enough to give away the winnings.

While Barry Greenstein struggled between the conflicting goals of focusing on ever more profitable poker games and devoting himself to making the world better, he would play some more tournaments and give anything he won to charity. He could do that much, at least, until he figured out his destiny.

While Andy Beal's past (and potential future) opponents became wealthier and better known, he began testing himself against several lesser, but still very skilled, players in heads-up games. His circle of friends and business acquaintances included many avid poker players, a few of whom kept their poker playing secret. Although such games in Texas were legal as long as no one took a fee or charged a rake for hosting the game—Beal had this carefully researched—these games were held in private and kept very secret. Between 2002 and 2004, Beal hosted approximately 600 hours of heads-up matches at stakes from very nominal to $20,000–$40,000.

On a rare road trip, he played a talented Phoenix amateur, who beat him and provided him insight on how an excellent player could read opponents. Andy began focusing on how to make himself as difficult as possible to read, especially because he figured he could level the playing field more in that way than by trying to read his pro opponents. Of course he would make the effort to read them, but that seemed at least as likely to mislead him as give him a clue on the strength of their cards.

Beal transformed his playing persona. He started wearing sunglasses when he played, shielding his eyes from the inquiring stares of opponents. He purchased multiple pairs just for this purpose, alternating to find the most comfortable and best at blocking out a view of his eyes. The largest pair looked like he ordered them from an Elvis Impersonator catalogue.

He also decided to block out noise. Apart from the distractions of the noisy poker room, Beal didn't trust himself to make small talk and maintain full concentration as well as the pros. The pros would routinely play hands in high-stakes games while chatting at the table, bantering with players at nearby tables, watching a sporting event, taking a phone call, eating, and conducting an interview—all during the same five-minute period.

In his early heads-up matches, especially against Howard Lederer, he would occasionally become engrossed in conversation and lose his focus. Lederer was genuinely interested in Beal's background and their common interests. It was not outside the realm of possibility that Lederer, an incredibly driven, smart computer science major back in 1985, could have finished his education and ended up at the same poker table, but as the live one instead of the pro.

But Andy would lose a hand on something he considered a silly error and say, "Okay, now we have to be quiet."

Beal found Howard interesting as well and enjoyed the conversations, but they interfered with the business at hand. If he was going to talk with Howard Lederer, it would have to be somewhere other than across a poker table.

Though Andy did not accuse Howard Lederer of this, he thought the pros might want to engage him in conversation to get him to give away information. Concerned that small changes in his speech could provide clues on the strength of his hand, he resolved to eliminate this possibility.

He bought several pairs of headphones designed to block out noise. To these, he added earplugs or connected an MP3 player programmed with instrumental music.

Closing himself off to the pros became an obsession with Beal and he went far beyond these conventional measures. Was the amount of time he spent deliberating before acting giving away information? He developed a way to randomize his decision time.

He built a tiny battery-operated motor that he placed inside his sock. The motor would issue a small vibration every eight seconds. Andy would make his decision—fold, check, call, bet, raise—in whatever amount of time it took to decide. But he would wait to act on the decision until the next vibration. That could be a half-second or up to eight seconds after he actually decided what to do. There would be no pattern to how long it took Beal to bluff, slow-play, check and call, or make other decisions during a hand.

Andy also tried to find ways to refine the accuracy of his decisions on pot odds. The biggest difficulty was figuring into the equation the likelihood that a bet would induce his opponent to fold.

For example, suppose he was holding king-nine suited, known by poker players as the dog hand (K9 = canine). In the small blind on the button, he had raised. His opponent reraised and he called.

The flop came ace-nine-four, all of different suits (or rainbow in poker parlance). His opponent acted first and bet. Assuming he had concluded that he shouldn't fold, should he just call or should he raise?

A determining factor would be the likelihood that a raise

would make his opponent fold his hand. Correctly determining that percentage would be the poker equivalent of proving Fermat's Last Theorem. Even guessing within 20 percent would be valuable and not beyond the realm of possibility.

Andy was on his own for figuring out that percentage. But what should he do once he figured it out? If an opponent would fold in this situation a certain percentage of the time if he raised, that percentage plus the amount in the pot would allow him to determine how often to raise. But if he decided to raise in that situation 75 percent of the time, was this hand in the 75 percent?

He used a special pocket watch as a random number generator. He would glance at the watch and, based on the position of the second hand, would determine whether this was one of the 40 percent of the times when he would raise, or one of the 60 percent when he would call.

He ordered several of these pocket watches from a friend. They had very clean white faces. He then had the second hand calibrated so that it would hit the minute and hour markers exactly and therefore be easier to see. Finally, he had the minute and hour hands clipped almost completely off so they didn't interfere with reading the second hand.

He attached the pocket watch to a large binder clip so it would stand upright. He would place it on his left and glance at it whenever he needed to make a decision based on a certain percentage that he could estimate.

The World Poker Tour debuted on the Travel Channel on Sunday, March 31, 2003, then began appearing on Wednesdays at 9:00 P.M. Steve Lipscomb was right: The hole-card camera turned a poker game into an exciting reality show. After the first few episodes ran, the tour wrapped up its tournament schedule with the WPT Championship, which became the finale of a new Bellagio tournament, the Five-Star. Although there were only a few weeks of ratings to judge the public reception to the tour on TV, poker players had responded enthusiastically with their bankrolls: The tour not only spawned new $5,000 and $10,000 buy-in events, it was also creating demand to support tournaments around the big buy-in events.

The Five-Star, which ended as the World Series of Poker started, consisted of twelve events, ending with the WPT Championship. The high-stakes players supported the tournament. Barry Greenstein finished in second place in the first event, $1,500 buy-in Limit Texas Hold 'Em (and donated the $59,000 in prize money to charity). Phil Ivey, a young tournament star increasingly playing in big cash games, won twice. Ivey, another successful player influenced by Barry Greenstein, had to live with "the Tiger Woods of Poker" as his nickname because, like Woods, he is a man of color. In addition, his aggressive style, outer cool, and habit of dominating tournaments with multiple wins invited the comparison. Howard Lederer won the penultimate event, $2,500 buy-in No-Limit Texas Hold 'Em, winning $220,000 over a field of 212.

The WPT Championship required a staggering $25,000 buy-in, though several entrants got in based on their finish in earlier events and the Bellagio held satellite tournaments during the Five-Star. As a result, 111 players entered. Doyle Brunson and Ted Forrest both made the final table, finishing fourth and fifth. Phil Ivey capped off an incredible Five-Star tournament by finishing third. Retired stock analyst Alan Goehring finished first, winning over $1 million, and Kirill Gerasimov, from Moscow, finished second.

As the Thirty-fourth World Series of Poker kicked off at Binion's Horseshoe in ever shabbier downtown Las Vegas, poker players had plenty of reasons to be optimistic. The live version of the World Poker Tour was a success and the televised version received early good reviews. Legends Brunson and Reese were playing more tournaments, and high-stakes stars Greenstein and

Lederer were making their mark as well, following the success of Jennifer Harman when she decided to play more tournaments a year earlier. The rest of the cash game players were following suit.

In fact, Doyle Brunson decided he was not going to restrict himself to a ceremonial appearance in the main event. He had won eight World Series bracelets, and Johnny Chan and Phil Hellmuth were right behind him with seven apiece. Hellmuth, in particular, publicized his quest for World Series superiority. Doyle told his friends he was going to try for number nine this year. Naturally, someone suggested a bet.

Plus, Andy Beal was thinking of coming to Las Vegas to play some poker.

8

Jennifer Harman's Wake-Up Call

April 2003

David Grey had been playing Andy Beal all morning and he needed to take a break. Grey had been a member of the group from the beginning, but this was his first session against the amateur.

The forty-four-year-old professional gambler was not considered a hold 'em specialist. His strongest game was Seven Card Stud, in which he won a World Series bracelet four years earlier.

The other pros considered Grey's strength not one particular game but consistency. He didn't go on tilt or let his ego get in the way if he was in a game that turned out to be especially tough. He often played more conservatively than his fellow pros and played all the games competently.

Despite his conservative style and appearance—he was bald and heavyset, but not big enough for gastric-bypass surgery like his now slimmed down colleagues Howard Lederer and Chip Reese—Grey had a mischievous streak. About five years earlier, at the Mirage, several players at the high-limit table were talking about dares they would take for $10,000, a conversation just begging to get someone in trouble.

David's friend Howard Lederer, then a vegetarian for about six years, said he would probably eat meat for $10,000.

Grey separated two flags from his stacks of chips. "Order the burger."

Once it was clear this was an actual bet, Howard went to poker room supervisor Donna Harris and asked her to order him a cheeseburger.

In many places, poker rooms offer food service. This tends to occur at venues where the poker room is a prominent part of the property, like in the Los Angeles casinos. The poker areas were built to accommodate food carts in the aisles, though watching poker players wolf down entire meals between (and during) hands is always a startling sight, no matter the locale.

In Las Vegas, the poker rooms are generally too crowded to allow food service and the casinos would rather have the players stroll through the gaming areas and work up an appetite on the way to a meal, preferably in some game where the house made more money.

The Mirage, and later the Bellagio, catered to the high-stakes players, both literally and figuratively. They could order from room service or any restaurant on the property. This kind of service doesn't come cheap, but the pros in these games had at least $20,000 in front of them, often much more, and a well-documented indifference to money.

Howard ordered the cheeseburger and told Donna to make sure they put on a lot of pickles, lettuce, onions, and tomatoes. Maybe he could convince his stomach it was a salad.

 While waiting for the food to arrive, Howard tried to talk

David out of the bet. "You don't have to do this. I don't want the burger, but I'll do it for $10,000."

When the tray arrived, Lederer repeated his offer to call off the bet. David wouldn't budge.

As Howard ate the cheeseburger, Grey said only, "I hope you get the worst case of diarrhea of your life."

Howard says, "To this day, David hates it that I didn't get sick."

This kind of thing was part of the texture of their friendship. Knowing that David despised olives, Howard gave his friend a chance to recover the ten grand by eating two of them. The offer still stands, unaccepted, but not unacceptable.

"If I'm ever down on zero street," he has told Howard, "I know where I can get ten thousand."

Once, when they were at a party that featured a relish tray loaded down with the hated olives, instead of blanching, David nudged Howard.

"There must be a million dollars' worth of olives on that tray."

When David Grey got up to take a restroom break, Lyle Berman moved over from the game at an adjoining table and sat in his seat.

Berman, the wealthy venture capitalist–casino operator–World Poker Tour founder, was a member of the group for the first time. He had a lot in common with Andy Beal, but they had never met. Both men were gamblers who had followed their instincts and curiosity, rather than conventional wisdom, to become successful in many different businesses.

Berman, in town for the World Series of Poker and the side games (now as high as $4,000–$8,000), bought a share of the action when Andy Beal came to town a week earlier. Lyle had heard the stories of how much the group had won and thought it seemed like a good investment. More important, it was something else he could do with his friends. He enjoyed the camaraderie at the poker table and this was an opportunity to participate further. He had recently failed to get Brunson or Reese interested in investing in his poker venture, and this was a chance to invest in something together.

David Grey was gone just long enough to run to the bathroom in the sports book and back. He didn't even know Lyle was taking over during that time.

Berman played four hands, two of which he immediately threw away, forfeiting the blinds. He lost $900,000.

Grey returned and saw Lyle sitting in his seat. His eyes traveled to the stacks of chips, now lighter by almost a million dollars. Before he could react—and he had a reputation for not mincing words—Doyle Brunson piped up from the next table.

"So, Lyle, did you have fun?"

Even Andy Beal, stone-faced behind dark glasses and his ears covered by noise-reducing headphones, started cracking up.

Lyle grinned sheepishly, as players at the adjoining table joined Brunson in a laugh.

Such good-natured moments among the players, so common during their 2001 battles with Andy Beal, were becoming few, far between, and (in this case) expensive.

After nearly six months of preparation, Andy Beal thought he was ready. He asked Craig if he wanted to come along to Las Vegas to keep him company, be on the lookout for potential cheating, help evaluate his play, and let him know if he was playing too many hours or letting his concentration slip. Craig accepted in an instant.

They arrived in Las Vegas on Sunday, April 27, 2003. It had been an enjoyable and exciting World Series for the high-stakes pros and followers of the tournament poker scene. To the amazement of participants and tournament staff, Doyle Brunson started showing up for preliminary World Series events. Brunson had bet Chip Reese $25,000 that he could win an event this year, and Reese gave him 10-to-1 on his money. Brunson finished out of the money in his first event and finished eighteenth in his second event.

On April 23 and 24, he grabbed his ninth World Series of Poker bracelet, winning a $2,000 buy-in event known as HORSE, where players alternate half-hour rounds of hold 'em, Omaha Hi/Lo, Razz, Stud, and Stud Hi/Lo. The event, also won by a Table One pro the year before (John Hennigan), attracted 113 entries, and won Brunson $84,000 (plus the $250,000 Chip Reese owed him from their bet). Media director Nolan Dalla's press release described the scene after Brunson's victory:

"The audience stood and watched in awe as Brunson fielded questions and reflected back on his fifty-plus years in poker. He told stories of his early days and conveyed what the game of poker (and the World Series of Poker) meant to him. Brunson closed off his shining moment in the twilight by saying he is determined to win a tenth gold bracelet. 'I'll retire when I stop winning,' he said. For all fans of the game of poker, and for anyone who was there inside Binion's Horseshoe on this day to witness history being made, it doesn't get any better than this."

Just four days later, Doyle was talking with Andy Beal, who was in town and ready to play a big game. On Monday, April 28, Beal had money wired to the Bellagio and asked the poker room to contact Doyle Brunson. They spent most of Monday negotiating over the stakes.

Andy wanted to play as high as possible to take the pros out of their comfort zone. Brunson explained that the players were busy with the World Series and their regular games, and suggested they play $20,000–$40,000. Andy wanted to play $50,000–$100,000. By the end of the day, Beal thought they had an agreement to play $30,000–$60,000. According to Brunson, however, the pros merely conceded that they were not inflexible about the stakes. Among themselves, they decided to make every effort to hold the stakes down, at least until they got ahead. But there was no reason to give in at the beginning. Andy was already committed to playing and they were "the biggest game in town." They would go up to $25,000–$50,000 to start, but even then, only if they couldn't get Beal to agree at the table the next morning to start at $20,000–$40,000. Doyle wanted to be called if they couldn't get Andy Beal to play at $20,000–$40,000 or $25,000–$50,000.

Brunson would have to scramble to get the players on board and coordinate the bankroll issues. The task was made much more complicated by Beal's timing.

There was no problem raising enough money for a $30,000–$60,000 game, $8–$10 million. Despite the close call at the end of 2001, investing in the top pros against Andy Beal was still a good investment. In fact, they would have the opposite problem. Smack in the middle of the World Series of Poker, every high-limit player in the world was in Las Vegas, and organizing that group would be difficult.

Andy Beal had always known that to beat the professionals, he would have to grab every conceivable edge. They were just too good at too many things—several of which he could not hope to match—that he couldn't overlook anything relevant to the game to find his advantage.

Giving as little advance notice as possible was part of that plan. He was correct that it helped him, but not for the reason he expected. Andy did not want to give the pros time to prepare for the particular demands of a high-stakes heads-up hold 'em match.

He didn't have to worry. The pros would not have done anything different if he gave them a month's notice. It had nothing to do with the stakes (which were large, but that had less of an effect on them than Beal thought) or his ability (which they considered substantial).

A common characteristic of high-stakes professional poker players is a confidence bordering on arrogance. Playing against other pros and skilled amateurs night after night was so competitive that players would crack under the constant pressure unless they truly believed that they were better than everybody else.

A story from the folklore of the first World Series of Poker illustrates this point. The 1970 event bore no resemblance to today's extravaganza. There were just six players, they played a variety of forms of poker in cash games for a week, and then voted on a champion. Supposedly, each of the six voted for himself. Only when Benny Binion told them to vote for the *second*-best player was the deadlock broken and Johnny Moss chosen as champion.

Eric Drache insisted this kind of arrogance was one of the many protections against pros teaming up to beat outsiders. "If you're going to be playing five pros and you somehow knew in advance that you were going to lose a million dollars, each pro is going to think their win will be more than $200,000."

The pros didn't practice. They played. Their preparation was the tens of thousands of hours they put in at the tables facing every conceivable situation. Andy was correct that they played by instinct rather than superior knowledge of fundamentals (though those instincts plus experience led to a deep understanding of the fundamentals), but they didn't develop or refine those instincts through study. The game with Andy may be different from what they faced yesterday, but yesterday's game was different from the game of the day before, which was different from the game before that . . .

Nevertheless, chaos reigned as Chip Reese and Doyle Brunson tried to organize the group. Beal had not planned this, but his timing could not have made the situation more stressful for the players.

Andy had reached Doyle Brunson during the $5,000 No-Limit Deuce-to-Seven Championship (with rebuys). This was the event in which Howard Lederer and Jennifer Harman had both won bracelets. It was also the event most frequently played by the big cash game players, though nearly everyone was playing more World Series events this year.

Brunson and Reese made the rounds of the Horseshoe and the Bellagio and called anyone they didn't see. Many of the players were in the tournament; some had already been eliminated and were returning to the Bellagio for the side action sure to start by that evening. Noon being an ungodly early time for a poker player to be at work (all World Series events started at noon), some had gone home or to their hotels. Those skipping the event were doing whatever poker players did when they were waiting for a game.

More important, the size of the group was sure to expand. Two years earlier, gathering the bankroll meant doing little more than asking around the table and having the players walk forty feet to their boxes to get the chips.

Getting players to join was no longer based on the likelihood of them walking into the game on their own, as Ted Forrest had done two years earlier. At the stakes Andy wanted to play, at least $20,000–$40,000 and probably higher, the universe of players who would buy in on their own was small to nonexistent. The minimum buy-in would be $400,000 to $500,000 and it would be courting disaster to start with less than $1 million. Few poker players in the world had a playing bankroll that large, and Forrest might have been the only one willing to bet it all in one game. There was, however, a slight possibility that some group of excluded players could pool their money and form a second group.

That was unlikely. Despite the hectoring of a few critics who think the pros team up against opponents, poker players are not team-oriented. In fact, most of them chose poker because they wanted to avoid the interdependence of conventional work.

 Howard Lederer's explanation of what he liked most about

being a professional poker player was representative of his fellow pros. "The thing I really like about poker is the lack of politics. You just sit down at the table and you're competing mind against mind. There's no pretense about it. There's no office, no backstabbing." According to Chip Reese, "If I wanted to work for somebody or let outside influences decide how hard I work, I could have done a lot of things with my life. But I like to do what I do, because I'm my own boss."

Ironically, playing Andy Beal as a group had put the players in precisely the situation they became poker players to avoid. The players repeatedly rose to the occasion in 2001, putting their common interests ahead of their individual ones, but it was far from clear whether they could do it again.

Everybody wanted a piece, or a piece of a piece. In sixteen months, the Andy Beal legend had grown and become distorted to the point that he sounded like an incarnation of the Easter Bunny, Santa Claus, and Monty Hall. No one seemed to remember him decisively beating Jennifer Harman, Todd Brunson, John Hennigan, Ted Forrest, and Chau Giang in succession.

The situation brought in politics, egos, and greed. The old group was just the Table One regulars in town whenever Andy showed up. Now, high-stakes amateurs like Lyle Berman took shares. Although Lyle was universally liked and respected among the pros, the irony was unavoidable. If Lyle woke up one morning and decided he wanted to play a certain game for especially high stakes, higher than anyone else wanted to play, would they ask Andy Beal if he wanted a share? Furthermore, despite Lyle's poker skill, no one expected that he would play Andy (and, other than a few impromptu sessions, he never did).

There was additional grumbling about Barry Greenstein, a regular in the biggest games in L.A., joining the group. Barry was winning big in the largest side games during the Series, establishing himself, along with Brunson, Reese, Giang, Berman, and Bellagio president Bobby Baldwin, as a regular in the $4,000–$8,000 mixed game. (Baldwin was not part of the group because of the obvious appearance of a conflict of interest, which was also why the group played at Sam's Town, a casino mostly catering to low-stakes locals, whenever Baldwin joined the game.)

But how could Greenstein be excluded? The two biggest recurring games in the world were the Series side games and Larry Flynt's $1,500–$3,000 stud game. Barry had a reputation of being the big winner in both.

The aforementioned Flynt game was a sore subject with a few of the pros. Until Flynt opened his L.A. casino in June 2000 and held the game in public, it was a private game, usually at his house, and players had to be invited. Eric Drache, who was staked by Flynt in the game but did not receive a fee for putting it together, turned down numerous opportunities to profit from his position as gatekeeper.

His decisions were bound to make some players unhappy. There were more interested players than spaces in the game. He also had to balance keeping the game challenging for the host but not *too* challenging. If the game was just Brunson, Reese, Drache, Forrest, Greenstein, and some other superstar stud player, what chance would Larry Flynt have? Flynt was a talented amateur, but he was an amateur. He could handle being an underdog, and even cheerfully lose in a challenging game and come back for more, but he would lose interest pretty quickly if his only competition was the six best stud players in the world, which is what the game would become if Drache invited only the best players who asked, or only his best friends in poker.

Chip Reese and Eric Drache went back thirty years and were good friends. Chip wanted to get into the game, but he understood. He certainly had no animosity toward Barry Greenstein just because Barry had been able to get inside. In fact, before Reese and Greenstein had played together much, Barry thought Chip was trying to hustle him into high-stakes games as an easy mark.

"Buddy," he remembers Chip saying in his most charming voice, "this is the perfect game for you."

At least one player took the regional rivalry personally. "That was their home game, so they didn't let me in. Fine. But this is my home game, so fuck you. You're not getting in mine."

Although most players were of the opinion that anyone willing to post at least $500,000 could join the group, the atmosphere was heavy with conflict. Poker players were comfortable in adversary situations, but that was usually because they could resolve their differences in the game. As Lyle Berman mentioned in an interview with poker player and writer Wendeen Eolis, "In poker, Jews, Muslims, and Arabs get along just fine." Players from conflicting backgrounds could get along in poker because they didn't take those conflicts to the table. These arguments, however, could not be resolved by a showdown of hands.

Some players looked at the avalanche of interest as cutting into their financial return. When the word circulated that someone had arranged for the Doc to have a couple of points without putting up money, a few players decided to make everyone not in the group from the beginning justify their participation.

Todd Brunson had a problem with this attitude. Todd was not a frequent presence in the ultra-high-limit side games during the Series. More often than not, he might not even be playing in the $1,000–$2,000 mixed game at Table One during the year. But it was not because of lack of skill or financial means. He did not live and breathe poker and played less than any of the other Las Vegas pros. An astute investor away from the poker table, when he did play, he often passed up the biggest game in favor of the *best* game.

When he thought his membership was in question, he was

ready to go to the mat. "I'll get my own group and play him myself."

Jennifer Harman thought this exclusionary attitude was nonsense. They should not be turning anyone down, especially a hold 'em player of Todd's caliber. The group was getting heavy with players who had big bucks but who she wouldn't take in a high-stakes hold 'em match. Despite Todd's one undistinguished performance against Andy in December 2001, she would have taken Todd over nearly anybody in the room to play Andy with their bankroll on the line. When he asked if she would contribute to his bankroll if he needed to play separate from the group to get a shot at Andy Beal, she said yes, though she didn't think it would come to that.

Doyle Brunson made a rare gesture on his son's behalf. "Either Todd is in or I'll give him some money and he can sit down in the game whenever he wants. He's in the group."

That resolved the matter. Few players actually favored limiting membership in the group, and this shut up the malcontents. The group had expanded from its original eight. Doyle and Chip Reese, obviously, were still members, as was Chau Giang. Todd Brunson was finally a member, along with Table One contemporaries Jennifer Harman, Howard Lederer, Ted Forrest, and David Grey. Barry Greenstein and Lyle Berman joined, along with some other high-stakes and tournament pros who bought partial shares.

Doyle Brunson had the task of lining up players to face Beal. Between the side games and the World Series, it seemed like everybody had something else to do. Howard Lederer was playing more World Series events this year than in years past. (He made it to the final table of the Deuce-to-Seven Championship that day and finished fifth.) All this was in preparation for the main event, which he was taking very seriously this year. Jennifer Harman was also playing more in the tournament. Even though Doyle had already won his bet with Chip, he was playing a few more events, as were David Grey, Barry Greenstein, and some others.

Then there were the cash games, which suddenly seemed to have gotten huge. Apart from the prospect of making a million dollars for a few days' work, the stakes had become so high, and so few players regularly played, that part of the fun was the familiarity, the camaraderie. There were seven-figure winners and losers over the course of the 2003 World Series, but everyone had a good time. Ultimately, even the losers looked forward to doing it again.

At the same time, they couldn't take their game lightly. It was a loose, wild $4,000–$8,000 mixed game, where they individually had more at stake than their 5 percent to 10 percent individual shares in the outcome of the $30,000–$60,000 game with Beal.

Besides, this was where the team concept could pay off. Let one of the players who specialized at hold 'em, someone not as interested in playing $4,000–$8,000, beat up on Andy Beal while they tried for a separate killing against each other.

That was Barry Greenstein's thinking. He was winning big money in the side games and didn't want to jeopardize that. But Doyle asked him on Monday night if he would play Beal on Tuesday morning and it was hard to refuse Doyle. There was also a shortage of players willing to play at Andy's requested time of 7:00 A.M. Usually, if a poker player was in action before noon, it was from a game that started the night before. But Barry would do his part for the team.

On Tuesday morning, April 29, Barry came down to the poker room to find Andy Beal and Craig Singer already waiting for him. Andy and Craig were surprised to see him. Greenstein had not been on the team during Andy's previous games and had no poker reputation to the outside world because he wasn't a Las Vegas character or a tournament star. Having carefully evaluated the styles of the players, Beal felt a bit unprepared.

After the introductions, Barry called for a supervisor to arrange delivery of his chips. The night before, Doyle Brunson and Chip Reese had gathered the group's bankroll and deposited portions of it in accounts of the players they expected to play the next day. (In addition to safe deposit boxes, which physically safeguarded money, chips, or whatever a player placed inside, individuals—but not groups—could establish an account with the cashier and maintain a balance, which could be accessed to obtain chips or a cashier's check.) Barry could handle the paperwork from his seat in the poker room, though he would have to go to the cage in person afterward to transfer the balance to the next player. They had deposited approximately $2 million in his account.

Before they started, Greenstein asked Andy what stakes he wanted to play, suggesting $20,000–$40,000. This was according to the group's plan, and it seemed like a reasonable place to start. It was the highest Beal had played previously, and it fit with Barry's estimate of the game his $2 million allotment would comfortably support.

Beal acted like he had been insulted.

"Twenty-forty? I worked this out with Doyle Brunson yesterday. I didn't come all the way from Dallas to play that low." Beal's tone was between a whine and a bellow.

Greenstein was at a loss. For somebody who was supposed to be so easygoing, Beal seemed very put-upon. Nor was he mollified by Barry's offer to go to $25,000–$50,000. It even seemed like Andy might walk.

Barry agreed to play $30,000–$60,000. Even though this was higher than the players had discussed the day before (by a margin that was itself higher than any of them, besides Ted Forrest, had ever planned individually), he was not going to call Doyle Brunson at 7:00 A.M. to get him involved.

* * *

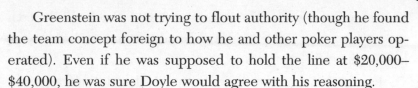

Greenstein was not trying to flout authority (though he found the team concept foreign to how he and other poker players operated). Even if he was supposed to hold the line at $20,000–$40,000, he was sure Doyle would agree with his reasoning.

Barry admired few poker players, but Doyle Brunson and Chip Reese were in that small group. They understood that you needed to give action to get action. It was no coincidence that Barry was closer with Ted Forrest than most other high-stakes players. Their approaches appeared very different—Barry, dour, quiet, and calculating; Ted, seemingly oblivious to what's going on around him—but they achieved precisely the same goal. They tried to create conditions wherein their opponents felt comfortable losing.

The men who lost money to high-stakes poker pros were intelligent and, by definition, wealthy. Nearly all were extremely successful at what they did. Barry Greenstein gave them credit for understanding that they were generally getting the worst of it. To insist on getting all the details your way when you already had the skill advantage was bad form and bad business.

While waiting for the paperwork and the chips from the cashier's cage, Andy and Craig carefully examined both decks of playing cards in the setup. They watched the breaking of the seals on the cellophane packages and carefully looked at the backs of all the cards as they were spread across the table.

This was part of a procedure Beal and Singer established before coming to Vegas. At Craig's urging, they had spoken with a consultant with experience in the casino industry about potential cheating. Beal had no reason to believe he was or could be cheated; he was just being prudent.

The consultant confirmed Andy's basic beliefs. Although the consultant acknowledged the possibility of "funny business" in the old days, the modern Vegas poker game was clean. He declined Beal's offer of a retainer to watch his heads-up games against the members of the group. There was nothing to be gained; the consultant knew and had played with some of them and they were honest players.

In addition, by playing heads up, Beal had eliminated just about all possible cheating opportunities, except for a crooked dealer or casino staff member bringing in marked cards. Again, that would be extremely unlikely.

As a precaution just the same, Singer picked up some books and videos on card marking and manipulation. Andy reviewed some of these, though Craig had the unofficial responsibility of inspecting the decks and observing the dealer with these lessons in mind.

Eventually, they abandoned all but the most perfunctory review of the cards. There simply wasn't any possibility, based on the property, the people, and the controls in place, that the pros, the dealers, or the casino could be cheating.

For the next several hours, neither player especially impressed the other. Greenstein's reputation as a hold 'em player was excellent, and he had been playing with tremendous confidence and success over the previous year, but Beal had never heard of him. Andy had worked hard on his game, but Barry felt the banker was staying in the match solely with lucky draws. On one hand, the pro started with seven-six, the amateur with six-deuce. The flop came three-four-five, making both players a straight. Unfortunately for Andy, he was in a horrible position because Barry had a higher straight. They kept raising, both after the flop and after the turn produced a blank (a card unlikely to affect the outcome of the hand). A seven—one of only three outs Andy had in his almost hopeless position—came on the river, forcing Barry to split the seven-figure pot.

Beal then quit Greenstein to play Chip Reese. Barry felt that Andy pushed him aside because he wanted to play a bigger name. Andy viewed it differently, switching players to someone he at least recognized. He didn't think he had Chip figured out by any means, but he had been practicing for months with Chip's style in mind. Beal won from Reese, not a huge amount, but enough to get him feeling comfortable playing again with the top pros.

Later that day, Andy played Howard Lederer, his chief nemesis (along with Ted Forrest) back in 2001. Lederer had taken a break from what had been to this point, the Deuce-to-Seven event notwithstanding, a disappointing World Series. Things didn't go any better for him against Andy.

Howard had an entirely different impression than Greenstein of Andy Beal's play. The banker had come a long way since he had been dominated by the pro in several matches in 2001. Other than the extreme aggressiveness that had become his trademark, he barely resembled the player the new members of the group were expecting. He had obviously devoted a lot of effort into making himself difficult for his opponents to read.

He looked exactly the same at all times during every hand. Immobile. Peek at the hole cards. No expression. Pause. Bet. Pause. Look at the flop. No expression. Pause. Bet. If not for the small hand movements on the cards or the chips, he could have fallen asleep at the table without Lederer knowing it. It was an impressive performance.

Playing Beal at $30,000–$60,000, Howard Lederer lost $1.8 million. Howard had a rule about ending a session if he lost thirty large bets. He would make exceptions, but he saw no reason to think things would change. He knew at the end of Andy's December 2001 trip that they had a game on their hands. Today, Beal was aggressive and in control. He ended the day ahead by over $2 million. It was an impressive return after a sixteen-month absence.

* * *

Barry Greenstein woke up early on Wednesday to play Andy Beal for a second consecutive morning. This time, Beal got the better of the match, winning $2 million. In addition, Andy left a different impression on Barry this time. He showed the pro a great deal of skill, both in general as well as in adapting his play to what he saw of Barry the day before. Greenstein played in the aggressive style that was typical of the pros in heads-up hold 'em. Naturally, he varied his play and tried to get into sync with Andy's style, but the banker seemed to be one step ahead. Beal was more aggressive, and when he drew back, it was to trap Barry or save chips on weak cards.

Aggression and mixing it up? That was how Barry had wanted to play but Andy got there first. It was an excellent, mature performance by the amateur. That was when it dawned on the L.A. pro that their edge was not that great. It was not a given that the pros were going to win.

Barry admitted to some of the other players that he felt he had been outplayed. He was being honest, and he wanted to warn the other players, especially those who had not played Andy, and naively thought that Beal had come to town to give his money to the pros.

A few high-stakes players reacted as if Barry had confessed to some ghastly crime. This just solidified Barry's view of the majority of poker players, even the big-money pros: some ability, not much backbone, and no understanding of what being a gambler was *really* about.

Barry Greenstein was not the only player declaring that the amateur had a chance to win. Ted Forrest also struggled in his first encounter with the 2003 version of Andy Beal. Ted Forrest took over for Barry on Wednesday afternoon.

Forrest was an obvious choice to play Andy Beal based on his past performance (though a few in the group still maintained that

Ted wasn't really a hold 'em player). He purposely kept a low profile and did not nominate himself to play at the beginning.

Ted felt if he played Andy early and won big, Andy might feel Ted had his number and would become discouraged and give up. Not that Forrest had some super-secret, never-fail strategy. Even if he had some incredible insight, he could act on it perfectly and still lose a session. But another big win by Ted might give Beal the impression that he had no chance, something the same result by another player would not necessarily do.

The whole issue became academic after Ted Forrest lost, too. In fact, he was lucky that it was only a small loss. Forrest got himself stuck $800,000 in a hurry and had to battle back to settle for just a small loss before Andy called it a day.

Ted agreed with Barry Greenstein that Andy was outplaying them. Beal had made himself hard to read, and was doing a good job at noticing when they changed speeds. He was always dangerous with his aggressive style, but if he could keep such tight control of himself and remain methodical, he had an excellent chance of winning.

Not all the changes in Andy's game were positive. The players may not have known the depth of his knowledge of pot odds, or recognized that the pocket watch he set on the table was a random number generator for making decisions based on odds and probabilities, but they immediately noticed another aspect of his mathematical approach. In fact, it would have been hard to avoid noticing.

Andy had at least 1,000 blue $1 chips with him at the table. He sat in Seat Four, around the corner to the dealer's left. The chips took up the space on the table in front of Seats One, Two, and Three. He was using the chips as a giant abacus to measure the likelihood of his opponent folding at each decision point in the hand.

That Beal had focused on trying to figure out an opponent's likelihood of folding demonstrated a very advanced analytical approach to the game. If you played passively, checking and calling, your chance of winning was precisely the same as the chance you would end up with the best hand. But if you took the lead in betting the hand, either opening or raising, you could win in an additional way: by getting your opponent to fold. That was the reason why aggressiveness was essential to every top pro's strategy, especially shorthanded. Having accurate percentages on such behavior would be a breakthrough and incredibly valuable to whoever had them and knew how to use them.

Gathering that information in this fashion, however, was a hopeless task. How many different decision points were there in a hand? There were four betting rounds, but play progressed differently depending on whether you were acting first or last, so add another four. For the last three betting rounds, the character of the community cards could have a significant bearing on a player's decision to fold in the face of a bet or raise. Even broadly characterizing the character of the board created a large multiple of the six decision points after the flop. Whether the player you were trying to induce to fold had themselves bet or raised at a prior decision point would create separate situations and the size of the pot would always figure into the decision whether to fold on a later betting round. In addition, the cards of the opponent obviously played a role and because they could vary, you needed a huge number of trials to have enough data from which to generalize. The exercise, though admirable in its goal, was a waste of time. Worse, it took a lot of effort and attention better spent elsewhere.

Before Andy and Craig left the Bellagio poker room on Wednesday night, Andy stopped by Doyle Brunson's table and asked, "Same time tomorrow morning?"

"Sure thing, Andy," Doyle replied without looking up from his game. Who would he get to play Andy at seven the next morning?

Barry Greenstein had made the sacrifice of coming down to play at seven in the morning for two straight days. He didn't particularly want to try for three, especially in light of Beal's performance on Wednesday. The early games also created the possibility that he could be worn out when the $4,000–$8,000 game next picked up. He wouldn't let down the team, but he was doing extremely well in that game during the Series, and didn't want to compromise his performance there.

Consequently, Doyle was back home at 2:00 A.M., still without a player for Thursday morning. He called Jennifer Harman.

Harman had the hold 'em credentials to handle Beal if anyone could. She had not distinguished herself yet against him but that had nothing to do with actual ability. Limit hold 'em, especially heads up, was a game of the long run. Individual hands, even individual sessions, were not necessarily indicative of a player's skill. Even relative to other poker players, however, Jennifer loathed waking up early in the morning.

"How would you feel about playing Andy Beal at seven?" he asked.

"Not good."

As proof of the differences between the lifestyles of poker players and the rest of the world, neither Doyle nor Jennifer thought there was anything unusual about him calling her at 2:00 A.M. In fact, she was where he expected she would be: at the Bellagio, in a poker game.

"Well, I guess I'll have to ask someone else," he said in resignation. Thinking out loud, he mentioned some other players in the group.

Doyle Brunson's genius about people manifested itself in so many subtle ways that you could overlook it if you weren't paying close attention. Making a joke at the table. Asserting vaguely defined authority to end an argument. Appealing to the right person with the right reason. This transcended poker. Whether it was natural talent or a lifetime of experience dealing with so many people in so many situations was moot. It was a rare and remarkable ability.

In this case, he hit the bull's-eye with Jennifer Harman. They had not spoken about how most members of the team were not especially good hold 'em players, and many of them had vastly underestimated Andy Beal's ability. Doyle just happened to mention a name or two that she would not want playing with her money in a big game.

"Well, okay, I'll be there."

Jennifer hung up, angry, and went home to get a few hours of sleep. She was angry that she had to leave her game, angry that she would have to play Beal on little sleep in less than five hours, and angry at being so thoroughly outfoxed by Doyle Brunson.

She slept less than three hours before dragging herself into the poker room the next morning. Like the first time she played heads up against Andy, all the problems associated with the game—the waiting around, the scrambling, fitting in with his schedule, the uncertainty about playing for such high stakes, other players' money riding on the outcome—disappeared when it came time to play. In fact, unlike some of her earlier sessions with Andy, and despite being dazed from lack of sleep, she came into this game playing well, loaded with confidence.

Harman was in control through the morning and early afternoon. When she was on her game, she could make an observer believe in extrasensory perception. Jennifer could sometimes feel when her opponent was weak and when he was strong. Despite Beal's many measures to prevent any attempt to penetrate his mind, Jennifer felt she had a good read on him.

In limit hold 'em, the match rarely turns on one hand. One player's superiority asserts itself in ways almost imperceptible to all but the closest observers. Harman and Beal played for about eight hours, during which time they played nearly 400 hands. When Jennifer left the game, she was ahead by $3 million. Because of the aggressive style of play, there was a lot of raising of the $15,000 and $30,000 blinds. Several pots were worth in the neighborhood of $1 million. But there were also plenty of hands where one player raised and the other folded. If the average pot was $150,000, this would be the equivalent of Jennifer winning just 5 percent more than Andy. (It probably was not even a matter of her winning *more* hands. Even more subtly, she was able, compared with her amateur opponent, to get an extra bet every so often on her winning hands or save a bet on losing hands.) The match was not like a brawl, where you could guess who the loser was by looking at one fighter's bloody nose or bruised face. It was more like a tug-of-war, where the flag in the middle moved only inches after hours of force.

Harman had actually gotten ahead $5 million, and lost a big pot. Then she misplayed a hand, and realized it was after 2:00 P.M. and she could barely make out her cards. During that short lapse—really just one hand of mistakes and one big one lost by the luck of the draw—she gave back $2 million. Ted Forrest was playing in a game at the next table, and she pulled him out of his game.

"You have to take over for me."

He immediately sat down in her seat and continued the game with Andy Beal, leaving her to take care of his chips and his spot in the game he had been playing.

For reasons only experienced players understand, Jennifer, though exhausted, sat in Ted's seat and played several hands. In variations of stud (including Razz and high-low), players pay the same ante to see every hand. In hold 'em, Omaha, and Deuce-to-Seven, however, they post blind bets twice per round and see the initial cards for free the rest of the time. Jennifer couldn't play

Andy anymore, but she thought it was unfair to make Ted leave his game while he could still see a few hands for free before the blinds came around to him. Generally, if a player leaves a game other than before being required to post the blinds, it is safe to assume that player is (a) new to the game, or (b) in serious physical distress.

And the physical distress had to be pretty serious. The following account is typical in Las Vegas poker rooms. A player moves from one game to another. Asked about why he moved from the other game, he explains, "This big gross guy sat next to me. You can see him over there. [Players turn to look.] Geez, don't draw attention to him. I feel bad enough already. When the guy sat down, he was so big that he just overflowed onto my seat. He had the worst body odor ever. His sweat was just percolating onto me. Then he had these sores all over his arms that he was scratching and picking. [Players act nauseated.] So you see why I had to get out of that game. As soon as it was my turn to post the big blind, I got up as fast as I could and came over here."

Therefore, Jennifer played in Ted's game until it was time for his big blind, then she picked up his chips and brought them over. In the meantime, Forrest's struggles against Beal continued. He lost $1.5 million of her $3 million profit, then clawed back to recover about half of those losses. He again felt like Andy was at the top of his game, and playing better than Ted.

Of course, Doyle Brunson asked her to play again the next morning. This time, Brunson's fifty years of experience in every conceivable situation were no match for Harman's stubbornness. She refused him the next day, too, though she agreed to try to make it into the room early to be on call.

When she arrived, she saw that Doyle was playing Andy. This was not where Doyle Brunson wanted to be on Saturday afternoon, playing hand after hand after hand of hold 'em with Andy

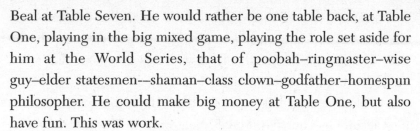

Beal at Table Seven. He would rather be one table back, at Table One, playing in the big mixed game, playing the role set aside for him at the World Series, that of poobah–ringmaster–wise guy–elder statesmen-–shaman–class clown–godfather–homespun philosopher. He could make big money at Table One, but also have fun. This was work.

Heads-up hold 'em was not Brunson's favorite form of poker. Brunson has admitted that, once, his no-limit hold 'em skills were so advanced that it was difficult for him to adjust to limit poker and he was not, by his standards, especially good. That was a long time ago, because even in his game, they played mostly limit poker and the fact that he still had the money to play meant he must have figured out how to play it very well. And even though he could play in a wild, loose shorthanded game with the best of them, the unrelenting action of playing heads up took a physical toll on him.

The force of Brunson's will could be unbelievable. He used to describe playing in games that went on for days, and how his leg might become sore or cramp up from being in an uncomfortable position. He would force himself not to work out the soreness, to use the pain to make him focus on playing better. Nearly seventy, with the accumulated aches and pains of age, especially the leg that became more painful and less useful with each passing year, he *could* force himself to do that. But would he want to? And would he want to force himself to play through discomfort instead of playing in a fun high-stakes game with his buddies, who gather here every year just so they can have a good time and try to take each other's money, one table over?

Harman took over and mowed through Andy a second time, winning another $3 million. She repeated the feat a third time a couple days later, relieving another player and winning $3 million during her session.

Other players won along the way, but it was Jennifer's consistent winning that sent Andy Beal back to Dallas a loser. Once again, he could only question why he stayed so long, why he played so many hours, and why playing this silly game had taken on so much importance in his life.

In fact, he even left Vegas for three days, then came back to play again. On Thursday, May 8, Beal went to North Carolina, to attend his daughter's graduation from Duke. On Sunday night, however, instead of returning to Texas, he came back to the Bellagio, thinking the time away would refresh him and return him to the careful form he displayed at the beginning of the trip. The next day, however, he got hammered by Howard Lederer and gave up trying.

Jennifer Harman did not consider her $9 million in wins a defining achievement in her poker career. (She considered her biggest achievements being the only woman to win two open events in the World Series of Poker and writing a chapter—limit hold 'em—in the updated edition of Doyle Brunson's strategic bible of poker, *Super System 2*.) At the same time, she recognized that, despite her impressive achievements from very limited tournament participation, she was a money player, and the only people who knew the accomplishments of the money players were other money players.

"That makes me feel good, that people like Doyle and Todd and Howard trust me enough to get in there and play. They actually trust my ability to play hold 'em that well to gamble their money. It gives you a sense of accomplishment, a sense that you are doing the right thing."

So the professionals were successful once again. Jennifer Harman rose to the occasion, like Ted Forrest and Howard Lederer before her, and validated the judgment of everyone in the group that the pros would come through in the end. The home team would always win.

Jennifer's triple play started a big month in poker in Las Vegas. The World Series ended in an explosion of excitement. Spurred on by hundreds of Internet players qualifying through online satellite tournaments, a record 839 players entered the main event.

For the second year in a row, an amateur took home the big prize, this time a tournament-record $2.5 million. More significant, he was one of the hundreds of Internet entrants, the improbably named Chris Moneymaker.

Howard Lederer ended his fifteen-year involuntary vow of poverty in the main event, finishing in nineteenth place. He was disappointed for days afterward, but looked forward to trying again in 2004. David Grey—allegedly not a tournament player and not a hold 'em player—outlasted his friend, made it to the final table, and finished in eighth place. Barry Greenstein was the tournament leader after Day One and also finished in the money.

The group had much to be happy about—so much so that they ignored some ominous signs. Especially as poker was becoming bigger, the games were becoming bigger, and *they* were becoming bigger, the incongruity of poker players in a team activity was threatening to erupt.

Increasingly, a class schism was developing among the players. The biggest side game during the World Series was $4,000–$8,000. Some members of the group always played in it: Doyle Brunson, Reese, Giang, Berman, and Greenstein. The other Table One regulars played it occasionally, or took on a partner when they played. The $4,000–$8,000 regulars generally wanted the players in the lower game, as if a $1,000–$2,000 to $2,000–$4,000 game could be characterized as "low," to do the heavy lifting against Andy Beal.

If two players had a 10 percent investment in the group's bankroll against Beal, their interest in the $30,000–$60,000 game would be the same as having 100 percent of the action in a $3,000–$6,000 game. If one of those players normally played $1,000–$2,000 and the other played $4,000–$8,000, the $1,000–$2,000 player was making a bigger investment relative to bankroll and expected profit. If the $4,000–$8,000 player had a positive earning opportunity in his game—and these players always thought they had a positive earning opportunity—they would rather have the $1,000–$2,000 player, who had relatively more at stake anyway, be the one who played Andy.

It was not an unreasonable position, especially because most of the players in the bigger game had not played especially well against Beal. Part of the package, however, was the ultra-high-stakes players' apparent indifference to the game. On one of the occasions when Barry Greenstein was playing Andy, he took a short break and let Mimi Tran, who was sitting watching him, play in his place. Tran, a high-stakes player in Los Angeles, was a protégée of Barry's and a former girlfriend. She had a reputation as a good hold 'em player, had made some World Series final tables, and was among the top five women in all-time World Series earnings.

She played about five hands while Barry was away, giving up the blinds in a few and losing showdowns in the others. That quickly, more than a quarter-million dollars was gone. Even though the same thing also happened to Lyle Berman during the series of matches, and the players knew Greenstein could have lost the same amount if he played the same hands with the same cards, it bothered some members of the group. At least one player suggested that Greenstein reimburse the group for Tran's losses.

Berman, at least, was part of the group. Lyle had also stepped in while several members of the group were watching from the other game, including Doyle Brunson. Berman's stunt bothered some of the same people. It was the appearance of indifference to the game that annoyed them.

The other development that Jennifer Harman's success allowed them to ignore was that Andy Beal was becoming a very talented heads-up hold 'em player. He had improved and adapted. Ted Forrest was a net loser on the trip, and Howard Lederer came out only a little ahead, and he wouldn't have done even that well had Beal not made his ill-considered decision to return to Vegas for a day after his daughter's graduation. Forrest and Lederer had been the most consistent winners against Andy Beal in 2001. Barry Greenstein also lost overall in his sessions against Beal. Had Jennifer and one other player not stepped up, could the group have lost? Who would be the go-to guy if Andy Beal, who seemed to have learned to beat Forrest, Lederer, and Greenstein, figured out how to win against their go-to girl?

9

A Lawyer, Not a Gambler

September 2003

The massive young man at the end of the table raked in another pot. He didn't say a word, dividing his attention among the cards, his cell phone, and the video monitors in his line of sight. His bearded face was expressionless. His brown hair was straight and neat, but a two-and-a-half-foot ponytail ran down his back.

The next night, the same man was at the center of the action. "Am I the only redneck at this table?" he asked. "If the Jews and the Arabs can agree on anything, it's how to take the redneck's money." He kept up the patter, deftly making fun of his opponents, but mostly himself. The only thing similar about Todd Brunson on these two evenings was the growing pile of chips in front of him.

Brunson was an enigma, even to most of his colleagues. Maybe this was part of the deal: You could succeed in the same business as your famous old man, but where everybody else thought they knew Doyle, nobody got to understand Todd.

On one thing, the high-stakes pros could agree: Brunson could play. He was a superb hold 'em player, especially in short-handed games. For some reason, however, before the 2003 World Series, Todd's position in the group was precarious. He missed the group's first go-round and became a member in December 2001 only because Andy Beal drafted him, asking if he could play Todd. Brunson then lost a million dollars in record time, albeit on a miracle river card making Beal an improbable full house. Granted, none of the pros put any stock in the results of one session, but it was not a good experience, and it didn't help that Brunson tried to pull players from the next table to show off his bad beat.

Then, during the World Series, he was in the middle of the fight over whether to limit membership in the group. He got in, but only after his father insisted.

That was the last thing Todd needed. At thirty-three, he was the youngest member of the group and almost always the youngest at the table in high-stakes games. He had dealt with the curiosity and the pointed questions about his father since he started playing professionally a decade earlier. He had developed a thick skin on the subject, especially because his peers knew that he was his own man and had made it to the top on his own. In a way, that made the disagreement during the World Series worse, because it came from his colleagues.

Although no one questioned Brunson's ability, most players would be surprised by his dedication to his profession. When Andy Beal came to Las Vegas in the spring, he did not let the pros know he was coming until he was already at the Bellagio. He did this to keep the pros from practicing, something they wouldn't have done anyway. But Todd Brunson practiced. He and Ted Forrest got together one day and played two freeze-outs with play chips, each taking a turn playing as Beal would.

Interestingly, "Andy" won both times. It was excellent practice for Brunson, who, like Howard Lederer in 2001, became a convert to Ted Forrest's way of thinking. Brunson usually believed in playing a very aggressive heads-up game but decided to follow Ted's advice to let Beal be the aggressor. "Andy's going to win generally. I've got to take advantage of the hands where he's going to screw up. He's so aggressive I just let him keep coming and keep coming."

It was also a reminder to both Forrest and Brunson that Beal could win.

After Jennifer Harman, Todd Brunson was the big winner against Andy in the spring. He was not wearing himself out playing World Series events, or wringing every bit of action out of the big cash games. (On any given day, Todd might tell you he was pacing himself or lazy.)

Brunson was the player who drove home to Andy the fruitlessness of his blue-chip abacus system. As Beal kept the tallies on the various piles of chips, Brunson silently followed the pattern of the movements with his eyes. As he figured out what the different stacks represented, he watched the hands where Andy would consult the stacks before acting.

When Todd realized that Beal was consulting the chips to decide if he would fold in response to a bet or raise, he started smacking Andy with raises after he looked at the stacks, both skewing the statistics and forcing Beal to fold hands where he had mediocre cards but expected to make money by inducing a fold. Those losses tended to be expensive, because they were pots that had been fattened by pre-flop raising and Beal had bet or raised after the flop. Brunson seemed to have a unique gift for taking advantage of his lapses in play.

As Beal stayed longer in Las Vegas and played more hours in May, it was harder to maintain his focus. He started compromising the rituals so carefully developed and rehearsed, sometimes just rushing through to play the hands, and play them even more recklessly as losses piled up. Todd seemed to sense those moods and take maximum advantage.

Todd Brunson had finally established himself as a player on the team. But the go-to guy?

The summer of 2003 was a momentous time for both Andy Beal and the poker community. Beal Bank continued expanding its business, finding what seemed like an endless supply of deals where it could pick up good debt at a discount. For the twelve months ending June 30, 2003, Beal Bank reported net income of $249 million, on assets of over $5.4 billion. The bank had paid cash dividends to shareholders (i.e., Beal) of $87 million. Andy could easily afford to take more lessons from the Las Vegas pros. In fact, with the money he had, it was increasingly questionable whether the pros, even with their edge, were playing a smart game by engaging Beal at his stakes.

The risk Andy Beal posed to their livelihood was the furthest thing from the minds of the Table One regulars during that summer. Poker, it seemed, had exploded onto the public consciousness. The World Poker Tour was turning into a TV phenomenon, on its way to becoming the highest-rated show in the Travel Channel's history. By the end of the year, five million people would watch it per week. NBC agreed to run a special WPT "tournament of champions" against Fox's Super Bowl pregame show.

Howard Lederer was the breakout star of the first season. By summer, both episodes featuring his victories had aired. He was becoming a celebrity outside the cloistered world of poker, as his careful, analytical approach contrasted with the growing audience's stereotype of a gambler.

As previously described, Howard also had a background that could sustain more than the allotted fifteen minutes of fame. Between his sister Annie's appeal outside the poker world and his other sister Kathy's August 2003 book chronicling their family's exploits and eccentricities, the idea was spreading that Howard Lederer and poker players in general could be unusual, exceptional, attention-worthy people.

In addition, the poker world was itself rapidly expanding. The outside world was gradually learning that Internet amateur Chris Moneymaker parlayed $40 into $2.5 million. This, in turn, fed the frenzy to sign up and play poker online. Part of this was due to the excellent and expanded coverage of the main event rolled out by ESPN during the summer. Even when ESPN reran portions of the seven hours of coverage after midnight, ratings remained significant. The combination of the World Poker Tour's and ESPN's coverage made casino poker so much more accessible that new players flocked to poker rooms. In particular, the new players wanted to try what they saw on TV, so no-limit hold 'em tournaments expanded to accommodate the demand. A lot of these players also stayed for the cash games, swelling attendance at long-stagnant poker rooms.

An expanded fall East Coast swing developed around the World Poker Tour and the attention. The Taj Mahal in Atlantic City had hosted the U.S. Poker Championships since 1996 at the end of the year. For 2003, they moved the date up to the first half of September. The Omaha and stud events drew the same number of contestants as 2002 but entries doubled in the preliminary $500 and $1,000 buy-in no-limit hold 'em events.

Ted Forrest, who had struggled in the biggest cash games throughout 2003, led the championship event, $7,500 buy-in No-Limit Texas Hold 'Em—not his best game, after the first day but was eliminated. Forrest had decided to play more tournaments, and spent some of this part of the year on the East Coast visiting his teenage daughter.

The Borgata, a new Atlantic City casino developed by MGM

Mirage and Boyd Gaming, hosted a World Poker Tour event as part of the tour's second season. Starting on September 20, immediately after the U.S. Championships, Jennifer Harman entered and almost won. She started in fifteenth place on Day Two, finishing in seventh, just one place from making the final TV table.

For Jennifer, it was almost a sweet ending to a disappointing and harrowing summer. In July, after getting off an airplane, she took off her shoes and noticed her ankles were swollen. Because she had had a kidney transplant twenty years earlier, she was trained to recognize this as a possible warning sign. She had a test done that indicated the transplanted kidney was not functioning properly. She spoke with doctors at the UCSF Medical Center, who changed her medication, but her kidney was beginning to fail.

At the stakes Jennifer played, it would not take much of a distraction to cause a six- or seven-figure swing in her bankroll. She managed to keep her head above water in the cash games while doctors tried to figure out how to save her kidney. Both the distraction and the physical discomfort made it difficult for her to maintain her focus. In retrospect, she was lucky to break even for the second half of the year.

The Tropicana in Atlantic City also jammed a poker tournament into the schedule that concluded on September 23 and 24. Barry Greenstein capped off a busy summer by winning the $3,000 buy-in stud event. A week earlier, he had also finished first in a $500 buy-in no-limit hold 'em event at the Taj. The two-week haul allowed him to give more than $70,000 to charity. He was going places and doing things he would not have considered doing in the past—entering a $500 buy-in tournament in Atlantic City?—but it felt good to spend at least a little of his time in poker toward a greater purpose. He was becoming actively involved in some children's charities and using the experience to teach his own children some valuable lessons.

If I could win one of these TV events, he started thinking, it would not only mean more money for charity, but could also encourage other people. Barry was not interested in trying to convert poker players or others to his way of thinking, but it would be certain to get some positive publicity. He didn't especially like the travel or the time away from his family (or the cash games) but he would continue.

Andy Beal had been working on his game throughout the summer. He was sure he was on to something, but executing it proved more difficult than he expected. During his last two trips, he had started out winning. His aggressive style and understanding of the fundamentals made him competitive. He felt his problem was that he was letting the pros get to him. With nothing else to do but play and no set times to finish or go home, he was staying too many days, playing too long, and losing his focus. Once he became fatigued, he was easier to read. He knew he was becoming careless in many little ways: holding his cards differently, moving his body and head differently, ignoring his signals to slow down and randomize some decisions.

One of the things he mentioned to Craig Singer before the last trip was for Craig to let him know if he was playing too many hours or getting sloppy. Craig did exactly that, but Andy ignored him. "Just another half-hour," or "Just a few more hands." He was learning the game, but he had not yet learned to manage himself. He would work harder on that, but it was not something he would be able to practice.

He continued to practice. A lot. During the spring and summer, he had numerous amateurs come to Dallas and play on the second floor. He and Craig continued to play as often as they could. As he played thousands and thousands of hands he felt that he was getting better control of his emotions. Or, more accurately, he wasn't experiencing those emotions to the same degree. The randomness of individual hands, of good and bad cards, was starting to matter less to him. At random intervals, he would try to conjure up the feeling of having aces in the hole, and then play his cards as if he had a very strong hand.

Despite all the planning, he made the decision to return to Las Vegas in late September on the spur of the moment. He had some open time in his schedule, so he came out, wired money, and called Doyle Brunson.

Again, Andy fortuitously had chosen a time that insured maximum chaos. Doyle resisted Andy's demand that they play a $50,000–$100,000 game. A lot of players were on the East Coast. A $20,000–$40,000 game might be the most they could get together.

Andy rejected playing for less than they had on the previous trip. He had yet to leave as the overall winner of these heads-up confrontations. How could they lower the stakes when they were ahead?

While they haggled over the size of the stakes, Andy told Doyle that, if he didn't get to choose the stakes, he would get to choose his opponents. Doyle rejected this out of hand. He wouldn't say this to Beal but he was good enough, and needed to be taken seriously enough, that their ability to switch players—finding different styles, removing fatigued players not used to starting their day at 7 A.M.—was an important part of their advantage. More important, Andy had no one he could substitute for himself. If he got tired, bored, or careless—an area where he was at a disadvantage to the pros, because they had spent years getting used to long, frustrating sessions where nothing seemed to go right—he had no choice but to play on in that condition.

Of course, he could always stop playing. But Brunson knew that the urge to gamble was tremendously strong. It could overcome an intelligent man's common sense. Professional poker players worked on controlling that urge, so it was unlikely they would "go off." Even if they did, they had a whole team to call on to take over, or to step in and remove them.

Andy Beal had only himself.

Craig had not accompanied him on this trip. Andy decided only at the last minute to come out and Craig was swamped with work. When Beal called him after he was in Vegas, Craig had to beg off. He came out toward the end of the trip, but could stay only a few days.

Beal and Brunson finally worked out arrangements. They would play $30,000–$60,000. Brunson and the group could play who they wanted and switch players when they wanted, with two exceptions. Andy would not play Todd Brunson or Jennifer Harman, the two players with the most success against Beal that spring.

With several members of the group still traveling back to Las Vegas, Andy Beal finally started playing on Wednesday, September 24, 2003. His first opponent was Chip Reese, who had not gone to the New Jersey tournaments. They played a close match at Table Three for several hours. Both men were in command of their games. When they stopped for the night, Andy was ahead by less than two bets. In a game with so much betting and so many hands played, it was a dead heat.

A dead heat with the most respected, best all-around big-money professional in the world? Not a bad start to a trip begun with so little preparation. Of course, he had been preparing to play at this level since the previous December. So what if he couldn't get the stakes as high as he wanted or impose more limits on his opponents? The game was what counted, and he was in control of his game.

Over the next few days, he won some matches, but had trouble with Chau Giang. Where were the players he had beaten last time? When he saw Barry Greenstein, he asked, "Barry, when are we going to play again?"

"I don't know, Andy," Barry said. "They don't want me to play you again for some reason." Greenstein could take the ribbing from Beal, but they weren't going to play again. Beal was too good to name his opponents and the group wanted to make him play whoever he was having trouble beating.

Greenstein could accept the ribbing at his expense. "I don't know, Andy. They won't let me play you again for some reason."

Barry was fine with Beal winning, even rubbing it in a little in jest. As long as the group won in the end, it was good that Andy felt he had a chance and was having a good time. Besides, this freed Barry up to play in the cash games. Those games weren't as big as during the World Series, but if he was going to stay in town and not play Beal, he might as well try to win some money. Andy's high stakes and aggressive style were almost contagious. In the spring, everyone was playing higher and looser. The prospect of winning all that money from Beal had made some of the local pros seem less concerned about losing to Greenstein at Table One.

Andy also struggled against Howard Lederer. At one point, he had Howard down a couple million dollars, but that was not very much at these stakes. Lederer, who was near his thirty-bet limit, this time had no intention of stopping. He had been thinking about Beal's improved play and how to adjust. He was sure he still had the edge in skill, especially in making decisions after the flop.

Did luck make skill academic? Or, consistent with the Branch Rickey quotation at the top of Chapter Four, did luck magnify skill? Howard Lederer got hit by the deck, making three consecutive full houses. He wiped out the deficit and left with a seven-figure profit.

Andy still felt confident. He was behind for the trip, but the money was secondary. Was he playing his best poker? He had to say he was at least close. Would his best poker give him a chance to win?

If his best poker wasn't good enough, there was no sense continuing. Yes, he believed, he could conceivably beat the best players in the world if he continued to play optimally. Lederer had played well, wringing the most bets out of his rush, but before that, Andy was the one wielding the club, and he also took a lot of bets.

Beal resumed his attempts to raise the stakes to $50,000–$100,000. Doyle Brunson wouldn't budge, so Andy tried a different approach.

Losing for the trip and low on funds, he refused to wire a large amount of money to the Bellagio. Over the first weekend, he played a series of the group's pinch hitters for relatively smaller stakes. The pinch hitters were high-stakes players who played mostly hold 'em. To play at the $1,000–$2,000 level and above, you had to be proficient in all the games. Below that level, however, there were many excellent players who stuck with their best game, usually hold 'em but sometimes stud or Omaha.

Andy Beal played heads up against some of these hold 'em specialists over the weekend, starting at $1,000–$2,000 and gradually moving up to $10,000–$20,000. Brunson contributed some of the group's bankroll to these players, though neither Beal nor most of the group knew the exact arrangements.

Andy generally mowed through these excellent hold 'em players. He had all his tools working: aggressiveness, control of himself, experience, and potentially intimidating stakes. The last two elements bear examining.

The players Beal defeated that weekend probably played more limit hold 'em over the past several years than Doyle, or Chip, or any of the members of the group. But, although Andy lacked the lifetime of poker experience his opponents shared, he was rapidly catching up in the specialized area of heads-up hold 'em.

Andy had played against the best poker players in the world for nearly 300 hours. He had spent at least that much time playing talented amateurs who visited him in Texas. Then he had at least doubled that total against Craig Singer. Despite the stories that circulated around poker rooms about the live ones that played too high—this record producer or nightclub owner or that sports team owner or pornographer—it was impossible to stick around against this level of competition and not improve. This year's live one might never become next year's professional, but the gap closed pretty quickly when the winners gave the losers such a good education. As for those losers who were untrainable, they quickly gave up.

Andy was nothing if not a quick study. The players in the group were unanimous in their belief that, except for them, Beal was a favorite against nearly every hold 'em player in the world, especially heads up. He proved it that weekend.

Even though the stakes were lower than in his games against Reese, Giang, and Lederer, they were still high enough to risk rattling his opponents. Put simply, if Doyle Brunson let you play cards with a half-million dollars, how would you feel if you had to tell him you lost the money?

The pros trained themselves to ignore the value of the chips during the game. Brunson himself said, "You have to be able to just sit down and play without realizing the value of the chips. I don't look at it as money until I get up from the table."

But an exception might be when they were someone else's chips. It was an adjustment, even for the most experienced members of the group. Todd Brunson has had no trouble sleeping after losing hundreds of thousands of dollars of his own money. " 'That's it. I've done the best I could.' But I've lost other times, when somebody else was involved, and it's a horrible feeling."

This renewed Andy's faith in the belief that he could rattle the group if he could get them playing high enough. He started playing members of the group again, but for slightly smaller stakes. He had built up his depleted bankroll with his wins over the pinch hitters and was trying to make a statement that he would not bring out the big bucks until they played him in a $50,000–$100,000 game.

On September 30, Andy lost against David Grey. Although some members of the group thought Grey's conservative approach to hold 'em didn't stand a chance against Beal's aggressive style, the result again suggested that matching Andy with even more aggression was not the way to win.

Beal got some revenge against Doyle Brunson that evening. Playing $20,000–$40,000, Brunson was running out of players and had to play Andy himself. He couldn't use Todd or Jennifer. Chau Giang had already put in two long sessions. Barry Greenstein showed up late from Atlantic City and wasn't volunteering to play. Grey had already played that day. Some other members had posted their money and were either out of town or unreachable.

Earlier, Doyle had a run where Andy felt like he hadn't picked up a playable hand for an hour. Whenever Beal would try to make a play at a pot, Brunson would raise him and chase him out or show down a big hand. He considered it a triumph of patience that he had managed to keep his losses to a minimum.

This evening, Andy was the one getting the cards, and Doyle was becoming frustrated by the combination of Beal's relentless raises and a lack of firepower to fight back. Brunson seemed short-tempered, though Andy thought some of that was a performance for his benefit.

On one hand, Beal raised and Brunson looked at his hole cards and threw them toward the dealer in disgust.

"I'm not playing these today."

They flipped up in the dealer's tray. Ten-deuce.

In poker, many hands have names. Everyone knows the obvious ones, like "pocket rockets" or "American Airlines" for ace-ace. A pair of kings are "cowboys." Two jacks are "hooks." Two queens? Before Roy Horn was mauled by a tiger, Vegas players called that hand "Siegfried and Roy." Generically, two queens are "the sisters," formerly "the Gabor sisters," occasionally now "the Hilton sisters."

Some of the less-well-known hands are part of the secret language of poker. The four of clubs and four of spades are "Darth Vader." (Black fours = dark force.) Nine-five is "Dolly Parton," though some players say the four of diamonds and two of diamonds (4d-2d) deserve that name. A pair of fives is known as "presto," supposedly after a place called the Presto Club in London on 55 Victoria Street.

Everybody in poker knows that ten-deuce is "Doyle Brunson." In both Doyle's back-to-back world championships, the hole cards of his winning final hand were ten-deuce. But he wasn't even going to try tonight.

Andy was tired and told Doyle he wasn't going to play much longer. He called for security to take his chips back to the cage as they played the final hands of their game. Jennifer Harman came by and she, Brunson, and Beal talked.

"So, Doyle," Andy asked, "how much did I win from you here?" He said it jokingly, rubbing it in a little.

"I don't know, Andy," said Doyle, acting as if it didn't matter in the least. "Not much for these stakes. A million something?"

Beal turned his attention to Harman. "When are we going to play a really big game, Jennifer, like fifty-and-a-hundred-thousand? For ten million?"

Jennifer giggled. "I can't play you for those kind of stakes. I'd go broke."

"But you're supposed to be the best hold 'em player in the world. That's why I won't play you unless we play those stakes."

They were sparring, playfully giving each other a hard time. "Maybe if you bought me a house. Or maybe if I had Doyle's money."

Andy became more serious and asked Brunson. "How about it, Doyle? I'll play Jennifer for ten million, fifty-hundred-thousand?"

As Jennifer walked back to her game, the last thing she heard was Doyle saying, "Maybe we can arrange it."

Beal and Brunson were both in negotiation mode. If Beal wired $10 million to the Bellagio, they'd give him his game. Beal wanted to limit the group's ability to substitute players. Doyle told him, at those stakes, he could use anybody he wanted, whenever he wanted. The way they left it, the group would be limited to two players a day, they would play at least six to eight hours, and Beal could stop whenever he was done for the day.

Andy was already supposed to play Chau Giang again the next morning. Would that be the start of the freeze-out?

Brunson told him it would. The security guard and the supervisor had arrived to verify the amount of chips Andy was having shipped to the cage. The largest denomination chip circulating at the Bellagio was $25,000. The high-stakes pros called it a cranberry, because of its color. Since their game in the spring, the casino had some cranberries available for the $30,000–$60,000 game.

Andy Beal was finally going to get his wish for an all-cranberry breakfast.

Between that night and the next morning, however, someone forgot to tell Chau. When he arrived, Andy told him they were playing $50,000–$100,000. Chau refused, consistent with the prior discussions about keeping Beal from kicking up the stakes. Andy, in turn, thought this was another tactic by the group to frustrate him.

They had to call Brunson and have him straighten it out. Yes, he told Chau, they had agreed to play Andy in a $50,000–$100,000 game, for $10 million, until one of them had the entire $20 million.

It was a spirited game, and Giang came out ahead, but not by very much. Beal was careful not to play too many hours and wear himself out.

The next morning, Andy Beal and Jennifer Harman started the second day of the freeze-out at seven o'clock. Harman had not picked up any appreciation for the early starting time. In fact, her malfunctioning kidney left her weak and tired, though she didn't fully realize it at the time.

Jennifer Harman and Andy Beal played the highest-stakes poker game in history from seven in the morning until three in the afternoon. Finally, after having to repeatedly look at her hole cards to remember what she had, she decided she was too tired to continue.

Andy had won more than $3 million. It was not a giant win, not even as many bets as any of Harman's three $3 million wins in the spring at $30,000–$60,000. But he had prevailed against one of the best limit hold 'em players in the world. He had again demonstrated that he had the game to compete at the highest level if he played his best.

Todd Brunson took over. Comfortable with his strategy and confident in his abilities, he nevertheless proceeded to lose over a million additional dollars before they called it a day.

It was a stunning development for the players. Beal's initial refusal to play Jennifer and Todd had given them a security in believing that trading their participation for higher stakes was a good deal.

It was a heady time for Beal, though he wasn't taking anything for granted. He was ahead by $5 million for the day. Even with Chau's win on the first day of the freeze-out, Beal was one-third of the way to winning. No one was going to lie down and just give him the rest of the $10 million, but anyone who thought he was in town to give his money away now knew better.

Each player in the group posted approximately $1 million. Putting aside the size of their nonpoker assets, that constituted (or exceeded) the entire playing bankroll of most of the pros. Several borrowed money just to post their individual shares.

It was not out of the question that Beal would win. In fact, winning $10 million at $50,000–$100,000 had to be regarded as much more likely than him winning $5.5 million at $10,000–$20,000 and he had improved substantially since he did that back in December 2001. Therefore, the players had to contend with the real possibility that Beal winning $10 million would just be the first round and they would have to scrape up another $10 million to keep the game going. Since poker players are ingenious financiers, they no doubt could accomplish that if necessary. But then what? Losses could rack up fast at those stakes. Whether you wanted to attribute the results to luck, skill, the stakes, or the random fall of the cards, simply sitting down to a game this size required the pros to acknowledge that they could be wiped out.

How did the members of the group take this reversal of fortune? Not only did each have a different feeling, but they each had a different feeling about how their colleagues were handling it. According to Chip Reese, "When Andy gets winning, there are a lot of jokes cracked that he's going to break everybody, that he's going to break the poker world, but nobody was really concerned."

Todd Brunson saw an entirely different scene. "It was like hysteria. There was crying. It was like, 'Jesus Christ, we have to win.' It was unbelievable."

The true state of affairs was probably somewhere in between, and it varied from player to player. Chip Reese and Doyle Brunson, with decades of success at high-stakes poker, could lose their share of the $10 million, dust themselves off, and keep going—not happily, but not broken. Barry Greenstein, the big winner in the 2003 cash games, could probably rebuild pretty easily but he didn't have millions of dollars he could lose without feeling the pain. His security, if you could call it that, was that plenty of people would loan him money so he could stay in action. Just a couple years earlier, in fact, a bad month of Chinese

Poker against Ted Forrest cost him over a million dollars and put him in the red.

That was the more likely scenario for most of the other pros in the group. The combination of high-stakes poker, high-stakes lifestyles, and thin capitalization had many players worried. Had the size of the stakes rattled Jennifer and Todd? If Beal won the freeze-out, they all imagined they would reup, but they would have to scramble to come up with a million dollars apiece. And what if he won again? Even though the group was still ahead (by a little) for the trip, these were the thoughts going through the players' minds. They were in uncharted territory.

When poker players joke about their profession, they sometimes say, "It's a hard way to make an easy living." No one knew that better than Doyle Brunson.

Despite the great highs of this lifestyle—playing games, making friends with unusual people, taking part in adventures around the world—he had not wanted this for his only son. It might seem like poker was a lot easier way to make a living than when Doyle was a young man, but Andy Beal had proven that wrong.

Doyle Brunson learned early about handling bad beats. Growing up in a small Texas town during the Depression, he ran everywhere. In high school, he set the state record for the mile run. At Hardin-Simmons University in Abilene, he was an all-conference basketball player. The Minneapolis Lakers, the first powerhouse of the National Basketball Association, considered drafting him.

An industrial accident at a summer job broke his leg so severely that he spent two years with it in a cast. But Brunson had no place for pity or regret. He dedicated himself to finishing his education, getting his master's degree, and preparing for a career as an educator. For competition, he would have to make do with golf, and maybe some poker.

Upon completing his education, he couldn't find a decent job at a school. He took a sales job at Burroughs Corporation and put his dream of becoming a school principal on hold.

In a customer's backroom poker game, he made a month's wages in a few hours. When the door had closed on his athletic career, he found a way in education. When there was no opportunity there, he moved to sales. Was poker a door that had opened for him?

In the mid-1950s, there was no such job as professional poker player. Few people had ever been to Las Vegas, then little more than a dust bowl 300 miles from anywhere with Bugsy Siegel's Flamingo, some Old West–type casino-saloons downtown, and little else.

Brunson would later tell of people in his hometown of Longworth walking on the other side of the street to avoid him because he gambled for a living. Gambling was illegal and viewed as immoral. No one saw gamblers back then as independents living on their wits, or as outlaws surviving outside the system. They were hustlers, lowlifes, crooks.

They were also perpetually on the run. It would be a decade before Brunson would play poker in a place where the game was legal—and then he and his colleagues were cheated out of all their money. Until then, he was "chasing the white line," driving around Texas to the places where insiders knew good games could be found.

Doyle Brunson had to be better than his competition to win, of course. Then he had to be savvy enough to avoid being cheated. He also had to stay ahead of the local law enforcement that tried to bust the game or shake him down. Finally, he had to get away with the money, because the circuit was at least as well known to thieves as to gamblers, and everyone involved knew the players carried a lot of cash and couldn't go to the law to complain if they were robbed.

Dewey Tomko, younger than Doyle but a veteran of the road

gambling days, said, "The kids today don't know how easy they have it, just having a place where they can show up, sit down, and play." (Tomko, like Brunson, was an educator-turned-gambler who channeled his competitive instincts into ultra-high-stakes golf betting. His exploits were chronicled as part of Rick Reilly's book *Who's Your Caddy?*)

During the late 1950s and early 1960s, Doyle met the men who took poker out of Texas and moved it to Las Vegas—Thomas "Amarillo Slim" Preston, Brian "Sailor" Roberts, Johnny Moss, Bob Hooks, Jack "Treetops" Straus. He allied himself with Preston and Roberts, traveling the Texas circuit together for several years, until they went broke together on their first trip to Vegas in 1964.

During the 1960s, Brunson married, had children, miraculously defeated cancer, and increasingly traveled to Vegas. He became close friends with Jack Binion, who, with his brother Ted, assisted their father, Benny, in running Binion's Horseshoe. He enjoyed the cycle of high-stakes golf during the day and high-stakes poker at night. The other regulars from Texas started migrating to this place where they could ply their trade without breaking the law or becoming prey to thieves.

For Doyle, Las Vegas was a city of dreams. He was respected as a skilled professional. His friends included casino owners and power brokers. Wealthy and influential men around the world came to play games with him, or invited him to join them in exotic locales. He was able to provide luxury and security for his family.

But this would not be the life for his son. Even in the glittering playpens of Las Vegas, gambling was not a lifestyle he wanted to encourage. He still had to remain wary of cheaters or phony friends who worked their way into his world to siphon off money from loans or business scams.

Gamblers were always one bet from oblivion. Maybe Brunson had been an exception, far ahead of his peers in skill and blessed with a wife who imposed financial discipline sufficient to provide a layer of security. But it was a profession where you either moved up or fell back. If you fell back, it was because you went broke. If you moved up, you were putting more on the line to risk going broke.

Not for Todd, he thought. Doyle could admit that he was a sick gambler who thrived in this outrageous environment, but he was going to use his success to make things better for his children. He would buy his son a better destiny.

Todd Brunson divided his childhood between family homes in Las Vegas and El Paso. While future peers like Jennifer Harman and Howard Lederer sharpened their competitive instincts as children over family card games, Todd had no such experiences. Poker was not a family activity in the Brunson home. In high school, he played football and joined the debate team. He had a quick mind and liked to compete. He wanted to be a lawyer someday.

While Todd was at college, he started playing in a local card game. According to an interview he gave to *Las Vegas Life*, he lost the money his father gave him for college expenses. Too ashamed to admit this, he took a job in a local restaurant to pay for school—and poker.

He kept playing and improving. His mother, Louise, handled the family's investments and had purchased a rental home in Orange County, California. The tenant had moved out and she was concerned about the house being vacant. Todd offered to live there during the summer. He did not say that he would also play in the local card rooms. By this time he was beating the local college games and wanted to test himself against poker room competition.

After the summer, he stunned his parents by telling them that he wasn't going back to school for his fourth year of college. He was going to play poker.

Louise Brunson was furious. But she couldn't blame her husband. Doyle's initial reaction was "I didn't even know he knew how to play."

Doyle was tremendously conflicted. On the one hand, Todd was an adult. He grew up in a loving, protected environment, but he was going to have to learn to make his own decisions, and this was one of them. On the other hand, his years of trying to save Todd from the hard parts of the gambling life had been in vain. Then, there was this hidden feeling of pride, which swelled when he saw Todd play and saw that he had a lot of talent.

Todd responded by asking his dad to share his wisdom. He had questions about all aspects of poker. He launched into a lengthy question, eager to be his father's student.

Doyle lost interest before Todd even got to the question. He paid his friend Mike Caro, a collaborator on *Super System* who also wrote a leading poker text on reading opponents, to give Todd about ten hours of lessons. After that, when Todd had a question, Doyle would say, "Go ask Mike."

Doyle never staked his son, either. Todd was going to have to learn for himself. Early on, Todd went broke many times in low-stakes games.

But he worked his way up, playing hold 'em in Las Vegas at every level, beating the game and moving up. If he got anything in poker from his father, it was inherited, not acquired. He did get his mother's common sense and financial savvy. He avoided the traps to which most young, successful poker players fall prey: drugs, high-stakes casino gambling, women looking for a free ride, hangers-on trying to do the same. Instead, he squirreled away money in stocks and real estate.

It had been a much easier road to the top for Todd Brunson than for his father. If Andy Beal beat Todd for the remainder of the $10 million, it wouldn't break either father or son. But this was still the hard part, the precarious life of the gambler. To get action, you have to give action. The unstated part of the equation, however, was that to give action, you could risk everything. If Andy Beal wasn't making Todd risk everything, he was certainly leading him along that path.

If anyone had more of an aversion to waking up early than Jennifer Harman, it was Todd Brunson. While Jennifer liked to wake up at about noon, it was unusual for Todd to get out of bed before 4:00 P.M. To play Beal at 7:00 A.M.. felt like torture.

To keep himself awake, he drank as many cans of Red Bull as he could. Without having eaten anything, it felt like the caustic liquid was eating away at his stomach lining. The whole experience gave him an ulcer (or aggravated it if he already had one).

They played for about ten hours. Andy continued playing a solid game, but Todd started getting the better of it. Even though Beal felt he could tell when Todd was changing his style and adjust, Todd, too, proved adept at reading Andy's changes in play. Over the course of the day, Brunson won back the money he and Jennifer had lost the day before, and then some.

By the next day, Todd was in agony from the pain in his stomach, but he was completely focused on poker. (Doyle Brunson is legendary for his retelling of the time Johnny Moss played for several days straight, and suffered a heart attack and was taken to the hospital. But he made it back to the game later that day. "It was only a *mild* heart attack.")

Todd wore Andy Beal down, then maximized his return on Beal's mistakes. He continued letting Andy be the aggressor. But when Andy overextended himself, the young pro trapped him and won a big pot. With his opponent playing less carefully, Todd was able to use the momentum on future hands. Having just gotten trapped for a bunch of chips, it was more difficult for Andy to remain aggressive in the face of Todd's increased aggression. More important, Beal was sure that Todd was having an easier time reading when he was weak.

For the last couple million dollars, Andy felt he just gave his money away. It was as if he could play only perfectly or terribly. Once his game slipped, he felt completely exposed.

It happened so quickly on that second full day against Todd Brunson—the eleventh day of his trip—that he couldn't look for an escape hatch. Andy had adopted the professionals' indifference to the money, and it came back to haunt him. According to Todd, he won the group more than $13 million over two days.

Affording the loss was no problem, but Andy Beal valued his money much more than he demonstrated at the end of the freeze-out. He would fly commercial to save $20,000 on a private jet; that was a no-brainer. He would even fly coach to save $500. But he sat there with Todd Brunson, not doing what he trained himself to do, not having fun, and gave away the last of the $10 million in the freeze-out.

He was disgusted with himself. He had done the very thing he knew led to his defeat in the spring: allowed himself to be worn down by playing too much, then playing badly in that condition. He didn't know whether he wanted to get away from poker forever or try again but without making such a stupid error.

10

The Big Game

It's like, oh goody. Now I get to be stressed all week. We just play so huge. We put so much at risk. But it's exciting stress, too.

—Jennifer Harman Traniello

May 2004

In February 2004, an interviewer asked Barry Greenstein about Andy Beal. Word of the game had been slowly spreading through the poker community and into the public domain. John Smith, a columnist for the *Las Vegas Review-Journal*, wrote in December 2001 about Beal's $5 million run and subsequent loss. Several Web sites devoted to poker news, rumors, and gossip occasionally mentioned when Andy was in town and what happened.

Greenstein was reluctant about going into detail. "It looks like he may have decided to pack it in."

It had been four and a half months since Beal had left the Bellagio red-faced with anger at losing the $10 million freeze-out to Todd Brunson. What about the rumors he would return?

"It would be nice if Andy did come back," Greenstein said. "He said $50,000–$100,000 was way too small, that $100,000–$200,000 would be next. Our bankroll is $10–$20 million. He wants to play a game so big that he can win that much."

That Greenstein was even giving interviews signaled how much the poker landscape changed since Beal's loss. Those changes probably affected no one as much as Barry Greenstein, who was fending off reporters almost daily. "Doyle gets this stuff all the time. At the table, we used to talk about girls or sports betting. Now it's all about who's interviewing you for what TV program."

On January 29, 2004, Barry won the $10,000 buy-in No-Limit Texas Hold 'Em Championship at the Fifth Jack Binion World Poker Open in Tunica, Mississippi. Greenstein had concluded that he was doing too well at poker to quit and get his Ph.D. He could change his mind someday, but even he regarded this as unlikely.

Medical research? That possibility was even more remote. If he was going to change the world, he would have to do it from the poker table.

That was why he went to Connecticut to play the World Poker Tour event at Foxwoods in November, to Tunica in January, and on a poker cruise later that spring. These were places he never would have gone without poker, and never would have gone even with poker if not for his commitment to donate his tournament proceeds to charity.

First prize was nearly $1.3 million, at the time one of the largest tournament poker prizes in history. After tipping the dealers, he gave it all away, mostly to Children, Inc., a charity that provided the necessities of life to children in twenty-one countries.

The Tunica finale was filmed as part of the second season of the World Poker Tour and would air in May. The media in Mississippi (where the tournament was held), Chicago (where he grew up), and Los Angeles (where he lived), along with poker publications, jumped on the story.

Giving over $1 million to charity? (He had actually donated more than $2 million by this time.) It was so incongruous with the image of poker players that the story spread even before the Travel Channel ran the episode. Members of the media had already started calling Greenstein by the nickname given on the broadcast: the Robin Hood of Poker.

In the rush to make the forty-nine-year-old into an overnight sensation, Barry's actual background took on the elements of myth. The basic facts were correct: brilliant math student, Ph.D. candidate, Symantec programmer, giving all his tournament money to charity.

Somehow, though, spinning that into a story led most people to believe that Greenstein was a wealthy computer programmer who lived off tens of millions of dollars of Symantec stock and that he took up tournament poker as a hobby. Tournament stars Paul Phillips and Phil Gordon had both retired young and wealthy from Internet-related companies, and people assumed Greenstein had simply done the same.

In fact, Greenstein had been in the opposite situation. He was a poker player who became a computer programmer and then returned to poker to earn a living. "Everybody thinks I made a fortune at Symantec. I was broke when I left Symantec." He had only a fraction of the wealth of those other high-fliers who turned to poker as a hobby. It was a case where the truth was harder to believe, and more remarkable, than fiction.

The Tunica tournament had provided a glimpse of how big poker had become. Jack Binion started the World Poker Open at his Horseshoe Casino in Tunica as part of a plan to build a gaming company beyond the family-owned Binion's Horseshoe in downtown Las Vegas. Although an uneasy public truce eventually followed the family fight that forced him out in 1998, most of the poker community was openly rooting for Jack's success and could barely contain their enthusiasm whenever a negative story surfaced—regardless of its truth—about Becky Binion Behnen and her husband, Nick. For Jack Binion, living well was sufficient, if not the best, revenge. Harrah's had agreed in September 2003 to purchase his company, Horseshoe Gaming, for over $1.4 billion.

The World Poker Open would never replace the World Series of Poker, but it was always well attended, especially by the Las Vegas pros. Jack Binion and his father were pioneers of poker in Las Vegas, and close friends with the Brunsons, Chip Reese, and Bobby Baldwin, the poker-playing president of the Bellagio.

Chip, Doyle, and a few other high-stakes players flew in a private jet with Baldwin to the tournament. This would be a reunion of several generations of poker elite. This also insured that the side action would be ultra-fast and ultra-high.

It also signaled a potential changing of the guard. Chip Reese, supposedly a big loser during the 2003 World Series side games, played in the World Poker Tour finale and made the final table. It was the first look that millions of new poker fans got of the legend. Reese never picked up good cards at the right time, however, and finished fourth. Barry Greenstein, the big winner in those 2003 side games, won the tournament and stole the show.

Barry's friend Phil Ivey also took down the money in the Tunica side games. Rumors swirled that Ivey won over $2.5 million. Only the players knew the actual amount, but it was clear that Ivey had a major league game to contend at the highest stakes.

The entire tournament was a poker lovefest. The event was so big that it needed two casinos, the Horseshoe and the Gold Strike, to contain it. The first hold 'em event, $500 buy-in limit hold 'em, drew 918 entries, the most ever for an event with a buy-in of $500 or more. That record lasted all of two days, when 950 players contested the first no-limit hold 'em event. In between the two hold 'em events, over 400 players turned out for an Omaha tournament. It was unheard of.

At the same time, unfortunately, the curtain came crashing down on the Behnen regime at Binion's Horseshoe in Vegas. On January 13, 2004, U.S. marshals raided the casino, closing it down for nonpayment of taxes. The timing could not have been worse. With poker in the gold-rush mode, the place that did so much to support the game looked like it would miss out on the party.

Just as Binion's was going through its death throes, poker rooms around Las Vegas sprang to life. The Mirage, which had struggled for years to rebuild its room after most of its business moved to its sister property, the Bellagio, had filled its room and was expanding, plowing under some adjoining keno space. In January 2004, the Mirage was short of dealers, cocktail waitresses, and even $1 chips.

The Palms, hosting a new cable program on the Bravo Channel, *Celebrity Poker Showdown,* had opened a poker room spreading middle-limit and no-limit games. The new owners of the Golden Nugget announced they were going to reopen their poker room during the World Series.

That was, assuming there would be a World Series. The Horseshoe shut down just three months before the Series was scheduled to start. By the end of January, Harrah's had reached an agreement to take over the property and announced it would run the World Series at the Horseshoe on the original schedule, but no one knew what to expect. A month before the scheduled first event, the Horseshoe was still closed.

The Bellagio and the World Poker Tour threatened to marginalize the World Series of Poker. At the beginning of April, the Bellagio hosted its second Five-Star tournament, concluding with the World Poker Tour Championship.

The Five-Star started with a bang. Tournament director Jack

McClelland had increased the minimum buy-in from $1,500 to $2,500. Despite the steeper price, entries for the first event rose from 203 to 361. It seemed nothing could stop the poker juggernaut.

And nothing could stop Howard Lederer. Lederer won that first event, along with $339,000 and a $25,000 entry into the tour championship. Two days later, his sister Annie won the third event, $2,500 buy-in limit hold 'em. Remarkably, it was the first major tournament win of her career.

On April 8 and 9, Ted Forrest won the $2,500 buy-in Seven Card Stud Hi/Lo event. Until recently, Ted Forrest had been thinking that maybe he "wasn't allowed to win." Traveling weekly to Larry Flynt's stud game at the Hustler, he had lost twenty out of twenty-two sessions. Barry Greenstein and Phil Ivey had been cleaning up in that game, and Flynt himself was a recent big winner. At the same time, Ted had lost over $2 million away from the poker table, in a combination of bad business deals, bad craps habits, and staking the wrong people.

Despite the high-stakes losses and other money drains, he had somehow kept afloat. He was regularly winning in lower-stakes games, paying off the winners at the Hustler, the casinos, and the players he was staking. He kept dedicating himself to the belief that his game would come around, his luck would change, and he could plug some of his leaks. He gradually cleaned up his business affairs, stopped staking other players, and imposed limits on his gambling in the pits. The tournament win was a sign that maybe his luck had changed.

On April 10, Howard Lederer threatened to turn the Five-Star into his family bank, finishing near the lead with twelve players left in the $5,000 buy-in no-limit hold 'em event. At 1:54 A.M. on April 11, Easter Sunday, however, the Bellagio lost all but emergency backup power. Over 2,000 guests had to be relocated to other MGM Mirage properties, and the next four days' tournament events had to be canceled. The twelve players received the remaining prize money in proportion to their chip position.

It seemed only a power outage could stop him. Two days after power was restored, the Bellagio ran the $5,000 buy-in Pot Limit Omaha event. Howard won this time, taking the first prize of $139,000. Although he went out on the third day of the WPT Championship, the Five-Star was a tremendous display of Lederer's tournament prowess.

He had become such a dominant tournament player that he had practically given up playing cash games, reversing the course of most top pros. In addition, he was capitalizing on his decision almost two years earlier to become part of televised tournament poker. Apart from the tournament success, he received offers to do color commentary on poker tournaments for Fox SportsNet. He also released the first of a series of instructional poker DVDs.

Finally, he had taken a significant role, both in development and marketing, for an online poker site called FullTiltPoker.com. In addition to Lederer, the site hired other well-known pros, including Phil Ivey, Erick Lindgren, Erik Seidel, Phil Gordon, and Chris "Jesus" Ferguson. Full Tilt was a late arrival in an increasingly crowded field, but its top-notch roster of playing professionals and marketing campaign gave it a shot.

Lederer and Forrest were not the only high-stakes pros to shine during the Five-Star. Barry Greenstein played in the tournament—he would stay at the Bellagio from the beginning of April to the end of May, leaving only during the outage and to make a few trips back to L.A.—and won the first event after power was restored.

His victory in the $2,500 buy-in no-limit hold 'em event was one of the most bizarre in the history of tournament poker. Barry started at the final table by playing in two tournaments at the same time. Late on April 5, play broke with him in tenth place in the $2,500 event and very low on chips. At noon on April 6, three hours before he would play at the final table—and be expected to make a quick exit—he entered the $5,000 buy-in Pot Limit Omaha event.

At three o'clock, he was leading in the $5,000 event. He walked across the tournament area to the final table of the $2,500 event and went all-in right away with ten-nine. After a flop of king-seven-six, he made a miracle inside straight on the turn with an eight. Later, he repeatedly stole the blinds, once trying to steal by going all-in with seven-deuce, regarded as the worst hand in poker. He was called by a pair of jacks. Jack-jack vs. seven-deuce? A seven came on the flop, and the turn and river cards were both deuces, making him a winning full house. Barry won $215,000, half of which he donated to Children, Inc., and the other half to Keep Memory Alive, an Alzheimer's charity supported by Bobby Baldwin.

It was almost noon when Andy Beal reached Doyle Brunson on Monday, May 10, 2004. He asked Brunson if the pros would play him in a really big game, "fifty-and-one-hundred, or one-and-two-hundred."

Brunson said, "Come on out."

Andy and Craig had already made their plans. They would be in Las Vegas by three.

Andy Beal had not given up on poker, nor had his losses hurt him financially. In fact, Beal Bank was having trouble finding things to do with all the money it was making. In a month and a half, its 2004 fiscal year would end, and it would report record net income of $282 million. In the post–Enron/WorldCom environment, reported earnings were always taken with some skepticism, especially because few people had the patience to comb through the details of financial reports. One bottom line, however, would put to rest any doubt about who could afford to lose more money playing poker, Andy or the group: Beal Bank paid cash dividends in fiscal 2004 of over $148 million.

He had even gone back to Las Vegas to play poker after losing to Todd Brunson the previous October. Less than a month later, he received a call from someone who wanted to back Johnny Chan, the two-time World Champion, against Beal heads up. Among the top pros and Vegas locals, Chan was a confusing package: phenomenally wealthy or apparently broke, a constant presence or mysteriously absent, patient and talented or impulsive and bored, kind and friendly or cold and angry. To the outside world, his legend transcended the current poker boom. He won the main event of the World Series of Poker twice in a row, then finished second the following year. He stroked a lucky orange for luck during his victories. His brilliant trap of Erik Seidel on the final hand of the 1988 Series was immortalized a decade later in the movie *Rounders*.

In November, Beal played Chan for three days and beat him. Like all stories about Johnny Chan, it was shrouded in mystery. Beal would not disclose who called him, but he said he was ahead of Chan after three days in a close, competitive match. The amount of Beal's win was probably under $500,000, and they played for stakes in the range of $10,000–$20,000 to $20,000–$40,000. They also played for a few hours on another occasion when Andy was in Vegas and Chan won that time.

Playing Johnny Chan for three days and winning even a small amount was an impressive performance. Chan, like Doyle Brunson before him, developed his reputation as a no-limit player and was once considered an easier opponent at Limit Texas Hold 'Em. But in the current environment where limit hold 'em was by far the more common game—and the big mixed games required not only skill at all forms of poker but all forms of *limit* poker—Chan had obviously adapted. Furthermore, few players in the world brought more of an intimidating presence to the table than Johnny Chan. Only about five-five, Chan still could glower at opponents with unbelievable intensity and his gaze immediately communicated the impression that he saw *everything*.

Beal also continued playing with Craig Singer and hosting talented amateurs at his office. One player he frequently matched up with for relatively high stakes was no amateur, though most people were not aware of his level of poker skill.

In the mid-1970s, Gabe Kaplan was a hot stand-up comedian with a hit television show, *Welcome Back, Kotter*. In the past twenty years, he has performed only occasionally. He has been making a very good living based on his investing skill, as well as his poker skill. A longtime poker enthusiast, Kaplan has been a fixture at the World Series of Poker and other high-profile tournaments and high-stakes games in Las Vegas and Los Angeles.

Other than the Table One pros, none of Andy's opponents had played as much high-stakes poker against world-class competition as Gabe Kaplan. They played on several occasions. Beal even tried out—mostly with embarrassing failure—some new strategies against Kaplan. But he continued to test himself and his theories, and to learn.

The delay between his October–November games and this May 2004 trip was primarily caused by business. Beal was especially busy, though, ironically, some of the bank's business involved developing a bigger presence in Las Vegas. The bank was reincorporating some of its operations in Nevada. In addition, one of the bank's projects involved participation in the loan syndicate financing Steve Wynn's new casino-resort on the Las Vegas Strip.

In early May, Andy saw an opening in his schedule and found out Craig Singer also had some time available. Maybe the time was right to take another shot at the poker pros. As usual, his timing was excellent.

* * *

The poker world collectively held its breath at the start of the Thirty-fifth World Series of Poker. Could Harrah's resuscitate the Horseshoe, shuttered since January? Even though they retained Binion's tournament staff, could they stage the tournament on such little notice?

The World Series exploded like a combination of Independence Day, New Year's Eve, and Super Bowl Sunday. The first open event, $2,000 buy-in no-limit hold 'em, on Friday, April 23, drew 834 entries. Only the main event the year before had a larger field, and no other preliminary event in Series history had 450 competitors. In all, five preliminary hold 'em events in 2004 exceeded the previous record.

The logistical problems were potentially enormous and unprecedented: having enough tables and dealers for over 800 players, running the conclusion of the previous day's event, conducting one-table satellites and super-satellites, holding nightly second-chance tournaments, and offering side games. Poker players are exceptional for their ability to find things to complain about, but there were very few complaints under the circumstances. Everybody's hobby/business/guilty pleasure was exploding on the public consciousness, and they were at the epicenter.

Ted Forrest won the next event, $1,500 buy-in Seven Card Stud. The entries for the event rose 50 percent since 2003 and it would be the first non-hold-'em event televised as part of ESPN's expanded package of coverage. It was Ted's first World Series bracelet since the three he won in 1993, and another sign that his slump was over. Forrest had made changes in his life and had dug himself out of the hole. Finally, it seemed, *he* was going to be the lucky one.

To the rest of the poker world, Forrest's win was a signal the cash game pros were getting ready to take over tournament poker. Less than a week later, Chau Giang won the $2,000 buy-in Pot

Limit Omaha event. On Friday, May 7, Barry Greenstein captured his first bracelet, winning the prestigious $5,000 buy-in No-Limit Deuce-to-Seven Championship. The final table also included Howard Lederer (who finished fourth), Chau (fifth), and Lyle Berman (seventh). The $296,000 first prize brought Barry's charitable contributions to around $3 million in less than eighteen months.

Andy Beal's arrival re-created the stress and chaos of his previous visits. He had called Brunson on the second day of the $2,000 buy-in Omaha Hi/Lo event. Howard Lederer had been eliminated late the night before but he was away from the Bellagio to watch his sister Annie at the final table. Todd Brunson also made the final table.

Annie Duke won the event, her first World Series bracelet and second significant tournament win, both of the year and of her career. (Many poker players, not recognizing her cross-over appeal to the non–poker world and the benefit it creates for everybody in poker, have resented the attention given to someone who had never won a World Series event. Rather than changing their tune, most now resent her for having won *only one* World Series event.) As with Jennifer Harman's win in Limit Texas Hold 'Em two years earlier, the victory ironically came on the same day as the women's-only event.

Brunson had the usual problems rounding up the players on short notice. At least he could reach Todd and Howard during the Omaha final on their cell phones. He was having no luck with Ted Forrest. Forrest, who rarely acted impulsively or lost his temper, had gotten in a fight with his girlfriend and shut off his cell phone. On this one occasion, however, it cost him his place in the group.

"If you don't get your money down, you're out." That was the rule, and there were no exceptions. Brunson had too much trouble in the past letting players slide about posting their money, and he had made it clear that the rule was now inflexible. Just when Forrest thought his luck had turned around, he was bounced from the biggest poker game in history.

That assumed the game would even take place. When Andy came into the poker room, Brunson, Reese, and several others were playing and kibitzing around a game of Chinese Poker.

Beal came prepared to negotiate over conditions for a $100,000–$200,000 game and start playing. He expected the group might try to talk the stakes down to $50,000–$100,000 to start.

He was shocked by what he heard instead. Doyle Brunson told him the highest the group could play him was $20,000–$40,000.

Andy was torn between ways of negotiating through this. Should he claim he was tricked into coming out because Doyle gave him the impression they would play him much higher? Or should he point out that it was unsporting to win all his money at stakes up to $50,000–$100,000 and not give him a chance to recoup at similar stakes?

Instead, he let his feet do the talking. He told them he was going to the cashier's cage to have his money shipped back to Texas, and then he walked out.

A spirited discussion followed, the players speeding it along based on the likelihood they thought Beal would follow through. Was Beal bluffing? Would he really leave after flying from Dallas to play? If he thought $20,000–$40,000 was too small, weren't they the only game in town? On the other hand, didn't they still have an edge potentially worth millions? And he had lost on every trip, so maybe he had paid for the right to call some of the shots.

Doyle finally decided the matter. "Okay, let's play him fifty and a hundred."

 He asked Marco Traniello to intercept Beal at the cage. Jennifer had been present for the discussion and Marco had brought his wife to the Bellagio that afternoon. If Marco went after Andy, none of the players would have to miss a hand.

Married to the world's highest-stakes female gambler, Marco had gradually become accustomed to the gambling life. Jennifer hadn't really given him much choice. For the games with Andy Beal, they were part of the team no matter what. Although his life outside poker kept him grounded in the value of a dollar (or a hundred thousand dollars), he was becoming more comfortable inside the poker world. He was nervous, but less nervous than he used to be.

Beal was already at the cage when Marco reached him.

"Come on, Andy. Let's go play."

Late Monday afternoon, Andy Beal started playing Chau Giang. Stakes were \$50,000–\$100,000. The composition of the team had changed since last year. Most of the players (except for Ted Forrest) from the original group were still in. A number of new players joined as they became part of the highest-stakes games, including Lee Salem, Gus Hansen, and Phil Ivey. There were at least fifteen members in the group this time, and several members had sold pieces to other players.

Andy won \$1.3 million before quitting at 10:00 P.M. He was trying to keep from tiring himself out.

Beal had played with Craig Singer sitting behind him. Most of the group played at an adjoining table or milled around. Giang, playing deep into the night in several World Series events while still active in the side games, looked like he hadn't slept since his last match with Andy the previous October. Gus Hansen, himself an ultra-aggressive player, thought Giang was playing Beal too conservatively. "My *mother* could beat Chau if he keeps playing like that."

Hansen wasn't the only one critiquing Chau's play. Each share in the group cost at least $500,000. At these stakes, in an aggressive heads-up match, that money could disappear fast. As high as everyone was playing in the side games, many players were stretched thin just taking that much of their bankroll out of play.

All the players standing around or watching intently from the second game created a tense atmosphere. Barry Greenstein, who later heard about the players hanging around, disapproved. "It looks bad if we win, like we're teaming up on him. And several people, I think it hurt their play to have other people watching them."

On the other hand, it was hard not to watch. The players could double (or lose) their investment in a flash. The stakes were so high that many members of the group would be seriously hurt by an Andy winning streak.

Chip Reese, usually difficult to rile about anything, quickly lost patience with all the watching and criticizing. If so many people had a problem with how things were going, he suggested, they should just disband, take a hit of $100,000 apiece, let Beal have his win, and refuse to play him.

Nobody wanted that. Complaining made many of the players feel like they got their $100,000 worth. Reese did not agree, but at least he made his point. When Howard Lederer played Beal on Tuesday, most of the players were gone.

Lederer regained his mastery over Andy Beal. Howard won $6.3 million, putting the group ahead by $5 million. Nobody was panicking when Chau Giang lost on Monday; $1.3 million was not very much at these stakes. But the atmosphere was more tense than on Beal's previous trips. Lederer had them all breathing easier.

Andy Beal wasn't panicking either. He felt good about his game, but had to conclude that maybe Howard had his number. Andy had struggled against other members of the group at various times—Ted Forrest in 2001, Jennifer Harman during the 2003

World Series, Todd Brunson during both 2003 trips—but he felt Howard matched up against him differently. For example, he was awed by Todd's gift for discovering and exploiting his weaknesses and lapses in play. But he could combat that by shoring up those weaknesses. Even if Todd continued to beat him, he felt there was always something he could do to improve. But against Lederer, he had no idea.

If Andy did not have to play Howard Lederer again, he thought he could win. Because he was down $5 million, he needed to wire more money to the Bellagio. He used the break in the game to negotiate with Doyle Brunson and the other players in the group on Thursday afternoon and evening.

Beal wanted to play the Big Game: $100,000–$200,000. He renewed his threat to leave if he didn't get his way. With Lederer's win, the pros had a taste of Beal's money and were hungry for more. Concerns from just twenty-four hours earlier—scenarios with Andy winning $10 million in a day and potentially wiping them out by doing it a couple more times—seemed remote. Barry Greenstein had the strongest opinion of the players at the table, and he favored giving in to Beal.

"We're ahead of him, so we should take a shot at playing bigger. If we win, we could win a hundred million dollars." To Barry, it was important that they had Beal's money, so they should leverage it into a potential bonanza. He also felt Beal was entitled to call the stakes. "You beat a guy out of $30 million and you're afraid to let him play for anything? That's ridiculous."

Greenstein was either very persuasive or the only one with an accurate memory. Afterward, Brunson said that he turned over the leadership of the team because of his involvement in the biggest side games, which took place not at Table One much of the time, but at Sam's Town or the Golden Nugget to accommodate Bobby Baldwin. Reese said later that he was not in favor of kicking up the stakes. Todd Brunson was playing in the Omaha Hi/Lo Championship downtown. (He was the last player eliminated that night, finishing tenth, but playing late into the evening.) Several others were playing in the event. Howard Lederer had left after playing Andy. Jennifer Harman was too sick to play.

Perhaps the only sour note of the World Series was the deterioration of Jennifer's health. By November, her doctors in San Francisco concluded that she would need a new kidney. For her blood type, the waiting list for a kidney was six years; she didn't have six years. Fortunately, she was able to find a compatible donor in her family. She was scheduled for transplant surgery on May 24, Day Three of the main event of the World Series. She was supposed to check in at UCSF Medical Center the next Monday, May 17.

Her situation was getting worse by the day. She had given up playing in high-stakes cash games; she just couldn't maintain the focus needed with that much money on the line. She tried playing in some World Series events but it became increasingly difficult, and she had to give up even that after trying to play in the Deuce-to-Seven Championship won by Barry Greenstein the week before.

Her face was becoming bloated and she was gaining weight. Her blood pressure shot up as high as 220/120. Other than visiting doctors and coming to the poker room to get her money down for the group the day before, she had done little but sit around her house, take endless medications, and call her father with instructions in case she died or suffered a stroke before making it to San Francisco. She also developed the flu, originally misdiagnosed as an allergy, further complicating her condition.

The members of the group negotiating with Beal agreed to let him have his way. They would play $100,000–$200,000. Over the course of the evening, they agreed to the following additional conditions: (1) Andy would have to play two days at these stakes, at least five hours a day; (2) each side would bring at least $10 million to the table; (3) the pros could use only one player per day;

and (4) Beal would not have to play Howard Lederer at these stakes.

Andy Beal got everything he wanted. The group demanded that he play for two days, at least five hours a day, and bring at least $10 million to the table. But he *wanted* to do all those things. He believed that raising the stakes to $100,000–$200,000 would take the players out of their comfort zone, so he wanted them playing as long as possible at these stakes.

He considered having gotten Howard out of the match to be important but even Beal didn't realize how significant a concession that would be. Despite having at least fifteen members in the group, they were seriously short of players. With Ted Forrest not a part of the group and Jennifer too sick to play, the only players with a good record against Andy were Chau Giang, Todd Brunson, and Howard Lederer.

Everybody in the group received a phone call Tuesday night, informing them of the new terms. Did they want to remain part of the group? When Jennifer Harman got the call, her immediate response was, "Who the fuck negotiated these kind of circumstances?" But she was still in, all the way, no matter what. In fact, no one dropped out.

On Wednesday, May 12, 2004, at 3:40 P.M., Andy Beal and Todd Brunson began the richest poker game of all time. How did Andy spend that day?

He started by wiring $15 million to the Bellagio. Then he went with Craig Singer to Binion's Horseshoe and joined thousands of poker players who were trying to get a discount on the $10,000 buy-in for the main event by entering a $1,000 single-table satellite.

Andy entered three satellites and did not win a seat. He played well in the first one. By the second, he decided he did not like no-limit hold 'em. By the third, he remembered why he hated ring games. It was a tedious experience, mostly pursued out of curiosity. If he really wanted to play in the main event—which he did not—he would have to come up with the $10,000 buy-in out of his pocket.

The other negative aspect of the trip downtown was that he was recognized by many of the players mobbing the Horseshoe. It was like Mother Teresa in the streets of Calcutta. Andy soon found himself fielding requests to loan or stake strangers the buy-in to play in the World Series.

Ted Forrest was also at the Horseshoe on Wednesday morning. To punish himself for missing the Big Game, he decided to enter that day's event, $1,500 buy-in no-limit hold 'em. It was a cattle call, with 834 players entering. Ted had decided to play more tournaments this year and was pleased with the decision, but he was playing this event only because he wanted to be someplace other than the Bellagio poker room. Watching the $100,000–$200,000 game and not being a part of it: That would be the real punishment.

Ironically, the one player Beal recognized did not recognize *him*. He saw Mike Laing, who had played him in his first games at the Bellagio more than three years earlier. Laing was not much changed: still gifted, still drinking, still erratic. He had been broke for a while, though he nearly made the final table of the main event in Tunica.

Andy had lost thirty pounds on the Atkins Diet and Laing didn't recognize him. Andy reintroduced himself. Although flipping pennies for $2,000 might not make the top-ten list of bizarre poker stories involving Mike Laing, of course Mike remembered Andy Beal. Some of his friends still ribbed him about offering to loan a billionaire $10,000. Laing was flattered that Andy remembered him.

As if anyone could forget Mike Laing.

* * *

After Andy's adventure at the Horseshoe, he attended a Las Vegas business meeting from 2:00 to 3:15. When he arrived back at the Bellagio, his $15 million was in the cage and Todd Brunson was ready to play. Andy signed for four racks of cranberries, $10 million in $25,000 chips. Brunson received $11.9 million in chips, but only two racks of cranberries. That was all the cranberries the Bellagio had. Security had also delivered Todd fourteen racks of flags, nearly $7 million. Stacked in a certain way, it would be almost the same amount as appeared in Andy Beal's photo from December 2001.

But the flags weren't for betting. Blinds would be $50,000 and $100,000—two chips and four chips. Bets would be four cranberries during the first two rounds, eight during the last two. If they bet with the $5,000 flags, it would be a twenty-flag–forty-flag game. They played with only the cranberries, and Todd could use the flags to buy back cranberries if he ran out.

If he ran out? Could he actually lose that much money in a poker game? He was not in favor of playing this high. Todd has said that it's a horrible feeling, losing someone else's money in a poker game. One member of the group told him, "If you lose, I'm going to kill myself." Todd thought he was joking but wasn't completely sure.

Later, Brunson described the encounter: "This is a guy who was battling a drug problem. I know he probably borrowed the money to get in the group because he'd been in the group before on his own money. I thought, that might actually happen. Then I got stuck $7 million." ("Stuck" is poker-speak for losing. Nobody "wins" at poker, either. They "get winner." Even a poker player who might have, without cards, become an English teacher, will say, "Doyle got winner for the third night in a row.")

Actually Brunson started on top. After thirty minutes, he was ahead by $3–$4 million. In a loose heads-up game where nearly every hand was raised before the flop, just one bet after the flop meant that at least $500,000 would be riding on the hand.

They also played a lot of hands. Table One had an automatic shuffler but the dealer would manually shuffle the deck if a hand had concluded and the machine was still shuffling. (When Beal hosted heads-up games at his office, he would hire two dealers: one to deal, one to shuffle the second deck. He had previously asked the poker staff at the Bellagio about paying for another dealer to shuffle the second deck while the primary dealer dealt the cards. Management declined, citing a lack of approved policies and monitoring procedures.)

Over the next hour, Andy took control, erasing the deficit and winning several million dollars. At least twice, Todd Brunson had to slide two racks of white $5,000 chips across to Beal, who gave him two stacks of $25,000 cranberries. The banker got ahead by as much as $7 million.

Brunson would not give in. Trained—if not bred—to play without a thought about the millions he had pushed to Beal during the afternoon, he staged a late comeback. He erased the deficit and actually took a small lead. (Everybody connected with the game regarded Todd's $1.1 million profit for the session as "small" at these stakes.)

At 9:45 P.M., Beal decided to call it a day. He was getting tired and he did not want to make the mistake he had made in the past of playing too long. He had Todd Brunson on the ropes, but he knew that Todd could crush him if he played too long and became careless.

Todd considered it a victory, more psychological than financial. "He thought he was really going to crush me. When I came back and finally won, he was real, real upset. He didn't say goodbye or anything. It's the only time I ever saw him do that."

Despite having over $6 million of Andy Beal's money, the pros were in trouble, more serious trouble than they dared admit. Who would play on the second day?

Lederer was banned. Todd Brunson was exhausted. Harman was too sick. Forrest didn't make the team. Chau Giang?

Chau informed the group that he was going to play in the $5,000 buy-in Seven Card Stud Championship starting at noon on Thursday. He was playing more events in this year's Series, mostly to answer his oldest son's questions about how he could be a professional poker player if he didn't appear on TV, and had won his third bracelet (and it would appear on ESPN during the summer).

Doyle Brunson wasn't going to play Beal on Thursday. Apart from the physical demands of staying on top of the constant action of the 7:00 A.M. game, Doyle had gastric-bypass surgery several weeks before the World Series. Although he had lost weight, he felt terrible. Even worse, he was going through the longest losing period of his poker career. It was not the time for him to step up.

Barry Greenstein would take one for the team, but no one was nominating him. He had yet to beat Andy, and the players angry about having let Beal raise the stakes had already designated Greenstein as the scapegoat if it ended badly.

Phil Ivey wouldn't play Andy Beal at these stakes. Whether it was because he had not played Andy and did not want to learn at $100,000–$200,000 or because he wanted to play in a side game or World Series event, he did not play Beal.

Chip Reese would play on Thursday morning. After Doyle Brunson, he was the oldest, most experienced, most respected, and the best guy-you'd-want-in-any-situation-if-your-life-depended-on-it poker player in the group, if not the world. He would also wake up and come to the Bellagio at 7:00 A.M., a secondary but not irrelevant qualification for the job.

They started Day Two of the biggest game of all time at Table One just after seven o'clock in the morning. Andy Beal sat in Seat Six. Like one of the Men in Black, everything about him was designed to leave no impression whatsoever. He wore a black baseball cap, black sunglasses, white dress shirt, and black slacks. He wore big headphones, listening to instrumental music. Craig sat in Seat Eight, in front of racks of flags and cranberries.

Chip Reese sat in Seat Three. He wore a powder blue sweatshirt and sunglasses. Sunglasses? What would Reese think Beal could read by looking in his eyes? Andy couldn't help but feel a little flattered that Chip thought that highly of his observational abilities.

Although Reese thought he had beaten Beal in most of their previous games, other members of the team remember it differently, as did Beal himself. In any event, Andy Beal was not intimidated by the prospect of facing Reese, despite Reese's well-deserved reputation as one of the greatest poker players of all time.

Beal started ahead and stayed ahead. The area around the table became increasingly active throughout the morning. At the beginning, David Grey was the only other member of the group present. Not really sweating Chip, he sat at Table Seven, facing away from the game, eating breakfast. By eight, David was watching the game, periodically making and receiving phone calls. Everyone wanted updates, and often. Lee Salem also watched most of the morning, mostly sitting in Seat One, looking somber in a dark sport jacket and white collarless shirt.

Doyle Brunson materialized and then disappeared, a difficult feat for a man using a crutch or a motorized wheelchair to navigate the byzantine floor plan of the poker room.

After nine, Gabe Kaplan appeared, wearing shorts and a T-shirt. Like Don King working both sides of the aisle at ringside, he sat between Beal and Craig Singer, then behind Craig, then behind Chip. As Reese's losses mounted and Chip traded in more chips, the racks accumulated in front of Craig in Seat Eight.

At ten, Gus Hansen came to watch the game. Hansen showed up in a white T-shirt and what looked like boxer shorts or swim trunks. A lanky, wiry presence, he radiated manic energy, sitting at the table, walking around, talking on the phone. A house phone was mounted upstairs on a pillar near the rail. Hansen talked on the phone, twisting the cord around his hands, then his arms, then pacing and twirling the cord. He almost wrapped himself in it entirely and had to disentangle carefully, not missing any of the conversation.

Andy was obviously doing very well. The signs around the poker room indicated the result: more phone calls, more players paged, more players arriving, some clearly wearing little more than pajamas, Beal frequently selling Reese back stacks of cranberries recently lost, the long-faced and slumped posture of the pros.

Then, at 11:40 A.M., it was over. They broke for lunch.

Andy Beal had all the cranberries. He won $8 million from Chip Reese. For the trip, he was ahead only $2 million, but he had nearly cleaned out the supply of chips the pros had brought to the table less than five hours earlier. Being the biggest game in history, it was, not surprisingly, the biggest winning session in history, and he did it against one of the greatest poker players who ever lived.

Beal was in a hurry to leave the Bellagio. He had a lunch date with the guy who built it. He whispered some instructions to Craig, spoke briefly with a couple of employees from the poker room, then left. Craig spoke with some players and some of the poker room staff before he, too, left.

The players stayed behind to pick up the pieces, convening an ad hoc meeting at Table One.

Chip was done. He had other business and wanted someone else to play. Some of the players made oblique comments about how the game had gone. He later said that three members of the team critiqued his play. One said he played exactly right. The second said he played too aggressively. The third said he was not aggressive enough.

The players debated who would play Beal, who told them he would be back at 2:00 P.M. He made it clear that this would be his last day in Vegas, though he did not say how late he would play. As they criticized each other, Chip, and other potential players, Reese repeated his message from Monday night.

"What's the big deal? Andy's been here all this time and he's never won. Let him take his win and we'll take our loss and go on."

No one else at the table wanted to do that. "Well, whatever everybody chooses to do is all right with me." Then he left.

As the players continued their discussion and the group gradually broke up, nobody did anything with the $20 million in chips on the table. Andy and Craig had put the Lucite rack covers over his chips and some players in the group had put covers over what remained of their chips. Everyone just relied on security and the cameras to make sure the money stayed there.

Andy had lunch with Steve Wynn at Wynn's office on the Strip. Beal Bank had been a large participant in a syndicated loan facility for his new casino. Andy had a great lunch and enjoyed Wynn's hospitality. He had a chef in the office who prepared lunch and the men visited for a couple hours, talking mostly about Wynn's plans for the new resort. Despite all the poker history made by these two giants of business—Wynn, over thirty years; Beal, over three years and, most significantly, over the last five hours—neither man brought up the subject of poker.

When Beal returned to the poker room from his lunch with Wynn, he was shocked to see a stranger in Chip Reese's seat. The man was about his age, fit, with dark eyes, dark hair, and a dark complexion. He looked European or Middle Eastern. The man introduced himself as Hamid and drank what looked like cognac.

According to Beal, the rules did not allow substitutions. Craig, also back from lunch, encouraged Andy to take it up with Brunson, who was in the room. Doyle pointed out that they also agreed that either side could quit whenever they wanted. Chip wasn't available and they wanted Hamid to play. If Andy didn't like it, he could quit. Or if he stood on protocol, he could say they quit.

Andy didn't want to quit. But who was this Hamid character?

Hamid Dastmalchi was a formidable presence at the poker table. He was the 1992 World Champion and a top high-stakes player, especially heads up. Although Hamid lived in San Diego, he had played all over the world since starting as a twelve-year-old in Iran. He smoked, drank, had a quick temper, and could play for days. He was Ted Forrest's adversary in the famous 100-hour $600–$1,200 "death match" at the Mirage, the one that ended only when Hamid had to be taken off the property in an ambulance.

As the match was starting, David Grey reached Jennifer Harman at her doctor's office with an update. "Hamid is going to play him."

Jennifer was nonplussed. "Hamid? What is that about? I'm on my way. I'll play him if I have to."

Hamid played Beal from 2:00 to 4:30 P.M. For the first hour he won back $5 million, more than half the money lost by Chip in the morning session. He was also drinking heavily, ordering and consuming several Courvoisiers and Budweisers. This was not unusual for Hamid but some of the players watching were horrified. Beal and Singer thought it was a ruse. How could someone play the biggest game in history and drink like that?

Jennifer Harman came into the poker room and saw Dastmalchi with a glass in one hand and a beer bottle in the other. This is great, she thought. She watched the cocktail waitress bring him another round.

Beal regained control of the match. By 4:30 P.M. Andy had retaken the $5 million from Hamid.

Doyle Brunson knew they needed to make a change. He told Gus Hansen and Jennifer Harman that one of them had to take Dastmalchi's place.

Gus said he was ready. "I feel good. I think I should play him." It would be his first time playing against Beal, so he wanted to set a limit for himself. "If I lose $2 million," he told Harman, "I'm done."

As he sat at the table, he put aside $2 million in chips, four stacks of cranberries. When they were gone, he would be, too.

Hansen, like his predecessor, immediately took the lead on his amateur opponent, quickly winning $2 million. Hansen's aggressive style, however, was not a good match against Beal. Gus was learning, like Ted Forrest, Howard Lederer, Jennifer Harman, and Todd Brunson before him, that you couldn't bluff Andy, and countering his aggression with more aggression turned the match into a showdown, where the experienced pros traded skill for larger pots going to the player with the better cards. By 6:00 P.M., the Dane had lost the $2 million back to Beal, and bluffed off another $2 million as well.

Hansen got up from the seat. He reached his limit and wasn't going to play anymore. Should Jennifer take over? She was so sick, from so many different causes, that she had to be the wrong choice. But it looked like she was the only choice.

Johnny Chan said, "Jennifer, go in. Just go in."

She had less than an hour to play. The last flight before the red-eye from McCarran to DFW left at 8:15 P.M. Andy was taking his twin daughters camping on Friday, and he would not risk being late by missing that flight.

Practically debilitated from fever, high blood pressure, and kidney failure, Jennifer Harman still managed to win $5 million from Beal in a half-hour. He called for security to take away his chips; he had just a few more minutes to play.

When security arrived at 6:45 P.M., he told them he wanted to play a few more hands. That turned into five minutes, then another five minutes, then another five minutes, then just a few more hands. He realized as the scene unfolded that Jennifer might assume that he would play even more wild during the last few minutes.

Andy used this to make the most of a run of good cards. On one hand, he raised before the flop with ace-queen. (It was a natural raising hand, but in a heads-up game played in such an aggressive fashion, he could just as easily been playing king-seven the same way.) A queen and two low cards came on the flop. He could feel Harman looking at him, trying to look *through* him. He paused a moment, tilting his head slightly. It was a rare attempt to shift gears, from trying to give the pros *no* information, to giving out *false* information. He bet, but Harman may have taken that small movement as a signal that he was trying to make a play at the pot. She raised him back.

She was the one making the play and Andy won, pulling in a pile of cranberries. With plays like that, he erased the $5 million deficit, and then won another million and a half before finally turning over his chips to security.

He quickly counted the chips before signing the forms from the supervisor and racing to the airport. He had a total of $21.7 million in chips in front of him. For the day, he had won $11.7 million. For the two-day $100,000–$200,000 game, he was quitting ahead by over $10.6 million. Even subtracting his losses at $50,000–$100,000, he made nearly $6 million for the four days.

There were only two nice things about this miserable time for Jennifer Harman, the last person to see Andy as he and Craig Singer rushed out of the Bellagio on the evening of May 13. The first was seeing how happy the experience had made him. "It's good, you know, that he wins. He's a nice guy. He's allowed to win." The second was, "I knew he'd be back. He was way too excited." There would be a time for finger-pointing and recriminations, but that wouldn't be for days. And Jennifer would have to take part by long distance, if she survived to take part at all.

The trip was a disaster for the high-stakes pros. Their losses came to over $300,000 per person. Their wins over Beal during the previous three years far exceeded that, but that money was long gone. In addition, several new members of the team never experienced those victories. It was a bad night to be a professional poker player in Las Vegas.

With one exception.

Ted Forrest kept plugging away in the $1,500 buy-in no-limit hold 'em event at the Horseshoe. With sixteen players left, he had an average amount of chips and survived to the final table. He got into a big pot with the chip leader, won, took over the chip lead, and never relinquished it. Frozen out of the Big Game, he missed out on a loss of over $300,000, and won his fifth bracelet. He also took home $300,000 in cash that night.

Ted's instincts from the early spring were correct: It was his turn to get lucky.

11

The Next Best Thing

The next best thing to gambling and winning is gambling and losing. The main thing is to gamble.

—Nick "the Greek" Dandalos (1893–1966)

Late May 2004

Jennifer Harman was correct about one thing: Andy Beal could not stay away. Feeling cocky and, in retrospect, a little stupid, he returned to the Bellagio on Monday, May 24, less than two weeks later to take another shot at the pros, and to let them have another shot at him.

When Beal arrived to negotiate over the stakes, he naturally met with resistance. The pros were adamant this time. They would have to concede that he won at the highest stakes of all time. They were afraid to play as high as he wanted.

As soon as Andy Beal left town on May 13, the players fell into dissension over the reasons for the loss. The first mistake was that they allowed Beal to reach his goal of raising the stakes high enough to make the pros sweat. The magic number to do that was $100,000–$200,000.

Doyle Brunson recognized it. "I think there was more pressure on everybody because it was so high. I could see the people playing in it were affected by it a little bit. That's what he wanted to do. Get everybody out of their element. And I think he did it a little bit with $100,000–$200,000 because after it was over, we all said, 'No, we're never going to do that again.' Twenty-forty is plenty big and if we're winning, we'll go to fifty-one hundred, but that's as high as we'll go."

For Jennifer Harman, the pressure of the stakes became magnified by the decision to let Beal exclude Howard Lederer from the match. "Ted's not in. Todd's played him all day the day before. Phil Ivey won't play him. I'm too sick. Chau was playing in the tournament. Doyle doesn't want to play him. Nobody wanted to play him. *And we're playing him as high as we can*. And we negotiate Howard out? Smart."

As the world's must successful professional gamblers, was there some element of losing face in turning down a big bet when they had the advantage? For Chip Reese, ego was not a part of it. "Sometimes, I know I have an edge but maybe the downside is so great that the edge isn't worth it. Those are business decisions."

Likewise, Doyle Brunson could live with Andy Beal saying the pros would not play him at his stakes. "The edge isn't big enough. When he first came, I thought we were a prohibitive favorite. He's made the gap so close that it's not that big a deal. He could win and damage the poker economy. I mean, you could lose $50 million or $100 million and it wouldn't be a big deal."

Doyle had a story to illustrate the necessity of even the consummate professional taking prudence over pride. "Benny Binion had a no-limit craps game. This guy came in and he got lucky and wanted to make such a huge bet he'd have owned the whole joint if he went on a five-minute run. Benny wouldn't let him make the bet. The guy said, "I thought you had a no-limit craps game?" Benny said, "I thought I did, too, until now."

The atmosphere created by so many players standing around watching also contributed, both to the dissension and the difficulty the players faced. Brunson, shuttling between the Bellagio, the Golden Nugget, and Sam's Town, where they played the largest side games during the Series, would not have allowed it. "It's a lot harder to play with all those people up there. I'd have chased everyone away and said, 'Get the hell out of here, you're bothering the player.' It's hard to play with someone critiquing your every move." Howard Lederer agreed. "It's one thing to be focused and try to eliminate from your mind the aspect of all these people you're playing for. It's another thing to see the people whose money you're losing. That can't help."

Maybe, just maybe, the pros had gotten a little lucky over the three years and wanted to close the betting window before their luck changed. Mike Matusow, a fellow Vegas professional who earned his nickname, the Mouth, for his outspokenness, believed, "They have no idea how good they're running. He could come in and win $10 million a day, every day for a month. If he's aggressive, he can win. And they've been very fortunate."

This was a view held not only by outsiders. Chip Reese surveyed the entire experience of playing Beal from 2001 to 2004 and concluded, "Andy played good enough to win. He should win sometimes. The truth of the matter is that he probably played unlucky to get behind as much as he did. He didn't even play that bad in the beginning and he could have easily won."

Ted Forrest also acknowledged: "The luck has probably broken in our favor."

For some reason, Barry Greenstein received a disproportionate share of the blame for the decisions made on the evening of May 11. Lederer, who recognized that the decision to raise the stakes was a close call and was not part of the debate, thought they got outnegotiated. "We let him get me out of the mix. We gave him everything. I know Barry was always arguing for 'Let him get his way. We should just gamble with him.' And that's a reasonable sentiment. But a lot of people were more like, 'What kind of idiots were we? We're the only game in town.'"

Todd Brunson, proud of his role as a winning player at the highest stakes in 2003 and 2004, nevertheless disagreed with letting Beal get his way. "They said, 'He's going to leave.' I said, 'Let him leave, he'll come back anyway.' Barry was the one who negotiated, along with Lyle [Berman], without anyone else's permission, and we're lucky something really bad didn't happen to us all."

Lederer's understanding was that "Doyle was the negotiator. Barry was the instigator. Barry was the do-whatever-he-says guy in the discussion."

To Barry Greenstein, those attitudes were antithetical to the fundamental philosophy of their trade. "We're gamblers. We try to get the best of it but we gamble when we don't have the best of it. We don't just play when we've got the nuts. You want the best of it, but when a guy loses money, he gets to call some of the shots."

Greenstein had no regrets, other than the attitudes of some of his fellow players. He believed in the basic plan of leaving people alone to play Beal, sticking with players who won, removing players who lost, keeping the stakes down when they started or were losing, and raising the stakes when they were ahead. "I didn't have any misgivings about playing him higher when we were ahead of him. But whenever something negative happens, you have a bunch of people whining. And let's say we're a two-to-one favorite. Two-to-one favorites don't always win. That's just part of it. If you lose, you shake the guy's hand. A lot of these people don't act like that."

Barry was in it for the money, because he thought the group had the edge. Philosophically, though, "I almost half root for Andy. I mean, what Andy has undertaken is, from the point of view of a gambler, really neat." Greenstein's decisions always had his, and the group's, financial interests at heart, but he could identify with Andy Beal more easily than with some of his fellow professionals. "Some of these people, the way they act, I feel almost like they deserve to lose. They really don't act like I think a professional should act."

Naturally, Andy Beal's decision to show up again during the main event of the World Series created disorder. Several members of the group were in the hunt for the championship, which would pay a mind-boggling $5 million. This year, 2,576 players had entered, a poker orgy so intense that the Horseshoe had to cancel super-satellites and split the field into two halves on May 22 and 23.

The big story of the Series on May 24 was Mike Laing.

Yes, *that* Mike Laing.

Out of nearly 1,300 players who started on Saturday, May 22, Laing was the chip leader with over 129,000 chips. No one exceeded his total on Sunday, so he started May 24 as the leader.

For anyone else, Laing's experience that day would be the most bizarre story of a lifetime. For Mike, it was just another day at the card room.

Early in the day, cameras focused on Laing, the chip leader, and tablemate Robert Varkonyi, the 2002 champion. Playing to the cameras, Varkonyi won a pot and joked to Laing, "What do you say we don't play another pot until the final table?"

Laing didn't miss a beat. "This *is* your final table, sucker. You just don't know it yet."

According to Laing, his concentration later faltered when his ex-wife showed up on the rail. As he drank, she drank. She also got access to some pills, and they argued because she wanted him to pay for them. Finally, he sent her home with a limousine driver he had hired to baby-sit *him.* After repeatedly calling her on the phone and receiving no answer, Mike said he called 911. When he learned she was being taken to a local hospital, he left the tournament, only to be told he could not see her or get information on her condition. (He said she later recovered.)

He returned to the tournament, drank a large quantity of Jack Daniel's, and found himself with ace-jack. As Varkonyi, still at his table, made a raise, a member of the tournament staff announced that there were only four former champions left in the field, and listed them. He did not mention Robert Varkonyi.

Robert complained to the others at the table, "Why didn't they mention my name?"

Laing called Varkonyi's bet, and said, "They must know I'm gonna bust your ass out on this hand." And he proceeded to do exactly that.

As his mind became increasingly addled from the whiskey, he made some playing errors, culminating in an ill-advised all-in bluff, which was called, eliminating him from the tournament.

Jennifer Harman wasn't in Vegas to see her prediction come true. Andy came back to town on May 24, a significant day in poker. It was Day Three of the world championship at the Horseshoe and transplant day in San Francisco for Jennifer.

Marco Traniello received the call on his cell phone while his wife was in surgery.

Was she in the group?

He thought about the emotional roller coaster of life with Jennifer over the past four years. He remembered the sick feeling in his stomach whenever he heard that Andy Beal was coming to town. There were all those times he told his wife that she had too much gamble in her. One of those times, he returned from Italy, came to the Bellagio, and marched straight to the men's room in the sports book so Ted Forrest could weigh him to settle a $3,000 bet he had with Jennifer over Marco's weight. (Jennifer lost that one.) He thought about Beal winning nearly $12 million in one day less than two weeks earlier, including a $6 million run against Jennifer in the last thirty minutes of his trip.

It took him only an instant to answer.

"We're in for the biggest piece we can get."

Today, Marco would be the gambler in the family.

He even offered to leave his wife during her kidney transplant to deliver the money. "If you need it, I'll come today. I'll fly to you and give you the money." They did not make Marco retrieve the cash from Jennifer's safe deposit box: This once, they could make an exception. But he had to offer. He knew that Jennifer would kill him if he let her be excluded.

Phil Ivey played Andy Beal on Monday and Tuesday at limits of $30,000–$60,000. Perhaps spurred on by the implication that he had ducked Beal during his early May win, Ivey wanted the first chance he could get to play the banker. Ivey was ultra-competitive and had established himself over the previous year as a successful player at the highest stakes imaginable. He was also wildly aggressive, a style that won him millions in cash games and tournaments, but did not intimidate Andy Beal at all. After two days, Ivey had essentially broken even. He was ahead by less than the amount of one contested pot.

To no one's surprise, a top contender for the world championship among the high-stakes pros was Howard Lederer. Dressed completely in black Full Tilt gear and looking in equal parts fierce, haggard, and exhausted, he was nevertheless eliminated on May 24 when another hot pro drew out on him, making a flush to beat his three of a kind on the flop.

Doyle Brunson.

Feeling every bit his seventy years and in the midst of the worst run of his career, Doyle nevertheless put on a poker clinic for thousands of players and observers at the Horseshoe and the millions who watched on ESPN through the summer and fall.

He finally busted out on Wednesday, May 26, in fifty-third place. His executioner? Bradley Berman, Lyle's son.

Beal knew he would have problems against Todd Brunson and Howard Lederer. Todd was superb at reading him and capitalizing on his mistakes; Lederer was impossible to figure out. Andy came to town ready to insist that he would not play either of them. As with limiting the stakes, the players had made it clear that they would rather pass up the chance to win his money than give in to his demands.

How could he be upset? No one was going to pat him on the back and say, "Good job, Andy," but they obviously thought their edge was not very big.

He got hammered by the group's two toughest players on May 26 and May 27. On Wednesday, at \$30,000–\$60,000, Todd Brunson won \$5 million in six hours. Beal stuck with his earlier announced decision to stop after that amount of play. In Todd's view, this was wise. "If I had two more hours, I'd have won another \$10 million. I just mowed him down from that point on. I was so sick when he quit."

Ahead by \$5 million, the players let Beal raise the stakes to \$50,000–\$100,000 for his match against Howard Lederer on Thursday. It was a concession that proved expensive, but this time for Andy Beal. They played for nearly eight hours and Lederer felt completely in command. "I ran pretty good that day," Howard admitted, "but I really feel like I worked some stuff out." He won another \$9.3 million.

Ted Forrest did *not* have his cell phone shut off when he received the call on May 24 asking if he wanted to be part of the group. Of course, he said yes. Because the pros won nearly \$15 million on this trip, he put himself in the enviable position of sharing in the win, without having to experience the \$6 million loss from ten days earlier. He also won the unofficial title, bestowed by David Grey, as "The Luckiest Man in Poker."

It was quite a turnaround from the beginning of the year, when Forrest thought he wasn't allowed to win. He referred to the trio of accomplishments—missing out on the $6 million loss, winning the hold 'em event, and cashing in on the $15 million win—as "dancing between the raindrops." More important to Forrest, however, than the money was the feeling that he was back in the mix. Best of all, Ted was increasingly getting that feeling of excitement from playing poker again. Sometimes it was a dangerous thrill, but he wanted to experience it nevertheless.

"If you never feel the pain of losing, you can't really experience the joy of winning," Ted has said. "We live life on the edge. Sometimes, we have to risk falling over the edge."

As Andy Beal left the poker room on May 27, he knew that his two toughest opponents had played their best game and claimed significant victories. But increasingly, his mind was occupied with a question he couldn't answer: Where am I going with this?

Poker was gradually taking over his mind, if not his life. He was spending a lot of time working on his poker game, something he recognized was necessary to have any chance against the pros. Even when he was doing something else, like taking his daughters for a walk or working on a $50 million business deal, his thoughts would wander to poker. He didn't want poker to become the focus of his life, but he couldn't see himself doing it halfway.

Almost as important, it was becoming less fun. The key to succeeding in being difficult for opponents to read, he realized, "isn't to hide your emotions. It's to not have them." After playing tens of thousands of hands, at stakes ranging from nominal to $100,000–$200,000, he had trained himself to be unconcerned about the money, as well as unconcerned about the quality of the cards. A pair of aces no longer filled him with a thrill he had to worry about hiding.

It became less fun. It didn't even seem like gambling anymore.

If Andy Beal had wanted to learn about how professional poker players thought, he finally knew. Like the pros, he was attracted to poker because it involved gambling. But developing skill made it less like gambling and more like . . . work.

Although Andy was supposed to play Phil Ivey again the next morning, he returned to the Bellagio poker room a few minutes later and found Howard Lederer and David Grey, still counting and racking chips and following the procedures for returning them to the cage and to the team's bankroll. He reached out and shook Lederer's hand.

"It's been a real pleasure playing with you, Howard. I thought I could master this game but obviously I haven't."

Lederer knew what was coming but he was at a loss for words. He had just won more than $9 million from Andy, so there was no sense saying, "Sure you have, Andy." But Beal was a talented poker player and an interesting guy. It wasn't losing out on a financial opportunity that made Howard suddenly sad.

Andy continued. "I hope to see you again, but it won't be across a poker table."

And with that, Andy Beal retired from high-stakes poker.

He shook David Grey's hand and said, "It was a real pleasure, but I'm not going to be back."

Grey pumped Beal's hand in return and replied, "I'm sorry to hear that, Andy. I'll see you in two weeks."

Epilogue

Caught by the Fish

Could David Grey have been right? Would Andy Beal be back?

To Howard Lederer, it was inconceivable that anyone could quit poker. "We all know as poker players that we couldn't breathe without poker, so how could you not play?"

Besides, the pros had heard it before. In December 2001, Beal told Chip Reese he was through with poker. He stayed away for sixteen months, but he eventually came back. He became disillusioned with the game a couple of times in 2003, but he still returned. How was this different?

A Las Vegas local who was friendly with Beal and had watched him play several times agreed. "Andy has it stuck in his head that he can figure out what it takes to beat these guys. He can't give up. He's hooked."

Beal insisted during the summer of 2004 that he was through with poker. "I'm officially retired from the game. I accomplished everything I set out to do. It wasn't about trying to win a certain amount. It was about experiencing it, and trying to adapt to the challenge. To continue requires a lot of effort and attention and, because I've already done it all, I don't think it's worth it. I don't want to do it halfway."

For Andy Beal, it was definitely *not* about the money. He could easily afford the eight-figure losses he had endured over the three years. When he walked away from the aerospace business in 2000, he had no trouble sleeping with an estimated loss of $200 million.

It was always unlikely that Beal would emerge an overall winner, and he recognized this. By continually raising the stakes, however, he improved his chances of recouping his losses and also increased the pressure on the pros. At $100,000–$200,000, they had trouble playing their best game. But they remedied this by refusing to play again at those stakes.

What, indeed, did he have to prove by playing $20,000–$40,000 or $30,000–$60,000?

In addition, even for a man who has always prided himself on keeping a full schedule, it was becoming too much. Though still young, healthy, and vital, it pained him to admit he no longer had the constitution of a crazy gambler.

"I learned that I'm getting old and lazy and complacent. Twenty-five years ago, when I was playing blackjack, I brought a lot more rigor."

Nevertheless, Beal left the door open a crack. As he focused on what went wrong—regardless of whether he played again, his brain would continue trying to figure it out—he became convinced that many of his losses were not due to the pros' superior skill, but his failure to manage himself. Because Andy never slept well in Vegas, he would play long hours and tire himself out. "I'd routinely win for the first day or two, then by the third day or so go downhill. Part of their edge is that I play too much, for too long. My tells show a little more, and I get tired more easily."

Consequently, through another writer, Beal told the group he would play one more game if they came to Dallas and played only four hours per day. My first visit to Beal Bank coincided with the aftermath of this offer. Although Andy repeatedly told me he had retired from poker, he excused himself from the interview a few times to check for an e-mail from Jennifer Harman. Most of the players did not favor coming to Texas; he heard she was trying to organize a bankroll to come down to play.

He never heard back from her, or, for that matter, anyone from the group.

In fact, the players had reached an agreement to play Beal together or not at all. Within the group, however, everyone had a different opinion. Jennifer Harman wanted to get on a plane and play. Jennifer's kidney transplant appeared successful. In less than two months, she was back at Table One and showing up on the tournament circuit, and playing well. She was itching for another shot at Andy Beal, "though it was actually kind of fun last time, being laid up in a hospital bed on morphine, making money."

Ted Forrest didn't care what the conditions were; they had the edge and should play. Ted was also back on his game. He was still commuting between L.A. and Las Vegas, with several trips back east during the summer, and loving it. ("I hear he's playing in some private game somewhere in Europe," a friend of his told me when I asked where I could find Forrest.)

"I can't wait until they perfect cloning," Ted joked to me. "I'd like to have one of me in every game."

On the other hand, several in the group realized the advantage over Beal wasn't very big. Maybe they should be careful about giving him everything he wanted. Ironically, Barry Greenstein, who was marked as the villain in May for taking that position, was part of the group not rushing to Dallas. Between the rapidly expanding tournament schedule, lucrative made-for-TV events, a charitable mission he and Phil Ivey took to Guyana, and playing in his regular profitable game, putting it all on hold to go to Dallas—possibly just to watch someone else play—held little appeal. "It's not guaranteed that we'll win. Andy's a pretty good player."

Earlier, Barry had told me, "When you play him, you're probably, at best, a two-to-one favorite, maybe even less. If you counted just wins and losses, we're probably ahead 57 percent to 43 percent or something like that. His losses have been bigger than his wins. When he's losing, his game deteriorates. That's something that's not as likely to happen when we're losing. Plus we have the advantage of putting in new players—fresh players, players with the most success against him or whose styles match up best. When you consider that we're the best in the world and we have those other advantages, it's pretty even. It's not really clear that, on skill alone, we're better than Andy."

Doyle Brunson believed Andy Beal outnegotiated the players during his first May visit, and was not going to let that happen again. He knew that Beal was smart enough to want conditions in his favor, but attracted enough to the game that he might play when the conditions were not in his favor.

At the Bicycle Club in late August, I saw Brunson several times just before the start of the main event, a WPT tournament with a prize pool of over $3.3 million. Despite his cooperation in an earlier interview and having introduced me to Andy Beal, he seemed not to remember me. This was particularly odd because I had seen him at the Mirage poker room a few weeks earlier, in advance of its WPT tournament, and he was very friendly.

I thought, Doyle Brunson is losing his mind. Here he is, playing poker for hundreds of thousands of dollars a night, and he is not in possession of his mental faculties. He must be just giving his money away.

My assessment proved about as accurate as Custer's about the Indians at Little Big Horn. Doyle spent the next four days plowing through the biggest field in World Poker Tour history, annihilating the final table and winning $1.2 million. I later heard from a couple of sources that Doyle was angry at another writer covering the Andy Beal game and figured the other writer's actions were complicating the arrangements. Brunson's mind is still stunningly accurate.

Because Beal never received a response to his offer, he continued to declare that he was finished with poker. Poker, however, was not finished with Andy Beal.

Word of the high-stakes games had been slowly leaking to the public since Andy's first trip to the Bellagio poker room in February 2001. Because so many of the participants in the game had allowed themselves to be interviewed for this book—especially Andy Beal—the floodgates opened. No one, it seemed, wanted to miss an opportunity to talk about Andy Beal and the $100,000–$200,000 poker game.

Just four days after Todd Brunson played Beal in that game, he appeared in an instructional poker video produced by Michael Berk, the creator of *Baywatch*. The video was hosted by former *Baywatch* star and 2001 Playmate of the Year Brande Roderick. She introduced Brunson, along with fellow instructors David Sklansky and Mike Matusow, as follows:

"Todd Brunson has won eight major poker tournaments and recently played in the highest-stakes poker game in Las Vegas history, with one- and two-*hundred*-thousand dollar betting limits, and pots building up to two and three million dollars each. Now, that not only takes a lot of money, it takes a lot of poker skill. Todd, I heard you once won thirteen million dollars in one day . . ."

In September, the New York *Daily News* featured a story about the Table One players. Several players discussed their success against Beal. Todd Brunson was quoted as saying, "I've beaten him for $20 million, $20.5 million to be exact." Chau

Giang said that he once beat Beal for $6 million. Referring to Jennifer Harman, the article stated that "she has pleasant million-dollar memories, too."

Andy Beal woke me up early in the morning after he saw the *Daily News* article, furious. Andy's memory for the amounts of wins and losses for individual sessions was hazy, but the numbers were not, for the most part, inaccurate. (Todd Brunson and Jennifer Harman both told me about their individual sessions with Beal, and others confirmed their accounts. Giang, however, declined to be interviewed. Although I heard that he had both winning and losing sessions against Beal, Andy denied that Giang ever won $6 million in one session, and no one ever described such a session to me.)

Beal was, however, correct in his assessment that the comments provided an inaccurate summary of the poker games. The players did not, for example, mention that Beal won nearly $12 million in one day when the stakes were the highest, and he won half of it from Chip Reese, one of poker's most respected and legendary players. "This makes it sound like I'm some kind of schmuck who lost a bunch of money and stopped playing because he lost so much."

It particularly bothered him that the attitude portrayed in the article was inconsistent with their apparent refusal to play him in Dallas. If they really believe they're so much better than me, he reasoned, why wouldn't they take me up on my offer to come to Dallas to play me?

Fortunately for me, I wasn't around Andy when he learned what Johnny Chan said about him in *Cigar Aficionado*. The October issue, featuring 2004 World Series Champion Greg Raymer on the cover, did mention that Beal beat Chip Reese for $6 million. But Chan refused to give Beal credit. "I guarantee you Andy got lucky on Chip. The deck ran cold [for Chip]. Andy started catching gut-shot straights and making flushes." Although the article did not mention it, and Chan may not have mentioned it, he was not present while Reese and Beal played. He also denigrated Beal's ability in general. "Let me put it this way," Chan was quoted as saying, "you can't bluff a sucker."

Beal wanted to go public, an extraordinary step for someone so private, especially regarding something like poker. He asked my advice, though I begged off. I genuinely like Andy Beal but what was good for him here was the opposite of what was good for my book. I told him a complaining billionaire wasn't likely to attract much sympathy, but the publicity would probably help me sell books.

I thought he might agree with my point about not expecting much public support until he asked, "What would you want to do if someone talked about you that way?"

His answer was contained in the next issue of *Card Player* magazine, dated October 8, 2004. A short article by the publisher, Barry Shulman, included a letter Beal asked Shulman to publish in the magazine, directed to sixteen of the players who had played Beal or been part of the group over the previous three years.

Beal started by pointing out that he won more than $10 million in the $100,000–$200,000 game, and that a majority of the sixteen players had overall losing records against him. He recognized that he was a net overall loser in the games, but "These stories have become like fisherman's tales, in which the fish is always getting bigger every time the story is told."

To illustrate that the matches were not as lopsided as some accounts made it appear, Beal asked the players to "put up or shut up." "Come to Dallas and play me for four hours a day and I will play until one of us runs out of money or cries uncle. If your play is so great and your wins have been as large as you claim, you should have plenty of bankroll and be jumping at the chance to come and play another $100,000–$200,000 game and win a lot more money." He said the players could choose locations, cards, and dealers, but, "You should provide a slate of any six or more of the above players and I will pick from your slate who plays."

The players did not accept his offer in October or November. This proved the point he was trying to make, and which players like Barry Greenstein realized from the outset: If the pros were better than Andy, it was not by so much that they could afford to give up any of their advantages. He wasn't some kind of sucker just begging to give his money away.

Doyle Brunson responded in the next issue of *Card Player*. He apologized for the fisherman's tales, though implied the actual responsibility for them was "the way the media can distort anything they write about." He proposed that the group play Beal, but on terms considerably more favorable to the pros: (1) Each side would raise $40 million; (2) stakes would be $30,000–$60,000, though if either side lost $20 million, it could raise the stakes to $50,000–$100,000; (3) the group would choose who would play and when; and (4) the game would take place in Las Vegas. Doyle said the first three points were nonnegotiable.

Through October and November, Beal and Brunson maintained contact. It would be unfair to characterize their talks as "negotiations" because Brunson wasn't giving in on anything. In fact, he lowered the size of the buy-in from $40 million to $12.5 million. Andy Beal continued to listen—and continued to insist that he was done with poker.

In mid-November, the discussions took another twist that could be called bizarre for a game played for three years under poker's version of omertà. Someone approached Doyle Brunson about paying for the TV rights to a heads-up rematch between the group and Andy Beal.

According to Beal, the amount was substantial, around $5–$10 million. He made an unusual proposal to Brunson: The loser gets the TV rights. His reasoning, though unconventional, was brilliant. "The rights will be more valuable if you lose. People will be a lot more interested in seeing me win than seeing me get beat up by the pros. And if you win, I'm going to bury the tapes and no one will ever see them."

In the meantime, I got a chance to play poker against Andy Beal. I was surprised he accepted my challenge to play. Like the members of the group, I wouldn't play him at stakes he considered high. We contested a nominal sum on my second visit to his office, a game of approximately five hours sandwiched between interview sessions.

I can't say that Andy took the game as seriously as, say, the $100,000–$200,000 match against Chip Reese. On the other hand, he was clearly motivated to keep me from being able to write that I thumped him heads up. He certainly *seemed* to take it seriously. He hired two dealers, set up the vibrating timer in his sock, put the binder clip with the random-number-generator/pocketwatch in front of him, and donned his sunglasses. A cigar store Indian would have been easier to read.

I started with the lead in our freeze-out, though it was simply because I picked up extremely good cards early. I had only rarely played heads up or outside a poker room. Although the conference room was large, the silence and intimacy of the surroundings gave me little to do during the play of the hands other than to stare at my opponent.

For a mediocre player, I am pretty good at reading my opponents. (Translation: I am a shade better than mediocre at it.) But there was no way to read Andy. What on earth were Howard Lederer, Todd Brunson, and Jennifer Harman finding when they looked across at Andy Beal? I saw nothing. But I kept staring.

Probably because I have a good poker stare—I just imitate Howard Lederer—and enjoyed a nominal chip lead, Beal was a bit rattled.

"I don't like the way you're looking at me, like you're seeing something."

He walked to a nearby table where he had several pairs of sunglasses in a bag and changed into the giant Elvis sunglasses.

Andy became satisfied with the change in eyewear when he took over the chip lead. I found two things difficult to handle about the game. First, Beal was so aggressive that I made the same mistake almost every top player has made against him: I became more aggressive. If some of the world's best players fell into the trap, I suppose I shouldn't be ashamed, but I spent months learning about what worked and what didn't against Beal, and for some reason I chose the latter.

Second, the level of focus necessary for such a game is significant. That Beal never spoke or moved made it even more difficult. During the last matches against him, both Howard Lederer and Todd Brunson brought their own music players and headphones.

As I continued to throw away chips on aggressive maneuvers, my mind wandered amid the silence. Keeping in mind that my opponent earned about a half-million dollars *per day* and was giving me a full day of his time—the second, in addition to numerous telephone interviews—I wanted to make the most of the time.

I started telling him stories from the book.

I told him about the four-day marathon match between Ted Forrest and Hamid Dastmalchi, which got us into a debate over whether Hamid was really pouring down cognacs and beers while he played $100,000–$200,000 hold 'em against Andy in May.

I won a couple big pots in a row.

"Okay," Andy said, "that's enough talking. Let's just play."

Ignoring his order, I mentioned the differences of opinion among the players about how they had individually fared against him. Although his recollection was generally not too good on particular sessions, he was surprised that Chip Reese claimed to have beaten him three of the five times they played.

While discussing this, I won a few more hands.

"That's it, Michael," he said in a voice more stern than angry. "If we can't just be quiet and play, I'm going to have to get my headphones."

Chastened, I shut up and proceeded to give away more chips. I tried too many fancy plays, too many bluffs, too many maneuvers. We each started with 300 chips and, in less than two hours, he had 500 of them.

The unusual thing was that I found it much easier to focus when I was low on chips. Whenever Beal came close to finishing me off, I would get up off the mat and fight back.

Three or four hours in the game, I started trash-talking, even though he had dominated the match:

"Come on, Andy. I thought you were one of the best heads-up hold 'em players in the world. Can't you finish off a guy who can barely play in a $20–$40 game in Arizona?

"Andy, I have a lot of questions left to ask. Could you please just win the rest of my chips so I can get back to something I know how to do?"

Finally, he had me down to just two chips. I was all-in on the blind and won. I was all-in on the next blind, and won that, too. Then I was dealt two kings and won that hand, too. Now, I had sixteen chips, still just a pittance, but after five hours, he had to be worrying that he'd never get rid of me.

"I swear, Andy, if you don't win these sixteen chips in the next five minutes, I'm going to get every chip you have and you'll have to live with seeing that in print for the rest of your life."

He laughed, but he had to be getting sick of this. He was clobbering me and I was still jabbering at him, and he couldn't close the deal. This game had no upside for him and we both wanted it over.

On the button, Andy started with queen-jack, both clubs, a good heads-up starting hand. He called the remaining two chips of my big blind and raised.

I had the ace-king of spades, one of the best starting hands you can have in hold 'em. It was a premium hand, potentially a monster, but the Texas road gamblers eschewed its common name, "Big Slick," for "Walking Back to Houston." According to T. J. Cloutier, probably the winningest tournament poker player in history, if you played ace-king too often or too aggressively in Dallas, you could find yourself walking back to Houston.

We went for a total of four raises before he just called. There were twenty chips in the pot, and I had six left.

The flop consisted of a ten of hearts, and a nine and seven of spades. It was exactly the flop I was looking for. I figured that Beal had an ace with an inferior kicker, which would mean he was drawing almost dead. I thought, correctly, that I wouldn't even have to improve to win the hand, but if I was wrong, I could probably still win it with any of the three aces, the three kings, or the nine remaining spades. I bet. (There was one flaw in my reasoning, which would not have changed my play of the hand had I realized it. The remaining kings would have made me the highest pair, but would have made Beal a winning straight.)

But it was a great flop for Andy, too. He had two overcards (cards higher than any card on the board) and an open-ended straight draw. He could win with any king or eight (for a straight) or jack or queen (for the top pair). Not knowing my cards, however, he probably guessed he would lose if he did not pick up one of those fourteen cards. Furthermore, some of those fourteen cards (like the king of spades, which was in my hand, or the eight of spades, which would make him a straight but give me a winning flush) weren't really available. But I had only four chips left, and the pot odds definitely favored him spending a total of six more chips (two to call my bet and the maximum of four I had left and clearly wanted to get into the pot) to win twenty-six chips (the twenty-two in the pot already plus the four more in my stack that were sure to join them). He reraised. I raised back, and he called, so I was all-in.

I made some gratuitous comment about how I was going to take those thirty-two chips if I won them and make him stay until I won every one of the 600 chips on the table.

The turn card was a three of diamonds, helping nobody.

The river card was the king of hearts.

For an instant, we both thought the same thing: I finished with the top pair and was somehow still alive.

Within a couple seconds, we and the dealers saw that was incorrect.

The suicide king had made Andy Beal a winning straight.

Not only did Beal outdraw me on the last hand—though he dominated the match and was leading 584 chips to 16 before that hand, so I can hardly cry that he won due to luck—but he refused to take my money when I tried to pay up. I wouldn't be walking back to Houston, but I would be slinking back to the Dallas–Fort Worth Airport the next morning, feeling that I played this hand right, but the couple hundred preceding it like a drunken refugee from the keno lounge.

Several of the players remain convinced that they will see Andy Beal again across a poker table. Some, like Ted Forrest, don't care much about the terms. "Our biggest mistake was originally not just getting on a plane and playing him in Dallas. Then we wouldn't have had to argue about choosing players and the size of the stakes." Others felt he simply couldn't give up the game and would, at some time in the future, just return to Las Vegas and say, "Who wants to play some poker?"

I spent nearly a year with the best poker players in the world. Andy Beal, if not part of that club, was certainly one of the world's best heads-up hold 'em players, and one of the world's most successful businessmen. In short, I had an opportunity to learn from some very wise gamblers.

I can say two things for certain. First, it will be at least several decades before there is a higher-stakes poker game than Andy Beal played against Todd Brunson, Chip Reese, Hamid Dastmalchi, Gus Hansen, and Jennifer Harman on May 12–13, 2004.

And second, I wouldn't bet you on it.

Bibliography

Books

Alvarez, A. *The Biggest Game in Town*. Boston: Houghton Mifflin, 1983.

Bellin, Andy. *Poker Nation*. New York: HarperCollins, 2002.

Bradshaw, Jon. *Fast Company*. New York: Harper's Magazine Press, 1975.

Brunson, Doyle. *Super System*. Las Vegas: B&G, 1979 (2nd ed.).

Cloutier, T. J. and Tom McEvoy. *Championship No-Limit and Pot-Limit Hold 'Em*. Las Vegas: Cardsmith, 1997.

Glass, Mary Ellen. *Lester Ben "Benny" Binion—Some Recollections of a Texas and Las Vegas Gaming Operator*. Reno: Oral History Program, University of Nevada, Reno, 1976.

Holden, Anthony. *Big Deal*. New York: Penguin, 1990.

Jenkins, Don. *Johnny Moss: Champion of Champions*. Las Vegas: JM, 1981.

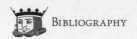

Konik, Michael. *The Man with the $100,000 Breasts*. Las Vegas: Huntington, 1999.

———. *Telling Lies and Getting Paid*. Connecticut: Lyons Press, 2002.

Lederer, Katy. *Poker Face: A Girlhood Among Gamblers*. New York: Crown, 2003.

Malmuth, Mason. *Gambling Theory and Other Topics*. Henderson: 2 + 2, 1999 (5th ed.).

May, Jesse. *Shut Up and Deal*. New York: Anchor, 1998.

McManus, James. *Positively Fifth Street*. New York: Farrar, Straus & Giroux, 2003.

Munchkin, Richard. *Gambling Wizards*. Las Vegas: Huntington Press, 2002.

Percy, George. *The Language of Poker*. 1988.

Preston, Thomas "Amarillo Slim," and Bill Cox. *Play Poker to Win*. Great Britain: Souvenir, 1974.

Preston, Thomas "Amarillo Slim," and Greg Dinkin. *Amarillo Slim in a World of Fat People*. New York: HarperCollins, 2003.

Rose, Ron, *Poker Aces: The Stars of Tournament Poker*. Dayton: Via Quinta, 2004.

Sheehan, Jack (ed.). *The Players: The Men Who Made Las Vegas*. Reno: University of Nevada Press, 1997.

Sklansky, David. *The Theory of Poker*. Henderson: 2 + 2, 2002 (4th ed.).

Sklansky, David, and Mason Malmuth. *Hold 'Em Poker for Advanced Players*. Henderson: 2 + 2, 2003 (4th ed.).

———. *How to Make $100,000 a Year Gambling for a Living*. Henderson: 2 + 2, 1998 (2nd ed.).

Smith, John, *Running Scared: The Life and Treacherous Times of Las Vegas Casino King Steve Wynn*. New York: Four Walls Eight Windows, 2001.

Smith, Raymond. *The Poker Kings of Las Vegas*. Dublin: Aherlow, 1982.

Spanier, David. *The Little Book of Poker*. Las Vegas: Huntington, 2000.

———. *Total Poker*. London: André Deutsch, 1990 (Rev. ed.).

Wiesenberg, Michael. *The Official Dictionary of Poker*. Inglewood: Mike Caro University, 1999.

Articles

Adams, David. "Big Furor, Tiny Island." *St. Petersburg Times*, October 18, 1999.

Alson, Peter. "Chan Is Bluffing (We Think)." *Esquire*, May 1989.

Bensman, Todd. "Dallas Entrepreneur Comes Closer to Building Space-Rocket Plant." *Dallas Morning News*, October 7, 1999.

———. "Dallas Entrepreneur's Rocket Plans Arouse Controversy in Caribbean." *Dallas Morning News*, March 18, 1999.

Berns, Dave. "Binion's Told to Pay Gamblers." *Las Vegas Review-Journal*, March 16, 1999.

Blow, Steve. "Math Lover Offers Winner Piece of Pi." *Dallas Morning News*, November 30, 1997.

Cochran, Mike. "Would You Bluff This Man?" *American Way*, February 15, 1993.

Dalla, Nolan. "From Longworth to Las Vegas and 70 Years in Between: Poker Legend Doyle Brunson Tells His Story and Shares His Views on Life as a Gambler (Parts I and II)." Pokerpages.com.

———. "Great Gamblers in History—Doyle Brunson." Gambletribune.org, October 22, 2003.

"The Deal with Beal." *Dallas Business Journal*, June 21, 2002.

Donovan, Doug. "Rocket Man." *Forbes*, April 17, 2000.

Eolis, Wendeen. "Lyle Berman and Steve Lipscomb's Confection: A Poker Tournament Season on National Television (Parts I and II)." *Poker Digest*, May 2002.

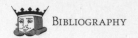

Files, Jennifer. "Dallas Banker Targets Market for Satellite Launching." *Dallas Morning News*, March 23, 1998.

Foust, Jeff. "Beal Aerospace Shuts Down; Cites 'Intolerable' Government Interference as Factor." Space.com, October 23, 2000.

Friess, Steve. "Power Out 13 Hours at Large Las Vegas Resort." *Boston Globe*, April 12, 2004.

"Frisco, Texas-Based Aerospace Firm Closes." *Dallas Morning News*, October 24, 2000.

Glanton, Eileen. "Where Are They Now?" *Forbes*, January 8, 2001.

Glazer, Andy. "A Princess Emerges from Poker's Aristocracy." Casino.com, September 24, 2001.

Green, Nick. "The Robin Hood of Poker." *Daily Breeze*, September 5, 2004.

Guberman, Mary Ann. "Poker World Roasts Doyle Brunson." *Card Player*, October 2, 1992.

Habal, Hala. "Plano Banks Fail to Impress Rating Agency." *Dallas Business Journal*, May 18, 2001.

Jaffray, Allyn. "Barry Greenstein: A Modern-Day Robin Hood." *Card Player*, February 27, 2004.

Johnson, Linda, and Dana Smith. "Interview with Doyle Brunson." Pokerbooks.com, 1998.

Kaplan, Michael. "All Bets Are On." *Cigar Aficionado*, July/August 2002.

———. "Hits and Runs." *Cigar Aficionado*, November/December 2000.

———. "Winner Take All." *Cigar Aficionado*, October 2004.

———. Young Guns. *Las Vegas Life*, August 2003.

Koch, Ed. "Doyle Brunson: Poker's Living Legend." *Poker World*, January 1995.

Kurson, Ken. "My War—Earn Cash While Working at Home!" *Esquire*, March 1998.

 Lanning, Rick. "Texas Dolly." *Nevada*, July/August 1983.

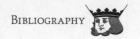

Lederer, Howard. "My 4 Day Diary of the 2003 WSOP." Gutshot.co, 2003.

———. "World Poker Tour Finals Report—A Look Back at the $25,000 Event," Liveactionpoker.com, 2003.

Lederer, Richard. "My Son the Poker Player." *19th Annual World Series of Poker* (tournament program), 1988.

Lent, Gary. "The $5,000 Olive." Finaltablepoker.com, May 4, 2004.

Mackenzie, Dana. "Mathematics: Number Theorists Embark on a New Treasure Hunt." *Science*, November 21, 1997.

Maudlin, R. Daniel. "A Generalization of Fermat's Last Theorem: The Beal Conjecture and Prize Problem." *Notices of the American Mathematics Society*, December 1997.

McNamee, Tom. "Power from Poker." *Chicago Sun-Times*, February 8, 2004.

Negreanu, Daniel. "Meet Jennifer Harman (Parts I and II)." *Card Player*, May 24, 2002, June 7, 2002.

Pappalardo, Joe. "Love and Rockets." *Dallas Observer*, March 1, 2001.

Phillips, Edward. "Beal Aerospace Developing New Launch Vehicle." *Aviation Week and Space Technology*, April 6, 1998.

Pienciak, Rick. "Getting a Taste of Ultimate Sin—Millions from Texas." New York *Daily News*, September 11, 2004.

Raghunanthan, Anuradha. "Beal Bank Plans to Leave Texas." *Dallas Morning News*, June 14, 2002.

Rice, Melinda. "Man on a Mission." *D Magazine*, January 2000.

"Rooms at the Top." *Player*, May/June 2004.

Ruchman, Peter. *The Fall of the Temple of Chance: Benny Binion's Legacy*. Gamblersbook.com, 1999.

Sexton, Mike. "Doyle Brunson—Part I." *Card Player*, September 10, 2004.

Shapiro, Max. "Meet Barry Greenstein." *Card Player*, November 21, 2003.

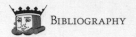

Shulman, Allyn Jaffray. "Doyle Brunson—Five Decades of Poker and Still Going Strong." *Card Player*, August 27, 2004.

Shulman, Barry. "Doyle Says, 'Let's Plan an $80 Million Freeze-out!'" *Card Player*, October 22, 2004.

———. "The World's Biggest Poker Game." *Card Player*, October 8, 2004.

———. "The World's Biggest Poker Game—A Proposed Compromise." *Card Player*, November 5, 2004.

Simpson, Jeff. "Big Games Bring in Big Money, Big Names." *Las Vegas Review-Journal*, April 13, 2003.

———. "Nevadan at Work: Doug Dalton—MGM Mirage Director of Poker Operations." *Las Vegas Review-Journal*, May 12, 2002.

Smith, Dana. "Interview with a Champ: Chau Giang." Poker-books.com, 1994.

Smith, John. "Former Aerospace Chief Suffers Rough Landing at Bellagio Poker Table." *Las Vegas Review-Journal*, December 21, 2001.

———. "Horseshoe's Sinking Fortunes Obvious to Many Toward the End." *Las Vegas Review-Journal*, January 16, 2004.

Surman, Matt. "The Call of the Cards." *Los Angeles Times*, March 27, 2002.

"The $20 Million Game of Hold 'Em." Masterbets.com, 2003.

Welch, David. "Profits Level Off for Beal Bank's Bad Loan Barons." *Dallas Business Journal*, September 20, 1996.

———. "The Thrill Is Gone: Beal Looks Beyond RTC Loans." *Dallas Business Journal*, July 12, 1996.

Wilson, Craig. "Poker Pays Off." *USA Today*, October 10, 2003.

Web Sites

Annieduke.com (profile of Annie Duke, information about Howard Lederer)

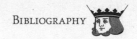

Bealaerospace.com

Bealbank.com

Bealconjecture.com

Bellagio.com (information about the resort and schedules of poker tournaments)

Binions.com (information on the history of the hotel-casino and the World Series of Poker)

Cardplayer.com (archives of *Card Player* magazine, player profiles, and tournament results)

Conjelco.com (World Series of Poker history and results)

Fdic.gov (reports filed with the Federal Deposit Insurance Corporation by Beal Bank)

Finaltablepoker.com (results of poker tournaments, stories, and columns by Andy Glazer)

Fulltiltpoker.com (profiles of poker players)

Gamblersbook.com (reviews and summaries of poker books)

Gamblingtimes.com (archives of *Gambling Times* and *Poker Player* magazines, player profiles, and tournament results)

Gaming.unlv.edu/WSOP/index.html (University of Nevada–Las Vegas retrospective on the World Series of Poker)

Gutshot.co.uk (articles and tournament poker results)

Homepokergames.com (profiles of poker players)

Playwinningpoker.com/wsop (information about the World Series of Poker)

Poker3000.com (results of poker tournaments)

Pokerclan.com (discussion and rumors about poker)

Pokerpages.com (results of poker tournaments and player profiles)

Pokerworks.com (results of poker tournaments and information about the nightly action in Bellagio's poker rooms, as seen by a dealer)

Rec.gambling.poker (discussion and rumors about poker)

Thegoodgamblingguide.co.uk (poker writings of Jesse May)

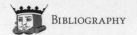

Thepokerforum.com (results of poker tournaments and background on the World Poker Tour)

Twoplustwo.com (Web site of 2 + 2, the company publishing Malmuth and Sklansky; poker information and discussion)

Worldpokertour.com (the World Poker Tour's official Web site)

Wptfan.com (fan site for the World Poker Tour)

Wptinsider.com (information on the World Poker Tour)

Acknowledgments

Although many people helped me during the course of writing this book, it could not have been written without the influence of two women.

My wife, Jo Anne, motivated me to pursue and complete this project, and was patient and understanding during my numerous "research" trips to Las Vegas, hours-long middle-of-the-night phone calls, and my decision to shoot craps with Ted Forrest. She has always given me the space to pursue my own path, no matter how difficult or foolhardy it at first (or later) appeared. That she is also a terrific editor with a laser beam for weaknesses in my writing is a freeroll.

At the beginning of this project, I met Linda Geenen, a poker dealer at the Bellagio. Her Web site, Pokerworks.com, is a remarkable account of daily life in Bellagio's poker room, one of the most interesting and bizarre work environments on earth. She was unbelievably generous with her knowledge, insight, and judgment.

I received so much help and support from so many sources that I must apologize in advance if I omitted anyone (possible) or did not adequately express my appreciation (likely).

Family: My children, Barry, Ellie, and Valerie, showed tremendous patience during the months I was away or preoccupied with this book, as well as considerable poker skill. My mom and dad provided encouragement and support, during the project and in the forty-five years preceding.

Friends: Steve Popuch, who introduced me to poker and deluded me into believing my interest in it was not abnormal. Ted Corse, who rekindled my interest in poker during early 2003 and told me during a Vegas trip in October 2003 an unbelievable story he heard about a $15 million poker game going on at the Bellagio. Ken Kurson, a tremendous writer, a tremendous mentor, and a tremendous friend. I would have no success in writing without him (ask him; he'll tell you). Hillary Schmulenson and Elena Wayne, who were instrumental in arranging my initial contact with Barry Greenstein. Elena's thirty-year friendship with Barry, which she was willing to place on the line to put me in touch during a period when everybody wanted a piece of Barry, started me along the way of penetrating the story from inside the group.

Howard Schwartz, owner of the Gambler's Book Shop, a remarkable Las Vegas institution that was my home away from home during several of my research trips to Vegas. Howard is a friend to all writers and students of poker, not just for his tremendous selection of books but his (completely unorganized) clipping files and heroic efforts to keep classic poker books from going out of print.

Poker player-writers: Wendeen Eolis, Max Shapiro, Nolan

Dalla, and the late Andy Glazer. Wendeen gave me good advice at the beginning of the project. Max has set a high standard for poker writing for years and his excellent account at Pokerpages.com of Mike Laing's win at the Reno Hilton's 2001 World Poker Challenge gave me background and insight into Laing's methods and madness. Nolan, who had a full plate with his own poker book and the World Series of Poker in spring 2004, offered help and friendship. Andy, literally and figuratively, was a giant among poker writers. He befriended me when I knew almost no one in poker, introduced me to Ted Forrest at the end of one of the most remarkable days in the history of poker, and showed me how an artist works his craft in writing about a poker game. I barely got to know Andy Glazer, but I miss him very much.

I expected at the outset that my research would be met with some hostility among players and poker room personnel. Despite the tremendous popularity of poker, the top players generally keep their business in the cash game secret. Industry sources said none of the Table One players would talk to me, giving reasons from fear of attracting attention from the IRS, to fear of upsetting Andy Beal (and future Andy Beals), to fear of demystifying their success.

I was thrilled that I have been able to approach nearly every one who played a part in the story, and nearly all of them agreed to talk to me. Some were eager. Some were reluctant.

I am grateful to two employees of MGM Mirage who placed their trust in me early in the project. They asked not to be named and were reluctant to provide more than background information, but I would not have been able to advance my research in some important ways without their help.

Later in my research, I received significant help from many people in the casino business, most notably the following: from MGM Mirage and Bellagio, Doug Dalton, Jack McClelland,

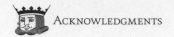

Debbi Callihan, and Karen Van Horn; from the Bicycle Casino, Yosh Nakano; and from Casino Arizona, Bob, K.C., players Shoes, Vegas Mike, and Bob Goldfarb.

I started this project with great respect for professional poker players. That admiration has grown during the past year. Although they had little to gain and plenty of reasons to be wary, nearly every player I contacted took me into his or her confidence and helped me understand their lives and games: Lyle Berman, Vince Burgio, Doyle Brunson, Todd Brunson, Freddy Deeb, Eric Drache, Ted Forrest, Barry Greenstein (and his friend, Alexandra Vuong), Mike Laing, Howard Lederer and his wife, Susan Lederer, Mike Matusow, Daniel Negreanu, David Plastik, David "Chip" Reese, Erik Seidel, Ron Stanley, and Jennifer Harman Traniello (and her husband, Marco Traniello).

Among this group, I can't express enough appreciation for the efforts of Doyle Brunson, Todd Brunson, Ted Forrest, Barry Greenstein, Howard Lederer, Chip Reese, and Jennifer Harman Traniello, who generally tried to keep a lid on the big games with Andy Beal, yet still cooperated, most of them in multiple interviews and by answering numerous queries by telephone and e-mail. Howard (for introducing me to Doyle and Jennifer) and Doyle (for introducing me to Andy Beal) helped this project tremendously when they could just as easily have killed it.

I'll let you in on another secret: Even though poker players spend their professional lives hiding what's inside, they are almost without exception the most open, trusting group I have ever met. I consider many of these people my friends. Even if they are really no more than merely sources who managed to bluff me, it has been a wonderful experience getting to know them. I understand how men who can afford it will lose huge sums of money to these players, enjoy the experience, and want to repeat it.

While working on this book, I received an opportunity to participate as one of several poker players in an instructional video produced by Michael Berk. My thanks go to Michael, Edna Dalton (who made it easier for me to approach her husband, Doug), Mat Sklansky, Eddie Novak, Brande Roderick, and everyone associated with the video for making it a memorable experience. It gave me a chance to meet Todd Brunson less than a week after he played the $100,000–$200,000 game with Andy Beal, as well as Mike Matusow and David Sklansky. Todd and Mike were both generous with their time in interviews.

Even though I gave his son Mat the proverbial shirt off my back—I'm not making this up—David Sklansky responded to my e-mail by saying, "I do almost nothing unless it is worth VERY big bucks to me." That was too bad, because Andy Beal and several players had very strong opinions about Sklansky and, even apart from that, it would have been interesting engaging poker's leading theorist on the application of his theories to this unusual poker game. But I wasn't offering him even SMALL bucks, so he was certainly within his right to refuse.

Finally, among my sources, I am indebted to Andy Beal. Even though he generally avoids publicity and I planned to write this book without his cooperation, the book is much better for his involvement. He was unbelievably generous with his time. Without exception, the players I spoke to early in the project stressed what a nice guy he was, something I assumed was code for "don't rile the pigeon." But Beal really *is* a nice guy, one of the nicest I've ever known. Thanks also to Craig Singer of Beal Bank, and Andy's staff, who put up with my frequent phone calls and requests for information.

This book would not have been written without the efforts of my agent, Eileen Cope, who stuck with me through failure and frustration and championed this project at Lowenstein-Yost Associates, and in the publishing world. I was lucky that she convinced Warner Books to publish it. Colin Fox, at Warner, kept me constantly fired up with his camaraderie and enthusiasm, and he made a beeline for the weakest parts of my writing, and helped me fix them up. Jamie Raab, Colin's boss, has been terrific in her support for this book. Getting a book published can be difficult, but not with people like Eileen Cope, Colin Fox, and Jamie Raab in my corner, and their numerous colleagues at Lowenstein-Yost and Warner who helped in ways too numerous to mention.

Several people helped in the preparation of the manuscript. In addition to many people I already mentioned, thanks to Linda DiFrancesco (who conducted the background research on Andy Beal in Texas), Melanie Croft, Joanne Schlesinger, and Kay Creighton.

Index